HANDBOOK OF PUBLIC RELATIONS IN INDIA

Handbook Of Public Relations In India

A STANDARD GUIDE FOR TEACHERS, STUDENTS AND PUBLIC RELATIONS PERSONNEL

D.S. MEHTA

ALLIED PUBLISHERS PVT. LIMITED
New Delhi Mumbai Kolkata Chennai Nagpur
Ahmedabad Bangalore Hyderabad Lucknow

ALLIED PUBLISHERS PRIVATE LIMITED

1/13-14 Asaf Ali Road, **New Delhi**–110002
Ph.: 011-23239001 • E-mail: delhi.books@alliedpublishers.com

87/4, Chander Nagar, Alambagh, **Lucknow** - 226005
Ph.: 0522-4012850 • E-mail: appltdlko9@gmail.com

17 Chittaranjan Avenue, **Kolkata**–700072
Ph.: 033-22129618 • E-mail: cal.books@alliedpublishers.com

15 J.N. Heredia Marg, Ballard Estate, **Mumbai**–400001
Ph.: 022-42126969 • E-mail: mumbai.books@alliedpublishers.com

60 Shiv Sunder Apartments (Ground Floor), Central Bazar Road,
Bajaj Nagar, **Nagpur**–440010
Ph.: 0712-2234210 • E-mail: ngp.books@alliedpublishers.com

F-1 Sun House (First Floor), C.G. Road, Navrangpura,
Ellisbridge P.O., **Ahmedabad**–380006
Ph.: 079-26465916 • E-mail: ahmbd.books@alliedpublishers.com

751 Anna Salai, **Chennai**–600002
Ph.: 044-28523938 • E-mail: chennai.books@alliedpublishers.com

Hebbar Sreevaishnava Sabha, Sudarshan Complex - 2
No. 24/1, 2nd Floor, Seshadri Road, **Bangalore** - 560009
Ph.: 080-22262081 • E-Mail: bngl.books@alliedpublishers.com

3-2-844/6 & 7 Kachiguda Station Road, **Hyderabad**–500027
Ph.: 040-24619079 • E-mail: hyd.books@alliedpublishers.com

Website: www.alliedpublishers.com

First Published, 1980

Edition, 2016

ISBN : 81-7023-334-8

Published by Sunil Sachdev and printed by Ravi Sachdev at Allied Publishers Private Limited, Printing Division, A-104 Mayapuri Phase II, New Delhi - 110064

Foreword

Public relations was once looked down upon as a lowly profession denoting, in a figurative sense, drum-beating on behalf of someone who was interested in promoting his wares.

In recent years, however, India has caught up in a big way with the western concept of public relations. In its widest sense, public relations now embraces virtually every branch of human activity – whether it is just promotion of products or image-building for individuals, corporate bodies, governments, and even political parties – who wish to project their activities or achievements or policies.

The public relations profession, once a neglected occupation, now has an ever-increasing number of practitioners. Quite a few of them know their ropes, many of them are at best half-baked, while quite a few of the practitioners are innocent of what public relations is or how it should be practised.

The value of public relations in India is now increasingly recognized. Public relations is no longer considered a luxury or a status symbol. However, progress towards professionalization of PR in India has been rather slow. This is a field for professionals and not for quacks who bring the profession a bad name. Universities and other educational institutions could usefully devote greater attention to this new discipline.

Against this background, the *Handbook of Public Relations in India* fills a void. I find in it virtually everything that a public relations practitioner may want to know. In fact, the *Handbook* contains reference material which could be useful not only to the beginner, but also to the seasoned public relations man who wishes occasionally to brush up his knowledge or check his techniques with what the *Handbook* lays down. It thus also serves as an excellent reference guide book on public relations.

There is hardly any book on PR written in the Indian setting. Mr. Mehta has been in this field for over a quarter century. I congratulate him on undertaking this pioneering work. Mr. Mehta's comprehensive book on the subject will be of great practical value to all those who have anything to do with public relations and related fields. Mr. Mehta has made a significant contribution to the cause of journalism and public relations in India through this and his earlier book "*Mass Communication and Journalism in India*. I am sure this will give an impetus to others to write books on public relations in India and enrich the limited literature now available on the subject.

G.G. MIRCHANDANI
General Manager
United News of India

New Delhi
15 August, 1980

Introduction

My book *Mass Communication and Journalism in India* published in 1979 has been well received in India and abroad. This is evident not only from the sales figures but also from the letters received from individuals and organizations welcoming the publication. A number of universities and educational institutions have included it in their recommended list of readings for courses in journalism and allied subjects.

Public relations is closely associated with mass communication and journalism. Yet with its growing importance in India, in government, in the public and the private sectors, PR has not only emerged as a separate discipline but has also become an important and necessary adjunct to management.

There is no dearth of books on public relations in the developed countries, particularly in the UK and the USA. There is, however, hardly any publication exclusively devoted to the Indian situation. Indian students have, therefore, to depend largely on foreign titles. Also, PR practitioners in India, in the absence of a standard guide on the subject, are handicapped in putting across their message in an effective and purposeful manner.

Our PR problems are different from those of the western countries. For instance, PR for public undertakings is a subject of special interest to us. It has not much relevance in the USA. We, therefore, need books on public relations written in the Indian context and in the Indian environment. The approach and the treatment of the subject have also to be different from what we find in foreign books.

There is, therefore, a definite need for books on public relations in India covering all these aspects. The present work is an attempt to meet these requirements and thus seeks to fill in an important gap.

The book is divided into three parts. The first part spells out the principles and practices of public relations, the problems of

PR in the Indian setting and Indian experience, the Indian PR scene and PR for the government, the public and the private sectors. The second part covers the use of different communication media, while the third deals with related subjects. A glossary of PR terms, a bibliography of books and periodical literature and other useful information given in the appendices add to its reference value.

I hope that students, teachers, new entrants, PR practitioners, senior executives and others associated with managerial functions in India will find in the book a friend, philosopher, and guide in their day-to-day work. The PR professionals abroad will also find it useful for a comparative study as it will give them an insight into the emerging PR profession in India – its problems, perspective, and operations.

D.S. MEHTA

New Delhi
15 August, 1980

Contents

PART I

PUBLIC RELATIONS SCENE IN INDIA

CHAPTER 1

What is Public Relations?

Public relations means different things for different people. Theoreticians consider it a philosophical and moral concept. The PR practitioners see in it nothing more than the 'art of getting things done'. The basic purpose of PR and PR techniques is, more or less, the same in all sectors – government, public and private concerns, and other institutions. Nevertheless, there are certain aspects of PR that are peculiar to a given class of organizations.

PR Defined

The following definitions give an idea of public relations and the scope of its operations:

- Art or science of developing reciprocal understanding and goodwill.
- Promotion of rapport and goodwill for a person, firm or institution, or other persons specially with the public or the community at large through the distribution of material.
- Establishing a bond of relationship and contacts between two groups of public.
- Plastic surgery to beautify the image of an organization.
- Lobbying for interests.
- Seeks to influence, solicit, or mobilize support for an idea, a cause, a problem, an institution, or an individual through communication and persuasion.
- Deliberate, planned, and sustained effort to establish and maintain mutual understanding between an organization and its publics.
- To develop and encourage attitudes and behaviour to nurture

the delicate plant of mutual understanding.
- Building of sound and productive relations with the organization's publics.
- A sincere effort to bring about harmonious adjustment between an organization and the community through dissemination of information, ideas about the organization to its publics – external and internal, and also providing a feedback from the publics to the management.
- Counselling management in dealing with public opinion and to plan and execute communication programmes to gain public understanding and acceptance of the management's point of view.
- Management of information.
- It evaluates public attitude, identifies the policies of an organization with public interest, and executes programmes for communication.
- Engineering consent.

In simple terms, PR is an attempt, through information, persuasion, adjustment, and contacts, to seek support for some activity, cause, movement, institution, product, or service.

Need for PR

Good public relations is no substitute for sound policy or good performance. False image cannot be sustained for a long time. Disillusionment will follow if the performance is not on par with the image. At the same time, right policy and good performance do not get automatically appreciated or even known without effective public relations. Therefore, the need for PR is obvious.

It is now recognized that money spent on public relations is a good investment. It is as money spent for good plant layout, good sales planning, or good legal practice. Sound, well-organized, and dynamic public relations is sure to improve not only the image of the organization, but also the profits of a business concern.

Effective public relations can win people to a certain cause or a programme. PR can motivate people to buy a certain product or a service. Good public relations attracts the right type of people to the organization. It can encourage investment from the public. Ineffective public relations or the absence of public relations can also do a lot of damage to the organization.

Essentials of Good PR

The best results are possible only if some ground rules are followed in PR work. The PR man should have a thorough knowledge of the organization. He should be well versed in public relations techniques. The management must have the highest respect for the PR man. PR is too fundamental and farreaching to be entrusted to anyone except to an effective and experienced executive. The PR man should be alert to public moods and public trends. He must be creative and thorough with details. Broad public relations experience is extremely necessary for his success.

No successful public relations is possible unless a well-thought-out public relations programme is drawn up on a long-term basis, keeping in view the present and the future corporate objectives of the organization. The objectives should be formalized in a public relations policy statement, and periodically reviewed.

The PR practitioner works through printed or spoken word and image. Broadly, he operates through two types of tools – one which is controlled by him, and the other over which he does not have any control.

In the first category are publications such as house journals, manuals, hand-books, bulletins; advertising; display and exhibits; motion pictures and slides; meetings; and conducted tours. The controlled tools are employed to reach specified publics of the organization. For instance, house publications can be used for internal circulation as well as for external audiences. Booklets can be introductory or institutional in nature or reference guides or brochures. Posters, play-cards, outdoor signs, stickers, institutional advertising, etc. are other controlled tools.

The news media – press, radio, and TV, are tools over which the PR man has no personal control. For successful PR, he has to gain and keep the confidence of the newspapers, news magazines, radio, and TV. This involves certain qualities on the part of the PR man. The PR dealings should stress on accuracy, integrity, performance, and providing of newsy, timely information and other material. In any case, the PR man should avoid begging or carping or trying to get pressure publicity through news columns and news casts by using advertising as a weapon. It is bad PR to ask a newspaper or a radio station to kill or suppress a particular story. News media expect from PR practitioners honesty, speed, frankness, brevity, cooperation, and supply of accurate and prompt information.

In India, the spoken word has a greater reach than the other media. It is also more compelling, more personal, more friendly, and more timely. The TV in India is still in its infancy. The cost of preparing and producing TV programmes is also prohibitive. The PR man has to keep all these aspects in view while selecting a medium.

What is not PR ?

PR is not 'lobbying' or 'fixing things'. It is not mere publicity, or bringing out publications. PR is not wining and dining or management of cocktail parties or carrying out *bandobast* or other ornamental functions.

Public relations is neither publicity nor propaganda nor advertising. Publicity is concerned with dissemination of information about an organization to attract attention or to publicize products or activities. The objective of publicity is to gain recognition, to build image, and to win the approval of the target publics. Propaganda is an organized effort to propagate a doctrine, an idea, or a cause. Propaganda may not have an ethical content. It is persuasion based solely on self-interest. Advertising is buying of space in print or time on air, to promote the sales of products, acceptance of ideas, or to earn goodwill.

PR has a much wider meaning. It is an all-comprehensive concept including several things. The objective of a PR programme is to promote mutual understanding between an organization and all those with whom it comes into contact both within and outside of the organization, to project its image, and to eliminate all sources of misunderstanding.

PR is not a wall between the truth and the public. Nor is it propaganda to impose a particular point of view, regardless of the truth, ethics, and public good. It is also not aimed directly to achieve sales though it does contribute indirectly to sales and marketing efforts. It is also not unpaid advertisement. It is much more than press relations. The PR programme should, therefore, not comprise stunts and gimmicks but be based on purposeful dissemination of information about the objectives and activities of the organization.

Public relations is both an art and a science. It has the beauty of art and the techniques of science. The substance of public relations is to develop understanding among different constituents which deal with the organization. The PR effort should be to earn goodwill, project correct public image and motivate publics in favour of the organization's policy, programmes, products, or services. All this, however, need to be done in a subtle and persuasive manner.

CHAPTER II

Major Areas of PR Activity

Public relations includes a host of things – press relations, advertising, publications, audio-visual and outdoor media, community relations, organization of conferences and seminars, hospitality and entertainment, financial relations, relations with the government, internal communications, etc.

More important than all these activities is the projection of the image of the organization in different media – press, radio, and TV – particularly in their news, features and editorial columns.

Press Relations

For a PR man, effective press relations is of crucial importance. In a democracy, with a free and vigilant press, press relations is not an easy operation. About half the space in the newspapers is filled in with paid advertisements. For the remaining half, there is always a keen competition among the government departments, public sector undertakings, local bodies, private sector, foreign embassies, etc. The PR man has, therefore, a tough time in getting his point of view reflected in the press.

Because of its pattern of ownership and for historical reasons, the press in India is sceptical, if not antogonistic, to the authorities. It considers failures particularly in the government and in the public sector as news and exposes their non-performance and other weaknesses with vigour. It acts as a watch-dog and seizes every opportunity to question their acts of omission and commission.

The PR man has, therefore, to keep a close watch on the press. He should not, however, lose his balance, if something unfavourable to him appears in the press. He can contradict major misreporting – but only when it is a must. Angry rebuttal, sarcasm, or snubbing the press must be avoided. A matter-of-fact, well-argued, logical explanation carries greater conviction with the readers. In no case should the PR man threaten with withdrawal of advertisements in such a situation. The rejoinder has to be prompt to have the desired impact. He should have close links at different levels – from the editor to the reporter to get sympathetic consideration to his releases on merit The reporters and photographers should be treated with respect and all facilities provided for the coverage. It is to be remembered that they are doing as much their work as ours.

Well-written and timely press releases, all assistance to correspondents to write their stories, easy approachability, ready communication, tolerance of press criticism, non-patronage, and avoidance of special favours to some papers at the expense of others are some of the important aspects of press relations work.

In projecting the work of his organization or of its products, the PR man should aim at creating a greater sense of public identification. The concept and the culture of the organization should be reflected while disseminating information about its products and services.

In developing effective press relations, the PR man should clearly understand that journalists need news. It is their bread and butter. It is their commodity to sell. They cannot remain in service without news. Also, the PR man cannot do without publicity. Therefore, there is the relationship of give-and-take between the two.

The PR man should also appreciate that journalists are nobody's fools. The press reporters have access to a number of sources of information. They always cross-check the information they receive. As such, any attempt to tell a blatant lie or to bluff them will only boomerang. The PR man can build confidence with the press only if he tells the truth and explains the situation in its proper context and perspective. He may also tell the press the likely consequences to the larger interests of the country or the society if the information is published in a particular form. The press may or may not agree with his point of view, which is its prerogative. But to suppress the truth, unless it is for vital security considerations, or to misguide a press representative would create in him a permanent enemy with disastrous consequences for PR effort.

Press relations work even in adverse conditions should be handled at normal temperature and normal pressure. Only then would it be possible to remove the aberrations and the distortions that tarnish the image of the organization. Press relations is not the projection of only personalities. More important is the projection of innovations, activities, and events. This is possible, if the PR man has something worth while to disseminate to the public. The effectiveness of dissemination is, however, dependent on proper presentation of material. The PR man's rapport, persuasive and pleasant approach can pay rich dividends when he is called upon to correct certain distortions, inaccuracies, and ill-informed criticism in the press about his organization. The PR man can be assertive and forceful in his attitude, depending on the circumstances, but he cannot afford to be offensive or aggressive with the press. He has to woo the public through different media, specially the press, as a young man woos a girl. Pleasant manners, sincerity, mastery over the subject, etc. will make all the difference in press relations work.

Advertising

Advertisement is another field of PR activity. The purpose of an advertisement is either to disseminate simple information or to motivate or persuade or influence people or to render an account or an explanation to the readers or the viewers. A product does not sell on its merits alone. The advertisement creates the demand and brings about an association between the demand and the product.

In preparing the advertisement copy, the PR man should employ the idiom that relates to his audience. In bringing out supplements in newspapers and magazines, the PR man has to weigh whether the supplement would serve its purpose, i.e. influence the target readers.

The PR man has, however, to guard against disproportionately high expenditure on advertising. He has to ensure that the engagement of advertising agencies does not lead to corruption, favouritism, nepotism, and other malpractices, besides wasteful expenditure. Radio as a medium of advertisement can render better service than the print medium, especially in the remote areas. The PR man has to keep these aspects in view while releasing his advertisements to the newspapers and other media.

Publications

Another important PR activity is of bringing out publications – brochures, folders, house journals, magazines, etc. These should be brought out only if there is a specific need for them and not as a prestige. In preparing these publications, it has to be kept in view that they truly reflect the concept and the culture of the organization. Clarity, easy comprehensibility, and straight forward approach is more important than the use of costly paper or colour transparencies. Expensively produced pamphlets do not necessarily result in better publicity. House journals should reflect the management's as well as employees' point of view. Direct mail material – leaflets, pamphlets, broad sheets, letters, telegrams – is also an effective PR medium of communication.

Other Media and Coordination

The use of audio-visual, traditional and outdoor media – films and exhibitions, hoardings, posters, puppetry, folk songs, etc. also come under the purview of PR activity. In certain areas, where modern media have no reach, the PR man can resort to oral communication as is being done by the field publicity units of the Central and State governments. Oral communication is an effective supplementary effort. The spoken word, the oldest means of communication between people, is still the most potent medium of PR. Good public speaking, courteous speaking over telephone, etc. can add to the PR image of the organization.

The PR man has also to ensure effective coordination with other publicity media, particularly radio and television. PR in the government and in the public sector must maintain a close liaison with the regional and branch offices of the Press Information Bureau and with the publicity units of the Directorate of Field Publicity and Public Relations and Information Directorates of the State governments. Proper coordination with these agencies would not only save considerable effort and money, but also result in a more purposeful projection.

PR with Constituents

For community relations, the PR man has to have a proper liaison with the local press and the local community. He has to understand and evaluate the local demands and work out positive programmes to interpret the organization's concepts to the community.

The PR man has also to provide professionally prepared information to the organization's financial publics including the financial press. He has to maintain a healthy flow and exchange of information with the financial analysts, bankers, major lending institutions, shareholders, and potential investors.

In the field of government relations, the PR man has to have a very intimate liaison with the concerned departments and personnel in the government so as to have an insight into government thinking on subjects in which his organization is interested.

The PR man is also in the best position to produce popular magazines, brochures, newsletters, bulletins, etc. He can initiate publications that have flexible contents such as periodicals for employees, special newsletters, etc. In all cases the PR man has to present the information in interesting and catchy manner. Apart from PR with the employees, the internal PR communication includes rapport with the Chief Executive and other senior personnel so that the PR man gets all information and keeps himself fully informed of all the important developments in the organization.

CHAPTER III

Public Relations in Indian Context

While the basic public relations objectives and the media that carry PR message are more or less the same everywhere, the PR approach and the use of PR tools and techniques differ a great deal depending on the environment – political, social, economic, cultural, and other relevant factors.

Public relations personnel in India have to orient their activity in their own setting. Therefore, a study of the special conditions that exist in India is of great relevance for successful and smooth PR operations.

A thorough familiarity with political, economic, social, and cultural environment of the country, an awareness of the emerging trends, and the direction and shape of things to come are absolutely necessary for the success of PR effort.

Land and People

India is the second most populous and seventh largest country in the world, with 62.58 crores of people (March 1977) and an area of 32.87 lakh sq. km. The average density of population per sq. km in 1971 was 177, varying considerably from State to State, being as high as 549 in Kerala and as low as 29 in Sikkim and 6 in Arunachal Pradesh. For any successful PR projection, it is necessary to decide the target area and the population so as to avoid wastage of PR resources.

The major religious communities in India are Hindus (82.72 per cent), Muslims (11.20 per cent), Christians (2.60 per cent), Sikhs (1.89 per cent), and others (1.59 per cent). The PR campaign must safeguard against hurting religious sentiments of any community.

People in India speak different languages and dialects. Fifteen languages have been specified in the Eighth Schedule of the Constitution. These are Assamese, Bengali, Gujarati, Hindi, Kannaḍa, Kashmiri, Malayalam, Marathi, Oriya, Punjabi, Sindhi, Sanskrit, Tamil, Telugu, and Urdu. Hindi in Devnagari script is the official language of the Union. But English is to be used in addition to Hindi for all official purposes. The multiplicity of languages gives a new dimension to PR activity in India. Therefore, expertise in different languages is required for purposeful dissemination of information in PR work.

Eighty per cent of people in India live in villages and 20 per cent in cities and towns . There are 5.75 lakh villages and 2,643 towns. Of these, 3.18 lakh villages have a population of less than 500 and 6,332, a population of 5,000 and above; 148 towns have a population of over one lakh each, nine have a population of more than 10 lakhs, while the four metropolitan cities of Calcutta, Bombay, Delhi, and Madras have a population of more than 30 lakhs. Therefore, knowledge in rural communication is of importance in PR work.

The population in India has been growing at a very high rate, nearly 2.5 per cent per annum, in the past decade. As a consequence, living standards are low. More than 15 per cent of the population is living below the poverty line. The PR organization in all sectors - government, public, and private - can take active interest to promote the nationally accepted family planning programme on voluntary basis.

Seventy per cent of people in India are illitrate. Media other than the print, particularly traditional media have therefore crucial role in PR work.

The Political System

India is a Union of States and is a sovereign democratic republic with a written constitution. It has a parliamentary system of government. The legislature of the Union, the parliament, consists of two Houses, viz., Rajya Sabha and Lok Sabha. The country is divided into States and Union Territories. In States, legislatures comprise one or two Houses - Legislative Assembly and Legislative Council. Parliament at the Centre and legislatures in the States are not only policy-making bodies, but also the most vocal institutions from the point of view of projection.

India has an elective system of democracy based on adult suffrage with the largest electorate in the world. Therefore, it should be the duty of all those who believe in democracy, rule of law, and other institutions in the country to direct their PR activities to inculcate and promote people's faith in the democratic set-up.

The parliamentary system, however, has yet to take firm roots in the country. The people's faith in the democratic institutions is at times shaken on account of large-scale political defections to attain personal power; wide-spread indiscipline in all sectors; inordinate delays and expensive administration of justice; steep poverty and slow economic development; rampant corruption; growing unemployment; communal and linguistic disturbances and power of money and appeal of caste and religion in election. The democratic experiment of over three decades has yet to stabilize though the people's faith in ballot is growing, as an instrument of change.

India is a land of contrasts. It is neither a developed nor a developing country. In fact, the country is in the process of transformation from age-old tradition to modernity.

Agriculture

About 70 per cent of the population is dependent on agriculture. Agriculture is in the main carried on by primitive and age-old method of cultivation, resulting in low level of productivity. However, a concerted effort is being made to apply modern techniques of cultivation so as to increase the yield.

The agricultural sector now contributes nearly one-half of the national income, provides livelihood to about three-fourths of the population, supplies the bulk of goods required by the non-agricultural sector and raw materials for different sections of industry. It also provides a substantial portion of the country's exports.

Better seeds, greater use of fertilizers and pesticides, more irrigation facilities, and application of modern techniques in cultivation have helped in the record production of foodgrains. All these developments are fast changing the face of rural India.

The PR activity by and large in India at present is urban biased. In view of the significant strides in the rural sector, it is necessary that PR effort has to be broadbased, covering the rural sector, particularly where development works are in progress. The rural people are potential buyers of many commodities and the PR campaign can succeed only if cognizance is taken of their requirements.

Industrial Sector

India is rich in natural resources and manpower. The resources have not, however, been exploited fully and are capable of greater utilization. In recent years, India has made phenomenal progress in the industrial sector. It has now a highly developed steel and heavy engineering industry, sophisticated petro-chemical complexes and refineries, and one of the largest railway networks in the world. In fact, India ranks seventh among the industrial nations of the world. There is a developed infrastructure of technical training institutions, scientific establishments, and laboratories. India has the third largest number of trained scientists in the world.

India has a free market economy. However, the government controls the strategic sectors of economy. According to the industrial policy of the government, some industries are the exclusive responsibility of the state, while some others are to be progressively State-owned. All industries of basic and strategic importance or in the nature of public utility services are in the public sector. Industries which are essential and require investment on a scale which only the state in the present situation could provide are also to be in the public sector. Private enterprise is expected to supplement the efforts of the state in this field. The future development of industries falling outside the two categories are in general left to private enterprise. The cooperative sector is also expanding.

Economic activity in India is divided into different sectors – government, public, private, and cooperative. PR activity has, therefore, to take into consideration the special problems in all these sectors and gear itself to cater to their specific and special requirements.

Socio-economic Changes

The spread of literacy, large-scale industrialization, inflow of modern technology, modernization of agriculture, contacts with the developed countries, influence of mass media network, etc. are having their impact on the social and cultural life of the people. There is a growing awareness among the woman-folk of their status and position in the society. Workers are increasingly becoming conscious of their rights. The joint family system is on its way out. Some of the old customs of *purdah* and arranged marriages are facing a challenge from the advocates of modernity. In brief, Indian society is in a ferment. A social and cultural upheaval has engulfed the country.

Because of the impact of science and technology, a tendency is growing among the people, particularly in the rural areas, not to accept blindly the customs, traditions, practices, and faiths. In the urban areas, social values and relationships are undergoing changes because of the stresses, strains, and tensions of city life.

Gaps between Demand and Supply

The public utility and social services – electricity and water supply, housing, medical, educational, and recreational facilities, and transport network – have considerably expanded since independence. However, they are nowhere near the requirements or expectations of the people. This is largely because of the increase in population, despite huge outlays on the family planning programme. The situation is further aggravated on account of the growing aspirations of the people. The gap between the demand and the availability of services is responsible for a good deal of dissatisfaction and frustration among the people.

Other factors that have added to the difficulties of Indian society are: staggering unemployment, particularly among the landless labour and the educated youth; widening disparity between the rich and the poor; and increase in communal, caste, and linguistic tensions among different sections of the people.

Politically, India has developed a sense of nationhood. Economically, the country comprises a single market. However, the democratic system has yet to stabilize. The country has still to achieve the desired economic development to raise the standard of living of the people. Also, India has yet to evolve a composite culture, bereft of linguistic, religious and cultural angularities.

Role of PR in India

A PR practitioner in India has to take into account these vast changes that are taking place in the country and the society. He has to remember that he is required to communicate with vast mass of people who cannot read and write, or who are living in almost inaccessible or remote or hilly areas, or with literate masses who have diverse cultural and ethnic backgrounds.

The PR man will be in an advantageous position if he is aware of the Indian scene as it exists today. This will help him grapple with his PR problems in a realistic manner. He can succeed in his work only if he has a modern and scientific mind, the will to work, the necessary flexibility, a missionary zeal, and the ability to adapt science and technology and new ideas and PR tools and techniques of the developed world to indigenous requirements and local conditions.

CHAPTER IV

PR for Government—Objectives and Organization

Communication with the citizens is necessary in any society and in any form of government. It is more so in a democracy where the government depends on popular backing. The citizens must be told of the governmental plans, programmes, policies, activities, successes, achievements, etc. so as to involve them and to get their willing participation in the governance of the country. Also, communication from the citizens – their reaction to the policies and programmes – must reach the policy-makers and administrators to enable them to modify or change the programmes accordingly. In the context of large-scale economic development in the industrial and agricultural sectors, the need for communication with the people through different media has assumed great importance.

National Objectives

The basic function of the government PR agencies is to provide information, education/instruction, and entertainment to the citizens. The effort should be also to motivate the people directly or indirectly. To discharge these functions in a meaningful and purposeful manner, it is necessary that the PR agencies are clear about their broad objectives which guide their work.

The national objectives should be non-political, non-controversial, and on which there should be a national consensus. The objectives should further the interests and the well-being of the people as a whole and promote the many-sided development of the country. The objectives should be long-term ones and need not necessarily change with political vagaries.

In a country of India's size and population, the diversity of religions, languages, regional imbalances, and several such other factors, it is not easy to evolve a national communication policy or information and public relations strategy acceptable to all. Nevertheless, such a policy is essential so as to give some direction to mass media effort. The country should also have the necessary infrastructure to implement the basic policy in the shortest possible time.

To discharge his functions in an efficient and purposeful manner, the PR communicator should have a clear idea of the basic ideals/values he has to promote. He should also know something about the available mass media infrastructure and the communication network.

Democracy and Development

The first and foremost objective of India's communication policy should be to preserve and strengthen the democratic way of life. PR communication effort should be directed to inculcate an abiding faith in the citizens in democratic institutions such as free and fair elections, the rule of law, independence of the judiciary, freedom of the press, secular character of the state, etc.

The PR man should also promote the understanding and involvement of the citizens in the socio-economic changes and developmental activities that are taking place in the country, so as to quicken the process of development. The point that needs to be emphasized is that development is possible in a democratic framework.

Other Themes

The PR communication should publicize the nationally-needed and the nationally-accepted themes that are basic to society. A few of these are: (i) planned development through the application of science and technology; (ii) national integrity and national unity, national cohesion, and common cultural heritage despite diversity in languages, regions, castes, and religions; (iii) family welfare and population control and stabilization of population at a level consistent with the requirements of national economy by reducing the present birth rate; (iv) use of improved methods of agricultural production – fertilizers, pesticides, modern implements, etc.; (v) spread of literacy through radio and TV; (vi) eradication of social evils such as consumption of liquor, dowry, etc.; (vii) citizens' need-oriented programmes – dissemination of useful information to the different sections of the citizens such as farmers, workers, artisans, students, and youth, information on housing, medical care and medical facilities, travel, prices of essential commodities, self-employment and employment opportunities, educational facilities, industrial relations; (viii) promotion of savings; and (ix) any other subject mentioned in the Directive Principles of the Constitution.

The government PR agencies also need to make a concerted effort to reach the poor and vulnerable sections of the community and the people living in remote and far-flung areas. This section of the people and the areas should be identified and disparity in communication facilities are to be minimized, if not ended. These sections and areas need information most and PR communication should satisfy this requirement.

The media available for PR communication in India are basically of two kinds: those which use modern means of communication, and those which are known as traditional media. In specific terms, the different media are: (i) Print – printed word, pictures, etc. which appeal to the sense of sight; (ii) Radio – sense of sound; (iii) Audio-visual – appeal to both visual and auditory senses – TV, films; (iv) Traditional media – puppetry, folk dance, folklore, community singing, rural theatre, etc.; (v) Oral communication – public meetings, group discussions, individual contacts, etc; (vi) Outdoor media – printed word and visual – posters, cinema slides, hoardings, neon signs, etc.

Organizational Set-up

The Ministry of Information and Broadcasting through its various media units keeps people all over the country informed of the governmental policies, plans, and programmes. The media also feed back information to the government about the people's reaction. They provide liaison with the State governments and other organizations working in the field of information and publicity. The ministry's mass communication set-up includes regional and branch offices as well as mobile units spread all over the country.

The media units under the I & B Ministry including the public sector undertakings and autonomous bodies aided by the ministry are : (1) All India Radio; (2) Doordarshan; (3) Press Information Bureau; (4) Films Division; (5) Directorate of Advertising and Visual Publicity; (6) Publication Division; (7) Song and Drama Division; (8) Research and Reference Division; (9) Directorate of Field Publicity; (10) Photo Division; (11) Registrar of Newspapers for India; (12) Central Board of Film Censors; (13) Directorate of Film Festivals; (14) National Film Archives of India; (15) Indian Institute of Mass Communication; (16) Film and Television Institute of India; (17) Children's Film Society; (18) National Film Development Corporation; and (19) Directorate of Evaluation.

The State governments and the Union Territories and the public sector undertakings including nationalized banks have their own departments/directorates of information and public relations/publicity. These departments undertake publicity of all types through different media and keep the State governments and the concerned organizations informed of the press and public reactions.

PIB

The Press Information Bureau (PIB) disseminates information about the policies and programmes of the Government of India through the medium of press. It also keeps the government informed of public reaction to these policies as reflected in the press. The PIB and its 30 regional and branch offices connected with a teleprinter network issue news, features, articles, backgrounders, etc. in English and Hindi and in 13 regional languages. The Bureau also coordinates publicity with the State governments and public sector undertakings and maintains a close liaison with the External Publicity Division of the Ministry of External Affairs. The 15-member Central Press Accredition Committee advises the Bureau on the accredition of press correspondents. The Bureau helps the correspondents with facilities such as housing, telephone, medical, travel, and customs clearance.

The PIB also runs Information Centres at New Delhi, Jullundur, Srinagar, Imphal, Aizawal, Kohima, and Port-Blair. It also publishes a single-sheet weekly wall newspaper *Hamara Desh* in English and Hindi and in ten regional languages, projecting the country's achievements and progress in various fields. The Bureau acts as a media coordinator in respect of national campaigns and highlights the governmental policies, programmes, and achievements laying stress on events and developments rather than on personalities.

The PIB's counterpart in the States are the State Government's public relations and information directorates. They keep close liaison with the local press and the representatives of newspapers at the State capitals.

External Publicity Division

The country's external publicity is handled by the External Publicity Division of the Ministry of External Affairs. The objective of this Division is to project the correct and objective image of the country abroad. The Division also seeks to promote understanding, sympathy, and support to India's external policy in foreign countries. Apart from press publicity, the Division undertakes audio-visual publicity including organization of exhibitions and cultural programmes. It produces small pamphlets specially for foreign readership and distributes other printed publicity material on various aspects of Indian developmental effort. It works in close cooperation with other ministries and departments of the Government of India, particularly the I & B Ministry.

Book Production/Promotion Organizations

The Government of India has set up some organizations to produce books at a low price and to foster book-mindedness in the country.

The National Book Development Board, set up in 1967, is the principal advisory body for the development of book industry and trade in the context of overall requirements of the country.

The Board, as reconstituted in 1970, has on it representatives of the different sectors of book industry – publishers, authors, printers, book-sellers, as well as of various governmental and non-governmental agencies.

The National Book Trust, set up in 1970, produces and encourages the production of good literature in different languages and makes it available at a low price. The Trust also subsidizes the publication of university-level books. It organizes book and periodical fairs and regional book exhibitions.

Books on the diverse aspects of national life, culture, and teachings of national leaders and 20 magazines are brought out by the Publication Division of the I & B Ministry. The Division also brings out the *Employment News* (weekly) in English, Hindi, and Urdu.

Books for children are published, among others, by the Children's Book Trust, the National Book Trust, the National Council of Educational Research and Training, and the Publication Division.

The Department of Tourism and several other government departments, the State governments, other organizations and private agencies bring out publications on a variety of subjects.

Under the Delivery of Books and Newspapers to Public Libraries Act, 1954, the copyright libraries are entitled to receive a copy of every new book and magazine in the country. There are four such libraries, namely, National Library, Calcutta; Central Library, Bombay; Connamera Library, Madras; and National Central Library, Delhi.

The *Indian National Bibliography*, published monthly with author, subject, and title index by the National Library, Calcutta, lists all publications published in India. It is an important source for the location of published literature in India.

The Sahitya Akademi, New Delhi, set up in 1954 for the development of Indian literature, translates and publishes literary works and popularizes the study of literature among the people. The Akademi also awards prizes to outstanding works in English and major Indian languages. An important publication of the Akademi is the *National Bibliography of Indian Literature*.

DAVP

The advertisements of all ministries and departments, excluding Railways, of the Government of India are released to the press by the Directorate of Advertising and Visual Publicity. The DAVP maintains a list of accredited or approved panel of advertising agencies. In the 33 years of its existence, it has grown into a government advertising agency with the widest multimedia coverage. Its activities are not confined to a single medium. It reaches a varied and diverse audience through the press, radio, films, photos, printed material, visual aids, and multi-dimensional representation of ideas.

The DAVP maintains a list of newspapers and journals. In selecting newspapers and periodicals for the release of advertisements, it keeps in view considerations such as: effective circulation (normally papers having a paid circulation of less than 1,000 are not used); regularity in publication (normally a period of six months of uninterrupted publication); class of readership; adherence to accepted standards of journalistic ethics; other factors such as production standard, the language and areas intended to be covered within the available funds for the advertisements; rates which are considered reasonable and acceptable for government publicity requirements.

However, the DAVP makes exception in the case of specialized journals, papers from backward and remote hilly areas, and newspapers published in Urdu and Sindhi. It gives special consideration to medium and small newspapers. There is a Rate Structure Committee, which determines the rates for advertisements released by the DAVP.

Classified advertisements released by the DAVP are for vacancies, tenders, etc. The display advertisements are for multi-media campaigns, to inform and educate the public on matters of immediate and long-term interest such as family welfare, small savings, agricultural production, cleanliness, prohibition, etc.

In the States, the directorates of public relations or information usually handle advertisements of the government departments. The public sector undertakings in most cases have their own public relations departments which release advertisements, both classified and display. There is an effective coordination between the DAVP and the State governments and the public sector undertakings in regard to the selection of media, rates for advertisements, placement. and other related matters, but there is no uniformity.

The outdoor publicity of the Government of India through panels, hoardings, posters, slides, display boards, etc. is handled by the DAVP, which has an art department to undertake visualization work. The DAVP also takes the help of specialized agencies in the field. The State directorates of public relations undertake such publicity on behalf of their governments.

Film Organizations

The Films Divison, set up in 1948, with headquarters at Bombay, records through the medium of newsreels and documentaries the contemporary history of India and the socio-economic progress of the country. Its main aim is to mobilize the film medium for providing audio-visual support in the dissemination of information to Indian and foreign audiences.

The Directorate of Film Festivals makes arrangements for national and international film festivals in India and participation of India in film festivals abroad.

The Film Finance Corporation, established in 1960, makes available finance for the production of films of good standard and for raising the general standard of films in the country.

The Children's Film Society, set up in May 1955, undertakes, sponsors, promotes, and coordinates production, distribution, and exhibition of films for children and adolescents. The Society functions with advice from educationists, writers, and film makers.

The Film and Television Institute of India, which became a Society in October 1974, receives grants-in-aid from the I & B Ministry. It imparts training in film making and television. Its activities can be grouped into two parts: (1) Film Wing – (a) film direction and screenplay writing, (b) motion picture photography, (c) sound recording and sound engineering, (d) film editing, and (e) film acting, and (2) Television Wing – training in production and technical operations in television.

Films are certified for exhibition by the Central Board of Film Censors. Set up under the Cinematograph Act of 1952, the Board consists of nine members and a Chairman, all of whom are appointed by the Government of India. The head-quarters of the Board is at Bombay, with regional offices at Bombay, Calcutta, and Madras. The regional offices are assisted in the examination of films by advisory panels, the members of which are appointed by the government and include educationists, lawyers, social workers, and others.

The government has set up a National Film Development Corporation to handle import and export, distribution, and exhibition of feature films, and allied functions. The export promotion of Indian feature films is handled by the Indian Motion Pictures' Export Corporation (IMPEC). The main objectives of the Corporation, inter alia, are: (a) to promote the export of Indian films, and (b) to serve as a corrective influence on such film trade activities as result in the loss of foreign exchange to the country.

Photo Division

The Government of India has an elaborate photo organization – the Photo Division, an independent unit under the I & B Ministry. It is the biggest production unit of its kind in the country. It meets the requirements of photographs of all media units of the ministry for internal and external publicity.

Apart from photographs for news and features, it undertakes photographic work for exhibition and printed publications. The Division has a large collection of photographs in black and white and also in colour. The collection includes photographs on development projects, industries, agriculture, places of tourist interest, etc.

Free lancers can obtain photographs from the Division at a nominal price. There is a photo library in the PIB where photographs are numbered and arranged subject-wise. The photographs and ebonoid blocks are released to the press by the PIB (Photo Unit) which is located near the Photo Division.

Most of the State directorates of public relation and information have their own photo section. They undertake news and feature assignments within the State and provide photographs for exhibition and publication. The public sector undertakings and large business houses have their own photo production units.

Song and Drama Division and Sangeet Natak Akademi

The Song and Drama Division under the Ministry of I & B with its 16 regional offices and through 41 departmental troupes and 400 private parties organizes programmes particularly in rural and border and forward areas to make the people aware of the social and economic ideals cherished by the nation. It runs an open air theatre 'Rabindra Rangshala' in New Delhi where popular feature films are screened at nominal rates. It also presents sound and light programmes with live action. The programmes are organized on occasions of national and regional importance, industrial exhibitions and agricultural fairs, religious festivals, etc.

The Sangeet Natak Akademi (National Academy of Music and Dance and Drama), set up in 1953, fosters development of dance, drama, and music. The Akademi has set up three national institutions – Kathak Kendra, New Delhi; Jawaharlal Nehru Manipuri Dance Akademi, Imphal; and the National School of Drama and Asian Theatre Institute, New Delhi – for imparting training in dance and drama. It also promotes puppet theatre in the country.

Field Publicity Directorate

The Field Publicity Directorate under the Ministry of I & B through its 221 field units and the field publicity units of the State Governments seek public support for national- and State-level campaigns. Mobile units equipped with vehicles, projectors, and generators operate in rural areas, particularly in remote border hill regions. The units conduct film shows, public meetings, seminars, song and drama performances, hari kathas, and qawalis and distribute publicity literature, in close liaison with the units of the Song and Drama Division and of the publicity departments of the State governments.

The objective is to mobilize people's involvement in the governmental plans and policies and their active support for campaigns for agricultural production, family welfare, prohibition, cleanliness, untouchability, national integration, etc. The units also feed back the government with people's reaction to the governmental policies and programmes.

Indian Institute of Mass Communication

The IIMC was set up in August 1965 as a centre for advanced study and research in mass communication. It has several faculties, viz. developmental communication; print medium; radio & TV; speech communication; visual communication; advertising and campaign planning; and traditional media and communication research.

The Institute is engaged in improving the professional knowledge, technical skills, and also the motivations of personnel working in newspapers, broadcasting and TV stations, information and publicity departments in the government, and in public sector organizations.

Apart from many special courses in specific subjects, the IIMC offers short-term courses for service officers of the Central Information Service, personnel of other ministries and State governments and the public sector organizations, banks, etc. It conducts an eight-month post-graduate diploma course in journalism and also in news agency journalism for developing countries.

The IIMC has a specialized library and documentation unit. It indexes and abstracts articles, maintains newspaper clippings, press releases, pamphlets, etc. and supplies bibliography on any aspect of mass communication. Its quarterly publication *Communicator* keeps the research workers abreast of the latest developments in the subject through research studies and papers. The Institute organizes seminars and symposia to focus attention on the problems of communication at national, regional, and local levels.

R & R Division/NDCMC

The Research and Reference Division under the Ministry of I & B., compiles *India – A Reference Annual*, and provides basic information material in the form of 'Background to the News' and 'Research Papers'. It also collects and disseminates information relating to mass communication studies and problems.

The Division has an excellent collection of books and periodicals on journalism. It indexes and abstracts selected newspapers and journals and maintains newspaper clippings. It provides reference information service, data compilation on mass communication, bibliography, and press clipping service.

The Division prepares a mass communication annual titled *Mass Media in India*. The annual provides basic information and statistics on different media of mass communication in the country. A *National Directory of Information Organizations* compiled by the Division provides information on the media organizations of the Central and State governments.

The National Documentation Centre on Mass Communication, set up in the Division, prepares bibliographies and other services such as bi-monthly service *Media Memory*, an archive of information regarding developments in various media of mass communication. The centre also supplies photo copies of reference material. The NDCMC is expected to become, in course of time, the nerve centre of all research on mass communication and allied subjects in the country.

RNI

The Registrar of Newspapers for India, prepares an annual report on the press in two volumes which is presented to parliament. The Registrar also allots newsprint and recommends import of printing machinery for newspapers. The Registrar clears newspaper titles, gives registration numbers, and carries out circulation checks. He also receives from every publisher in the country an annual statement in respect of each newspaper.

The two important media – All India Radio and Doordarshan – have been dealt with in separate chapters.

CHAPTER V

The Government and the Press

The government is the biggest source of news. In the absence of regular flow of governmental information, the press just cannot discharge its responsibility to inform and educate the citizens or mould public opinion. Similarly, no government, much less a democratic government, can do without the press. Therefore, there has to be a good working relationship between the two.

Relationship in Democratic Set-up

The relationship between the government and the press is a fairly simple one in single-party states. There the press and the other media are the instruments of the ruling party, which is also the government. They tell the citizens what the government directs.

In countries with a democratic system, the concept of the press reporting directly to the people, performing an independent public function, is apt to come into conflict with formal political institutions. In democratic countries – or in pluralist societies such as India – the relationship between individual newspapers and parties and politicians is far more complex.

The relationship in India between the democratic government and the media, particularly the newspapers, has yet another dimension. Although newspapers have only a limited reach, the impact of the press is far more than the circulation statistics suggest. In view of the powerful influence the press excercises on the minds of the people, all democratic governments are deeply interested in getting into newspaper columns.

For a proper development of mass media in India, the correct relationship between the government and the press is of crucial importance. The real question, however, is, should the government have any policy at all on press medium except that it does everything to strengthen the press freedom and to provide the necessary facilities for the coverage of governmental activities?

In India, the relations of the press with the three branches of the government have been rather nebulous. During the freedom struggle, the press functioned as the advance guard of the nationalist forces. When the nation became sovereign, a sense of mutual trust and regard continued between the legislature and the press. Rajagopalachari's Press Bill came as a shock to journalists. But confrontation between the press and the government was avoided mainly because of the enlightened and liberal outlook of Jawaharlal Nehru and his colleagues.

In the wake of the Emergency in June 1975 the freedom of the press was restricted. In March 1977, the censorship practised during the Emergency was abolished; the Publication of Objectionable Matter Act was repealed; to ensure a faithful publication of parliamentary proceedings, the Feroze Gandhi Act was re-enacted; Samachar was dismantled; the Press Council was revived with powers to consider complaints even against the Central and the State governments; the Press Commission was appointed to go into all aspects of the press and a new advertising policy was laid down. The freedom to publish the proceedings of parliament and State legislatures is now guaranteed under the Forty-fourth Constitutional (Amendment) Act.

Governmental Interference

Despite this, governmental interference is alleged in the working of newspapers and news agencies. It is pointed out in some quarters that the PIB is a hindrance to the press in having free access to official sources of information. The press should have freedom to get information directly from the concerned government personnel and not through government information wings. The Government of India's policy to control the sources of information through the PIB is considered violative of the freedom of the press.

The DAVP and the State directorates of public relations, it is argued, should not have the right to fix government advertisement rates. Each department may be left free to negotiate with the advertising media in regard to quantum, rates for advertisements, etc.

The monopoly of the State Trading Corporation in regard to import of newsprint and newspaper printing machinery also comes in the way of freedom of the press, according to some leaders of the newspaper industry.

It is alleged that the government media men try to influence the newspapers in regard to publication of articles, news stories, etc.; they interfere in the working of the news agencies by asking them to withdraw a particular story which may not be palatable to a particular department; they exert pressure on editors in regard to transfer of inconvenient correspondents; in some cases, proprietors are threatened if newspaper organizations try to resist the pressure of the government.

The press freedom in India has recently led to a big outburst of journals dedicated only to mud-slinging and titillation. The yellow clouds which mushroom over the Indian press are a matter of concern to the government and the society. This aspect also affects the relations between the government and the press.

The important question, therefore, is what more need to be done to strengthen the freedom of the press. A calm and dispassionate consideration of the subject to pinpoint areas, if any, where governmental interference in the working of the press still exists is necessary so as to take measures to safeguard the freedom of the press.

The Role of the PIB

Let us examine in concrete terms whether the existing government institutions in India dealing with the press media interfere with the freedom of the press. Is the PIB necessary? Similar questions can be asked in respect of information and public relations departments of State governments.

The PIB is a two-way pipeline for the dissemination of information to the media and through them to the public, as also for providing the government with a feedback on what the newspapers are saying about governmental policies. To the extent the newspapers reflect public opinion, the PIB's feedback service can also be regarded as a mirror of public opinion. In this respect, the PIB is different from other media units and has to assume additional responsibilities and has to be treated with greater confidence.

There are principally two kinds of users of PIB material: (a) the accredited correspondents in New Delhi and the newspapers and the news agencies they represent, and (b) the large number of small and medium newspapers published in different languages from different centres. As far as the latter are concerned, the PIB's effort is limited to providing them with day-today press releases and background material put out from time to time in different languages as promptly as possible. In addition, whenever the correspondents and the editors of these publications visit Delhi, the PIB arranges briefings and meetings for them with ministers and senior personnel. The PIB also organizes conducted tours of journalists from the regions to developmental projects.

The basic question to be answered is whether the PIB, as it is now constituted, acts as an institutional impediment to the flow of information from the government to the print media. It can, no doubt, be improved and made more effective to ensure better flow of information, but, will its abolition yield the desired results?

The idea of the PIB is to ensure that the ministries and the departments of the government have professionally trained and full-time information officers so that they can (1) advice the government on the manner and the content of dissemination of government information; (2) provide press representatives with information sought from the government; (3) clarify doubts and also enable the accredited correspondents to have access to senior personnel who can brief them; and (4) provide the government with the feedback of the reporting and comments by the press so that (a) any criticism or misreporting on account of inadequate supply of information can be remedied by giving out that information either generally or to particular correspondents and (b) the government knows the public reaction in respect of governmental policies, programmes, and performance.

Any set-up that replaces the PIB will have to perform all these functions. One of the ideas often suggested is that the ministries/departments could have their own public relations officers without the PIB acting as a coordinating agency. It is alleged that the PIB is an instrument of news management and so it should be disbanded. News management in ordinary times, on the face of it, is impossible. On the other hand, a PRO attached to a ministry/department will be in a better position to withhold information or colour it because the individual ministries will then be accountable to the actions of the PROs. Under the present arrangement, the slightest lapse by the PIB officer is brought to the notice of the Principal Information Officer and the Ministry of I &B. It is directly linked to the concept of freedom of the press which is the responsibility of the I & B Ministry to uphold.

More importantly, the small and medium newspapers which have only one correspondent at the headquarters and those which cannot afford to have a correspondent at the headquarters will be disadvantaged functionally if the PIB is not there. The PROs can keep them at their mercy and acquire a clout which the PIB officers do not have. A close examination of the difference in the functioning of the PROs attached to industrial undertakings, both private and public, and the PIB officers reinforces this point.

The advantages of the PIB set-up in respect of simultaneous distribution of material in different parts of the country through its network of regional and branch offices and arrangements for translation of the material into regional languages are obvious.

While from the academic point of view, a centralized arrangement may be distasteful, in practice, it is of immense advantage to correspondents engaged in the work of collecting information and projecting it in their own way.

It is also not correct that the PIB officers attached to different ministries/departments prevent correspondents and others with contacts to meet ministers and senior personnel on their own. In fact, in many cases correspondents meet especially the ministers by themselves, sometimes even without the knowledge of the PIB officers. Similarly, in the case of secretaries, while some may go by the advice of the PIB officer, others readily meet correspondents provided they know them and they have the time for meeting the correspondents. As far as the PIB officer is concerned, it is his constant endeavour to ensure in-depth briefings (sometimes off the record) by senior officials for correspondents specializing in their respective subjects. The PIB is, therefore, not an impediment to correspondents in this aspect.

In the absence of the PIB, should various departments of the government of India be left free to organize their own press publicity? Should the press have free access to government personnel at all levels? Is it feasible for the government officials of different categories to disseminate information to the press correspondents? Will it not mean 'free for all' and result in information chaos? In a situation of this kind, can there be any coordination of information even within a department? Will this arrangement be convenient to the press itself? Will the press make similar demands from the private sector organizations? Will this arrangement be a practical proposition?

Other Government Media Organizations

It is also a moot point whether it is advantageous to canalize government advertisements through a centralized agency such as the DAVP. Should the government departments be left free to release advertisements of their own without any uniformity in rules? The public sector undertakings where one hundred per cent government money is involved are free to decide their advertisement media, the quantum, the rates for advertisements, etc. Has this freedom been utilized for public good? Should this freedom be extended to government departments? Any decision to dispense with the DAVP or similar organizations at the State level should await examination by an expert and impartial body. Again, it is doubtful whether a step such as this would be in the interest of medium and small newspapers, particularly those published in regional languages.

Newsprint and newspaper printing machinery are largely imported items. Big newspapers may have the capability and expertise to import but other papers may find it difficult. Also, the present happy foreign exchange position may not remain forever. The question has to be viewed on a long-term basis. Some form of regulation by the government may be necessary. If scarce newsprint is distributed among the newspapers by the government on some rational formulae, can this be considered an act of interference with the freedom of the press?

The government's responsibility to ensure the free functioning of the press is clear. But no amount of constitutional and legal safeguards can guarantee the freedom of the press. In the ultimate analysis, it depends on the calibre, the stature, and the character of the media men themselves. Healthy conventions, code of ethics, or guidelines can be evolved to mutual advantage. It is nobody's case that all is well with the government media. There is considerable room for improvement. Constructive and practical suggestions can go a long way in developing a healthy relationship between the government and the media.

Confrontation or Cooperation?

What should be the nature of this relationship? It cannot be that of an 'adversary' or an 'unquestioning ally' in all circumstances and in all situations. The press in a democracy has to be a watch-dog, a vigilant watch-dog. To perform this function, the press has to have contacts with the government's sources of information.

If the relationship is necessary and in public interest, where is the question of the 'touch-me-not' attitude on the part of the newspapers or the government media men? It is as much the duty of the government media men to suggest to the press certain articles, items, stories, etc. for possible use, of course without coercion, threat, or inducement, as it is the right of the editor to throw it in the dustbin. In this game, there is no question of violating the freedom of the press. There is no conflict.

A continuous dialogue is necessary between the government and the press at different levels so as to ensure a better appreciation of each other's point of view. While the government should not be unnecessarily touchy about press criticism, the press also should not smell foul in all governmental actions. If there is any misunderstanding or difference of opinion, it should be resolved, but this is possible only if the government comes out with more and more and timely information and establish not only rapport but also its credentials with the press. The press, on the other hand, must eschew character assassination, yellow journalism, and cheap sensationalism.

Just as the government has a clear responsibility not to do anything directly or indirectly to interfere with the functioning and the freedom of the press, the press too has, in a democratic country, certain obligations. For instance, it is in its own interest if the press does everything to strengthen the democratic way of life. Similarly, it has to play its role in the economic development of the country by disseminating technological and scientific information relevant to agriculture and industry to the people. It can also make significant contribution towards eradication of social evils.

Any confrontation between the government and the press is not in the national interest. The role of the press in a nascent developing country such as India should be that of friend, critic, and guide, always keeping in view the larger public interest – accelerating the development of the country by the removal of economic and social backwardness, strengthening of democratic institutions, communal harmony, adult education, planned development of population, etc. These are non-political, non-controversial subjects but are vital to our national life. These basic ideals can be pursued by the press irrespective of the change in the government at the political level.

Threats to the Freedom of the Press

The freedom of the press cannot be safeguarded by only constitutional provisions nor the threat to it is only from the government. Constitutions are not self-enforcing. Legislatures, executives, and courts must be assiduous in safeguarding the principles a nation cherishes. So should the non-formal political institutions, such as the press. Freedom is not given, it is taken. Freedom of the press depends on the courage and the persistence with which the press asserts that freedom, not by the benevolence of the legislatures and the executives. The courts, too, may not be able to always side with the press.

Another aspect of the freedom of the press is that threats to freedom of expression do not arise only from the government. Any fanatical group of people who resent criticism are a threat to the press – be they followers of a particular religion, ideology, caste, or economic interest or be they plain rowdies.

The freedom of the press is also threatened by proprietors and editors. Not all newspaper publishers are in the publishing business only for profit. Many of them are avowedly a part of the power game – throwing their weight behind particular parties, policies, or politicians out of either conviction or convenience. There are very few parties and politicians that do not seek or welcome the support of newspapers.

To some, the freedom of the press is the freedom of the editor. This proposition is largely a myth. In several cases, the proprietors of the newspapers have a major say in regard to the policy of the paper and in some cases also about the inclusion of material. The directives from the management to the editorial staff and others may be direct or indirect depending on their relationship.

What is true of owners is also true of editors. Editors rarely are saints who are unelated by success and undepressed by defeat. They relish the role of advisers to those in power. They too play the power game. Alliances between newspapers and politicians are common. But it is also true that seldom are they long-lasting.

The present idea of the press being an adversary of the government has a long history. The executive has always resented the claim of the press that it is a watchdog, reporting directly to the public. In actual fact, proprietors and editors have often wished to share power and have been adversaries to some politicians in office rather than to government as a whole.

The freedom of expression is also affected by dominant economic and financial interests. A great deal of honest expression of opinion is today inhibited by the fear that the owner and the circulation manager, not to speak of the advertisement executive, will not like it. Even those editors who courageously oppose the government and political authority turn timid when matters of religious and linguistic jingoism are involved. They are afraid of groups of political activists raiding their offices. The freedom of press, is therefore a complex phenomenon and not a simple proposition as many trend to think.

CHAPTER VI

Perspective for Government PR

Integrated Thinking

A public relations officer attached to a ministry/department of the government will not be able to discharge his functions adequately and properly if he does not know the problems of the government in its entirety. It is necessary for him to have an integrated thinking and approach. He must have a clear concept of the country's socio-economic development, economic plans, and an overall view of the different sectors, their long- and short-term perspective. For instance, in the railways the PR man must have a clear idea of the different sectors of economy, the role of other modes of transport, the movement of essential items such as foodgrains, coal, fertilizers, petroleum products, priority in investment, and other relevant aspects.

PR Approach

The PR man has to develop a technique to get over the reluctance of the policy planners and administrators to part with information. Many of the latter are either tradition-bound or afraid or shy or too busy to spare time for PR aspects. It is the duty and the responsibility of the PR man to get information and, where advisable, disseminate it to the media. He must also know when to withhold a particular piece of information. The extent, manner, timings, style, etc. are important aspects on which he has to take clear decisions, while dishing out information.

In some cases, the PR man has also to guard against the VIP publicity – own photograph, own speech, and own story. He has to impress the VIP that in a democratic society with a free press it is not possible to mount any personality-oriented publicity campaign by feeding the media with personal achievement stories. He has also to avoid the tendency of issuing long hand-outs, particularly when they relate to personal achievements or speeches of the VIPs. It is not the kind of food that the media will take. The media have the option to throw the stuff in the dustbin. In any case, such food cannot be swallowed by the media day after day. The long releases in other cases also are a waste of effort. The PR man should write virtually what the correspondent would write, just that much and no more.

The PR man in government will not be successful unless he works as a professional journalist. He has to accept the ethics and rules of the game of the profession of a journalist. If he wants success in his work, he has perhaps to make a nuisance of himself to get a story to feed the press and other media. At times, he has to cajole, bully the minister or the secretary to get information. If he decides to wait to be invited for information, he will be a dismal failure.

Another point to remember is that no newspaper is going to take PR material if it is dished out late in the evening. It is a better strategy to hold over the hand-out for the next day, if it can wait. If it has to go, then the story should be pruned to contain only operative paragraphs. The PR man should clearly distinguish between the story, the full text, and a backgrounder for the purpose of release.

Press Contacts

Another effective way of projection is through press briefings. Nothing is more welcome to a press correspondent than an exclusive story, which will be his own story. The PR man can certainly help, and in certain cases also write for him. The giving of information on exclusive basis is a delicate work. It is a skilful game. With moderation, with restraint, and within control, this is a game worthwhile for any PR man to play provided he does it on the basis of non-discrimination and non-patronage to any correspondent/class of correspondents.

Another aspect on which the PR should lay stress is in regard to frequent meetings with correspondents, editors, senior column writers, commentators, sub-editors, assistant editors, etc. Such meetings can be extremely rewarding. It provides an opportunity for the PR to read their minds, their thinking on important subjects. The PRO can also brief them on some aspects. It also helps in establishing rapport with the press. The PRO can develop a relationship where the news and editorial staff not only check up critical stories but at times project also the government point of view along with their stories.

There is a tendency on the part of the ministers and the administrators to ask the PR man to issue denials for distortions, untruths, gossips, scandals, inaccuracies, etc. In these matters, the government and the PR man should develop a thick skin. It is not only futile but counter-productive to chase every little untruth, every little distortion, or every little scandal that somebody has written. A newspaper may be indulging in such writings deliberately, as a matter of policy. There are also yellow journals which print this kind of news. In some cases, the denial gives such stories a wider circulation. The denials should be resorted to only in exceptional cases.

The feedback to the government is yet another important function of the PR. The feedback is in regard to what is written in news and editorial columns, comments, etc. Adequate, timely, and almost a running feedback of what is being written and what has been said about a certain policy/decision of the government is very important.

The PR man has to create an atmosphere in which press people are automatically attracted to him as a source of information, rather he has to always seek them out or invite them. He should not work on the wave length of a civil servant. The regulated and uncommunicative approach, use of administrative jargons, bureaucratic reaction to the problems, etc. are fatal to PR work.

Publicity for Government and not for Parties

Another important thing to remember is that the PR man in the government should give publicity to the government and not to individuals as such, unless the activities of the individual concerned are connected with the discharge of his official duties as minister or senior officer of the government.

Public relations personnel in the government should not offer any publicity services to any political party or its leaders and office-bearers unless the activities to be publicised are directly connected with their duties as ministers in the government. The distinction between the party and the government has to be recognized in the PR work.

Channel of Communication

In the context of the enormous increase in governmental activities through developmental, socio-economic, and welfare schemes, the need for giving adequate and timely publicity to the policies and achievements of the government assumes special importance.

All news about the Government of India is generally communicated to the press through the information or PR man. The PR man is normally also the channel of communication to other news media such as radio, television, etc.

In all ministries, no one except the minister in charge and the secretary should give any information to, or be accessible to, the press representatives, i.e. correspondents accredited to the government of India. The minister may, in special cases, authorize an additional secretary or joint secretary, or another officer to give information to the press representatives on any particular subject. But there is no general authorization. Any other official, if approached by the press representative, directs the latter to the information officer.

It is the function of the information officer to give publicity to the policy and programmes of the ministry to which he is attached and to keep the ministry informed of the reactions of the public thereto as reflected in the press. In order to discharge his functions effectively, the information officer should get all facilities in keeping with his functional responsibilities.

Since the information officer is the ministry's official spokesman to the press, he should have access to all sources of information and be briefed by senior officials from time to time. On his part, the information officer will not release to the press any information without obtaining clearance from the appropriate quarter. At interviews with accredited press correspondents, the information officer is normally present.

The information/public relations officers have thus an active and important role to play in projecting the image of the government through the media. For obtaining better publicity results, it is essential that he should be fully conversant and be associated with all that is happening in the ministry/department to which he is attached. This enables him to draft his releases with a better grip and knowledge of the subject and further satisfy the queries that keep on flowing from the press correspondents for elaboration, clarification, and for more detailed information. In other words, the closer the association, the more effective will be his service.

The information officer should attend all internal meetings dealing with policy decisions, progress reports, reviews of past performance, and future planning and projections. Similarly, he should attend as many meetings, discussions, etc. as possible connected with the work of the ministry/department. He should also receive on a priority basis all the background and agenda papers for all meetings as well as the minutes/proceedings of the meetings and statements of follow-up action taken, the replies to all parliamentary questions, and also the note for supplementaries, the background papers, reports, etc. prepared in reply to a specific questionnaire, etc. of the Estimates Committee/Committee on Public Undertakings in connection with their studies.

Modes of Dissemination of Information

The form in which information is to be released to the press is to be decided by the information officer, that is, whether it is to be a press note, an official hand-out, an unofficial release, or in any other suitable form. A press communique is issued only to announce appointments of high dignitaries or joint statements with foreign governments. The press release is drafted by the information officer from the material placed at his disposal by the ministry.

When any official report, resolution, notification, etc. comes up for publication, the information officer should decide well in advance about the date and the time of its publication. This will enable him also to prepare the press release explaining the salient features of the publication.

A public notice or any other matter which should appropriately issue in the form of an advertisement is not issued as a press release. Material of this kind is advertised through the Directorate of Advertising and Visual Publicity. However, in suitable cases, there is no objection to a press note or a press release being issued in addition to the advertisement to explain the subject.

If the information received from the ministry is found to be in conflict with that already released or about to be released by another ministry, the information officer holds back the release of such information to the press and immediately consults the ministry concerned in order to reconcile the conflict. Publicity given to the material is decided on the basis of these consultations.

Communication with the press may also take the form of a press conference or a press briefing. Such press conferences or press briefings are generally held to:

(a) explain to accredited correspondents and selected editors the scope and purpose of an important report or an official statement, etc. which is likely to be of widespread public interest; or
(b) give the press a general review of the policies and activities of government; or
(c) explain to the press any specific important development.

Press conferences may be held by the minister only, or under his direction, by the secretary. Press briefings may, however, be held by other senior officials, specifically authorized in this behalf. Information given at such briefings is attributed to an 'official spokesman' or 'official source' but not to anybody by name.

Whenever it is proposed to hold a press conference, the information officer should decide in advance about the date and the time of the conference. He also makes suggestions for holding a press conference or a press briefing when, in his opinion, this would help to put forward the government's point of view and clarify details of policies. He obtains material to prepare a handout for distribution at the press conference.

The PR man in government has thus three basic functions – to disseminate information and to project the image; the official spokesman; and the public reaction evaluator.

PR Problems in Government

PR in the government has a serious problem to overcome in the case of the Delhi-based journalists, especially those connected with metropolitan newspapers. They want exclusive 'stories' and are loath to publish hand-outs. Where the press releases concern a policy pronouncement or an important announcement, there can be no exclusiveness. They go in for 'inside stories' often based on incomplete information and sometimes even distortions. With free access of correspondents to officials at different levels, there is practically no limit to such reports. Sometimes it becomes physically impossible for the PR man to chase such reports and issue denials. In most cases, the tendency of officials is to advise against joining issue with publishers of such reports, because they may contain a grain of truth which is regarded damaging. Secondly, denying a report does not always amount to undoing the damage done by the publication. So the PR man should be discreet in issuing denials.

The best PR antidote to incorrect and sensational reporting is more and more information. There is plenty of it which is not of a classified nature, and which can be given to the media. The PR man should not reduce himself to a mere producer of press releases. His position as the original source of information to correspondents should never be eroded, otherwise, he will lose credibility and leverage with the press.

It is, therefore, necessary that the PR man should be fully in the know of all matters of importance concerning the ministries/departments he or she is connected with. While this has been accepted in principle and put down in circulars, the practice leaves much to be desired. There is a need for a well-defined procedure for providing such information. In this respect, he should be treated as a member of the inner circle in the concerned ministry and not merely as a recipient of information which officials decide should be made available to him. Of course, he has also to exert and 'make a nuisance of himself'. It is necessary to institutionalize the flow of information from the ministry to the PR man. It is not necessary that all information should be put out through formal press releases or put out at all. Once in the know of things, the PR man can release it selectively and build up leverage vis-a-vis correspondents.

In the case of economic ministries, there is an absolute need for the projection of government policies as an integrated package with linkage affecting different ministries and departments. Whenever a policy decision of an economic nature is made, such studies should be made available to the PR man, so that individual officers do not issue material concerning their ministries and departments in piecemeal.

CHAPTER VII

Projection of the Public Sector

In the case of the public sector in India, the PR man will not be able to conduct a purposeful campaign unless he is aware of the (i) magnitude of operations of the public sector as a whole; (ii) the concept, the culture, and the philosophy of the public sector in our economy and in democratic framework; and (iii) the inherent difficulties of PR work in the public sector in the context of the coexistence, competition, and hostility of the private sector.

The government's industrial policy has been first laid down in the Industrial Policy Resolution of 1948, and further clarified in the Industrial Policy Resolution of 1956. The PR man in the public sector undertakings should know from these sources the basic philosophy of the government's industrial policy.

Enormity of Operations

The public sector in India has grown in size, depth, and extent since independence. It has emerged as a major factor in the country's economic growth. In a wider context, the public sector in India comprises public utilities such as railways, road transport services, ports, posts and telegraphs, power and irrigation projects, and departmental undertakings such as Chittaranjan Loco Works, Diesel Loco Works, Integral Coach Factory, and various defence production establishments.

The Central public sector undertakings as commonly understood are, however, statutory corporations and companies with 51 per cent or more of Central government share-holdings. There are 164 such undertakings under the various ministries of the Government of India.

These enterprises can be divided into two broad categories,

namely, (1) those producing goods such as steel, minerals and metals including coal, petroleum, chemicals, and pharmaceuticals, heavy, medium, and light engineering, transport equipment, consumer goods, and agro-based products, and (2) those rendering such services as trading and marketing, transportation, contract and construction, industrial development, technical consultancy, small industries, and tourist and financial services.

The total investment, turnover, gross profit, generation of internal resources and foreign exchange earnings of the 142 running undertakings amounted in 1977-78 to Rs.12,851 crores, Rs.17,556 crores, Rs.947 crores, Rs.731 crores, and Rs.1,561.85 crores respectively.

The total number of employees was 16.38 lakhs with a wage bill of Rs.1,645.51 crores. The annual expenditure on social benefits and housing amounted to Rs.112 crores.

The public sector employs two-thirds of the workers in the organized sector. The share of the public sector in the total profits and dividends in the economy was 32 per cent in 1975-76. The public sector accounted for 37 per cent of the capital stock, i.e. reproducible tangible wealth.

As on 31 March 1978, the Bokaro Steel Ltd. topped all public enterprises in terms of investment (Rs.1,436 crores) followed by the Fertilizer Corporation of India (Rs.1,299 crores) and Hindustan Steel Ltd. (Rs.1,212 crores). In turnover, however, the first three enterprises are: Indian Oil Corporation (Rs. 3,006.98 crores), Food Corporation of India (Rs.2,848.74 crores), and Hindustan Steel Ltd. (Rs.1,188.41 crores). In respect of profits, Indian Oil Corporation tops the list (Rs.100.24 crores) followed by ONGC (Rs.58.72 crores) and Bharat Heavy Electricals Ltd. (Rs.54.52 crores). The Eastern Coalfields Ltd. has the largest number of employees (1.87 lakhs), followed by Bharat Coking Coal (1.70 lakhs) and Hindustan Steel Ltd. (1.30 lakhs). The IOC also tops in terms of payment of tax (Rs.51 crores), followed by Bharat Heavy Electricals (Rs.29 crores) and Mineral & Metal Trading Corporation (Rs.28.19 crores).

Among the top giant industrial units in the country in terms of annual sales, the first seven are the public sector enterprises of the Central government. The IOC ranks first with the sale of Rs.3,000 crores, followed by SAIL with Rs.1,271 crores, whereas the topmost unit in the private sector, namely TISCO, has an annual sales income of only Rs.363 crores.

Special Features of the Public Sector

Some people pose the question of public vs. private sector. In reality, they complement each other. However, in actual practice, the public sector has to operate under special circumstances.

1. The public sector exists not to earn profit as such, but to meet a social need, the fulfilment of which requires it, inter alia, to earn profit.
2. The public sector has to compete with the private sector on equal terms (no special price of purchase preference is shown to the public sector).
3. The public sector belongs to the people and is financed by the involuntary savings of the people, including the poorest sections thereof, who pay indirect, if not direct, taxes. Therefore unlike the private sector, where the share-holders alone are financially interested in the undertaking, the public sector has to be responsive to the financial interests of the public at large.
4. The performance of the public sector creates greater interest than that of the private sector, e.g. failure of a furnace in a public sector is news, while a similar happening in a private steel plant goes unnoticed. The public sector has to be responsive to the public opinion, while the private sector need worry only of the share-holders.
5. Powerful propaganda media at the command of the private sector are turned on to create doubts about the efficiency, integrity, and the basic justification or the existence of the public sector (e.g. lack of expertise in management, corruption, etc. are criticized in the public sector, while 'sickness', corruption, etc. in the private sector are ignored).
6. Motivated criticism is directed to prove the unsuitability of the public sector as an instrument of development. An image of corruption, of inefficiency, and of intolerable burden on the resources of poor tax-payers is projected to discredit the public sector.
7. Some losses are endemic in the very nature of the public

sector, e.g. public utility services, production of items of strategic importance, etc. The public sector is concerned with basic industries such as steel and coal involving huge investments, long gestation period, initial losses, and lesser return to the capital.

8. The public sector offers maximum employment and looks after the employees well. This is reflected in subsidized education, canteen, electricity, water, and other welfare services.
9. In the selection of sites, the need for removing regional and economic imbalances is an important factor. It overlooks to some extent technical feasibility for setting up an industry in a particular region.
10. The public sector takes over 'sick industries'. This is yet another drag on its performance.
11. If the public sector has to discharge its public obligation and social good, it cannot run on purely commercial lines. These obligations, however, should not be left vague. They should be spelt out in writing and limits laid down. If an enterprise is asked to undertake obligations which are not usually discharged by the private commercial organizations, they should be accounted for separately. Some of these are: employment of more staff than what is absolutely necessary, inconvenient locations of the projects for political and other reasons, non-introduction of labour-saving devices, concessions to certain categories at government directives, etc.
12. The public sector, unlike the private sector, is always in the public gaze. Its policies, operations, recruitment, pricing, quality of products, profitability, etc. are under constant public scrutiny. The public sector, because of its ownership, is accountable also to parliament. People are concerned with the functioning of the public sector. PR is also therefore necessary with members of parliament. The developing of cordial relations with MPs is a specialized PR activity in the public undertakings.
13. Public sector employs a very large work force. A positive PR approach is therefore needed to deal with a large number of people. The PR man is required to create a feeling of identity and of common purpose among the workers.

Greater sharing of information in a participative manner with the workers is necessary to establish cordial relations. With proper PR, the management decisions such as new work methods, redeployment of workmen, etc. can be implemented without confrontation with the workers.

14. Consumer protection group movement may also grow in India. In the future the consumer may also seek a status on par with the trade unions.
15. Operations in foreign markets has exposed the public sector to competition and conflict with the established multi-national organizations.

PR in Public Sector

The public relations in the public sector has, therefore, to take into consideration the above special features associated with it. The public sector PR effort has to be directed to remove the distortions of one-sided publicity that prevails at present. This task needs to be performed by public undertakings collectively and not by any undertaking singly and in isolation. The government has also a responsibility in this matter as it has to answer criticism in the parliament.

The point the PR man needs to stress is that the public and the private sectors are complementary to each other. Both are engaged in the common task of country's economic development. However, the public relations in the public sector cannot overlook the fact that there is a conflict between the two sectors. They compete for scarce resources – capital, foreign exchange, skilled manpower, etc. The PR man in the public sector, however, should not run down the private sector but should explain and highlight the pioneering work assigned to the public sector. He should not join issue with the private sector in mutual mud-slinging.

In view of the nature of public relations task in the public sector, it is necessary to have dedicated and talented professionals fully committed to the philosophy of the public sector. They should not only be well versed in publicity techniques but should have a clear grasp of the basic objectives for which the public sector was created, its concept, philosophy, and culture.

Public relations is an essential adjunct to the public sector. The PR effort should not be used for non-productive purposes. The PR man should be associated with the decision-making processes in the enterprise. He should be deeply involved in its affairs. Only then will he be able to provide a bridge of understanding between the enterprise and the public.

The public sector units should have professional PR set-ups. The PR set-up should not be saddled with non-PR jobs. The PR chief should have direct access to the primary sources of information in the organization. He should attend all meetings where policy decisions are made. The PR department should be adequately staffed and functional facilities such as transport, telephone, entertainment expenses be provided.

PR in the public sector should be directly under the chief executive and not under any other functionary – personnel or sales manager or company executive. Also, public relations should not be burdened with the functions which do not require professional training, education, or skill. Jobs, such as arranging parties, looking after guests, attending to rail or air reservations, receiving and seeing off VIPs and other *bandobast* duties, should be avoided so that the PR is not downgraded.

Apart from projecting individual public sector organization, the PR effort should be to stress that without the public sector, India would not today be among the front rankers in the world in industry or technology. Be it nuclear or space technology, heavy engineering, aeronautics, ship-building, steel, energy, machine tools or such essential consumer goods as pharmaceuticals, textiles or bread—the contribution of the public sector to national development has been tremendous.

Also, the Indian public sector has been able to compete with the best in the international market to secure prestigious contracts. Again, the public sector has stepped in where the private sector has sought to escape from its social responsibilities. For instance, the public sector has taken over textile mills and engineering units which had been declared not only 'sick' but 'dead', and these abandoned units have now started generating profits.

A charge repeated ad nauseam against the public sector is that it is losing money. In any case, it is not making adequate profits. PR in public sector should bring out that it is misnomer that the private sector is doing nothing but earning profits. Hundreds of crores of rupees have been sunk in the sick private units by nationalized banks and other financial institutions. The low return on capital employed in public sector is a reflection of the fact that a large part of public sector investment is in steel and coal where pricing has been deliberately such as to reduce the rate of profits. This aspect can be properly explained through PR.

It is easy to criticize the functioning of the public sector because it is always completely open to public gaze. It is also subject to controls of various types—control by Government, accountability to Parliament, and above all, its responsibility to the people. On the other hand, the private sector companies often get away with all kinds of malpractices which do not come to light. Also, most newspapers are a part of big industry, and where they are not, they depend upon big industry for patronage. All these factors make the public sector more vulnerable to criticism, particularly by the press. The PR has to take into account these aspects in planning any campaign.

Apart from socializing the means of production in strategic areas, the public sector provides a countervailing power to the growth of large houses and large enterprises in the private sector. It is not only the producer of important strategic goods of a basic nature, but is also used effectively as a stabilizing force for maintaining essential supplies for the consumer. The public sector undertakings have thus vital role to play in the coming years. Therefore, the debate about the need for or the rationale for the existence of the public sector is not only meaningless but a totally sterile one. This point needs to be forcefully brought out by PR while publicizing individual undertakings.

CHAPTER VIII

PR for Private Sector

Impact on Business Management

Public relations 'tends to flow over the whole gamut of business and management'. Each department or aspect of business and industry has its specific PR problems and tasks. The sales department is concerned with distributors, dealers, customers, and with sales promotion activity. The personnel department deals with recruitment and welfare of employees, while the production department is anxious about the quality and output of the product. But in all these spheres, public relations has a part to play. It can make a visible impact on all operations.

Share-holders

Public relations in the private sector has to deal with the share-holders. The goodwill and support of share-holders is of vital importance to the existence and success of any business concern or industry. A new class of people are entering the investment field in India. The subscription to the shares of the industrial concerns is no longer the monopoly of the people from the urban areas. Public relations effort, therefore, has to be directed to attract the affluent rich sections from the rural areas and motivate them to invest in the industrial concerns. For this purpose, techniques of communication, relevant to this new class, have to be employed.

The pubiic relations in a private concern normally does not have any direct responsibility for the preparation of the annual report, the balance sheet, audit reports, or directors' report. The PR man, can however, help a great deal in projecting the organization's image with the share-holders by advising the management on the overall approach in the annual report, its main theme, the format, the style, presentation, illustration, etc. and also in ensuring that the report gives as complete a picture of the organization as possible in simple and attractive manner to the share-holders and other financial publics. A report with a 'PR touch' can have a much greater impact and effect.

The popularizing of the annual report, however, has its limitations because of its legal and financial contents, but the PR man can supplement the report with informative, non-technical booklets. The PR man can also organize visits of share-holders to the company's factory or works.

Distributors/Dealers

All manufacturers depend on distributors and dealers for the sale of their goods. Dealer relations is a key element in any commercial organization. It is the dealer who stocks the merchandize, promotes, and finally sales the product. The dealer is the last link in the marketing operations where product is finally exchanged for cash. The dealer represents the manufacturer to the public. An unscrupulous dealer can bring the producer to disrepute by selling products at an inflated price and by indulging in other malpractices.

The PR man can contribute a great deal towards cordial relations between the manufacturer and the dealer. Through dealer education and training programmes, dealer magazines and bulletins, seminars and symposia, dealer conferences, publicity campaigns including demonstrations of products, etc. the PR man can make the dealers active partners in the concern.

The PR man has a twofold role – to convey the difficulties, experiences, successes, etc. of the dealers to the management, and to keep the dealers informed of the developmental plans, production schedules, etc. of the company.

The PR man can impress upon the dealers through suitable publicity material and also orally about the importance of after-sale service, promptness, courtesy, etc. in building up sales.

Though the PR man is not directly concerned with non-payment or delay in payment of commission, etc. to the dealers, he can certainly bring to the notice of the management specific cases of serious lapses on the part of the concerned departments.

Customers

For a business organization the customer is an important public, the focal point. The survival and prosperity of the company depends, to a large extent, on the customer satisfaction. The customer is satisfied with the product or service only if it reaches him at the right time, at the right place, and at the right price. Public relations has, therefore, to make an all-out effort towards customer satisfaction.

PR is an aid to marketing all along the line, right from the stage of planning of a new product to its effective selling. The PR man can evaluate the customers' attitude towards a product and provide valuable clues to the marketing department so as to enable it to take corrective action and to decide about the continuation, modification, or dropping of a particular product or service.

Public relations can also provide the right orientation to the marketing department as well as to other departments of the company. It can provide guidance to those who are making, testing, dispatching, selling, or servicing the product. The objective of PR is to win the customers' good-will on a long-term basis. It can do so by providing effective pre-sale or after-sale service.

It is true that the quality and the price of goods are important from customers' point of view. However, the PR man can through research, surveys, and probes can find out the customers' buying habits and their reaction to the new product and pass on that information to the production department. At times, the total personality or the corporate image of the firm is more important than the product. As such institutional advertisement and other PR activity can help win customers.

The PR department should be also fully alive to the customers' complaints. It cannot afford to ignore the complaints, however trivial they may be. It is true that individual complaints are normally handled by the marketing or the complaints' department, but the PR man has to be closely involved in this work as it affects the image of the organization.

A complaint directly received by the company or voiced in a letter to the editor in a newspaper or a grievance made by a member in the parliament, or legislative assembly in the course of debate or discussion has to be taken note of by the PR department. The PR man has to go through these complaints and initiate prompt action. A thorough investigation and remedial action is necessary. The PR department must give reply to all such complaints. Even in the case of groundless and frivolous complaints, the PR man should write a polite letter to the customer. If the complaint is true, it is advisable to tender an apology and replace or repair the product. There should not be any hesitation in admitting lapses or failures. The tendency to cover up failures does not serve any purpose. The admission of a shortcoming and corrective action help establish credibility and rapport with the customers.

It is necessary for the PR man to make a concerted effort in cooperation with the production and marketing departments to project a new product or a new service. This can be done through features in house journals; by bringing out folders, brochures, and newspaper supplements; by organizing symposia and seminars; by producing sales literature and instruction manuals; by conducting advertising campaign through press, radio, TV, film, outdoor media; through issue of press release; and if necessary by organizing a press conference; by displaying the product through demonstration; and by participation in exhibitions and trade fairs.

The PR man can also serve the customer though customer publications, which not only give information about the product or services of the company, but also contain news and articles of interest to the entire industry and related subjects.

The customer can also be motivated by sponsored programmes on radio and TV and in some cases through fashion shows organized by the manufacturers in cooperation with some organizations or magazines. Beauty contests for Miss India conducted by the manufacturers of textiles and others motivate the potential customers through an interesting spectacle which combines sound, light, music, and dance.

Government & Parliament

Public relations in a private enterprise has an important role to play with the government and the parliament. The proper functioning, growth, and in some cases, the very existence of a business organization depends upon governmental policies and actions.

The political and administrative wings in the government are represented by the ministers and the permanent officials respectively. Communication with both is very important, though the day-to-day PR work in a business organization is mostly confined to the government officials at various levels.

PR through 'personal contact' is the most effective means of communication. On such occasions as the opening of a new plant, the observance of an anniversary, VIPs – ministers or government officials – can be invited. The visit of the dignitaries would enable them to have a first-hand knowledge of the company, its product, its services, its management, etc.

The 'direct mail' is another method of communication. The annual report and other important literature including folders, brochures about the company can be mailed on a regular basis to ministers and officials.

The most effective way to reach the government is, however, through the columns of the daily press. It has a much greater impact than the material mailed out to them.

Parliamentary proceedings receive wide publicity and therefore it is in the interest of a company or business organization to communicate with the MPs and keep them informed of its performance, problems, and activities. The approach has to be on a selective basis. Apart from leaders of various parties, the PR effort should be to brief members of the concerned Consultative and Select Committees of the parliament.

Close liaison and personal contact with MPs should be supplemented by supply of memoranda, background papers, etc. either direct or through the chambers of commerce and trade and industry associations.

The PR man should ensure that communication is organized in a planned, sustained, and imaginative way with ministers, officers, and members of parliament and legislatures.

The public relations department can also present calendars,

diaries, souvenirs, etc. to the MPs. However, care has to be taken that the articles presented are appropriate for the occasion and of the kind that are likely to be retained and used by the recipients and not distributed to others. And also the articles presented should not be conspicuous in terms of cost.

The PR department of a large business organization has also to keep in touch with the Planning Commission – the programme as well as the technical wings. The PR man can provide relevant data to the Technical Division and the Task Force and apprise it with the issues which the company would like to bring to the notice of the Planning Commission.

Internal Communication

The projection of the image of the organization among its employees is an important PR function. The purpose of PR's internal communication is twofold, viz., to convey management decisions, policies, and programmes to the employees at different levels, and to feedback the management with the reactions of the employees.

The correct policy should be to disseminate more and more information and establish management's credibility with the employees. Only that information should be withheld which may lead to speculative activity or may create problems for the company with its other publics. When information is given out, it has to be ensured, that the message is not distorted while passing through different channels. It is better if the workers receive the information in their mother tongue. In no case should the channels of communication be clogged. Otherwise, the employees will rely on gossips and on unreliable sources of information. Secretive atmosphere can do positive harm and give rise to suspicion, misunderstanding, and lack of faith in the management.

The PR communication with the employees can be carried out orally and through audio-visual and visual media. The information of relevance to the employees is disseminated through carefully planned meetings and conferences, through visual and audio-visual media such as circulars, manuals, newsletters, pamphlets, posters, publications and films, slides, etc.

The PR man can also make an excellent impact on employer-employee relations if he organizes the celebration of religious festivals and other community functions. PR can also make its presence felt on occasions such as marriages, birthdays, deaths, illness, etc., of the employees. The PR touch on these occasions can make all the difference.

The house journal is the most effective medium of internal communication. It provides a two-way communication between the management and the employees besides incorporating useful information for dealers, suppliers, etc. It can be in the tabloid or in the magazine format. The magazine format with monthly frequency can provide up to date news about the organization. It is easy to handle and preserve.

The house journal should include information from headquarters and despatches from the regional and branch offices. It should cover the company's activities, plans, policies, programmes, major campaigns, etc. The journal should be properly edited and judiciously illustrated. Employees' participation through contributions, letters to editor, etc. in the house journal is of crucial importance. The journal should be well produced with professional lay-out and also promptly despatched, preferably from the printing press itself so as to avoid delays.

The contents should include features not only about the top management, but also about the employees including marriages, births, sports, cultural activities, informative material, etc. The management should also get feedback from the employees. The journal should provide education and entertainment to employees. As such, it should include cartoons, short stories, quiz, write-ups in lighter vein as well as educative material written in popular style on family planning, safety, savings, prohibition, etc.

If it is necessary to provide the journal in more than one language, the language version should not be the literal translation. The translation must convey the spirit of the message and not its letter.

The employees make a number of demands. The demands have to be considered in the light of resources and other factors. Normally, the personnel department handles the employer-employee relations. However, PR has a silent role here also. The PR man should maintain a sustained flow of information about the amenities provided to the employees such as educational, health, recreation, housing and other facilities.

The PR man can also motivate employees on nationally accepted programmes such as family welfare, savings, safety, etc. through printed and visual material.

Local Community

Industrialization in an agricultural country such as India has its own peculiar problems. When a plant is set up in the rural area, the management has also to provide, in many cases, health, education, welfare, and recreation facilities not only for the workers, but also for the local people or the community around, the group of people who reside in a particular area.

The villagers recruited to the work force have to be integrated with others, and adjusted to the new environment. They have to be provided not only jobs, but also other amenities associated with industrial way of life.

No company can succeed if the local community is hostile. Local public opinion is of vital importance. The company has to take interest and to give support to local causes, to local fairs, celebrations, exhibitions, clubs, etc. It can lend a helping hand in setting up parks, hospitals, schools and in promoting sports and cultural activities for the local community. In some cases, the entire responsibility of development of the area falls on the company. It can help the local people not only through employment, but also by offering assistance in the setting up of ancillary industries and providing opportunities in its marketing operations.

PR can play an effective role in inculcating a sense of belonging and unity among the workers and also in the local community. Through community relations, PR can project the effort of the management in developing the area and in some cases even towns.

PR can project the image of the organization that the plant is not merely concerned with production and profits but is also equally keen to develop the area and organize and support services beneficial to the community.

Good community relations or to build up a reservoir of goodwill with local people can pay rich dividends to the concern in times of adversity. It can, in that case, depend on their sympathy and goodwill to tide over the crisis. Adverse public opinion can make things very difficult for the organization. The image of the company in the local press gets projected in the national press. Since the company or the organization derives a number of benefits from the local community, it is only proper for the organization to give something in return. The company's growth and prosperity is dependent, to a large extent, on the goodwill which the business enjoys with local people.

For effective PR with local community, it is necessary to fully know all the aspects of the community – the historical background, geographical factors; composition of the population – age group, customs, language, culture, etc.; other business and industries in the area; political, social, and cultural organizations, and other government welfare agencies; existing schooling, medical, recreational, and other facilities; and leaders of the community.

One way to involve the community in the company's affairs is to periodically invite a cross-section of the community to the factory or to the plant. The visitors can be acquainted with the processes of manufacture, the usefulness of the product, and other aspects such as cleanliness, sanitary arrangements, welfare activities for the employees, etc. Informative leaflets, sample of products can be given at such visits. The visitors to be invited should include representatives of students, press, local leaders, officials, families of employees, etc.

At times, the company can make a gesture by lending its premises for local meetings, programmes, etc. It can offer advertisements to promote community interests. Other steps to be taken by the organization to identify itself with the community are: observance of local holidays, advising local students about employment opportunities, helping local authorities in their effort to improve the lot of the community.

In fact, of late there is a tendency among industrial houses to 'adopt' local communities and villages and provide all facilities and amenities for the people. The PR man has to be the key figure in this set-up to project the image of the company.

To sum up, community relations is a social obligation of any business. This aspect is extremely important. PR activity in respect of community is essential for company's survival and prosperity.

CHAPTER IX

Communication with Rural Community

Communication with India's rural masses is of crucial importance. It not only informs and educates, but also motivates the people. People's involvement is possible only if the message of development, modernity, scientific, and technological changes in various fields is given out to rural people in concrete terms and in simple and clear language and symbols.

The Government of India's declared policy, programmes, and development strategy are for more and more stress on rural development. Banks, financial institutions, research organizations are now evincing increasing interest in rural transformation. They are discovering new ideas, avenues, and opportunities to deepen their involvement in the rural sector.

Industrialists in India are coming forward to set up new industries in rural areas. They are no longer allergic to the idea of going to backward regions. In fact, many manufacturers now realize that the rural world offers unlimited opportunities for them. The rural people are potential customers of plant, machinery, and consumer items. The development of rural India has opened up new markets. It is therefore very much in the interest of the government, the public and the private sector to devise ways and means to effectively communicate with this upcoming community in all possible ways.

The Press

Mass media agencies in India are accessible largely to people who live in cities and towns. Take, for instance, the most powerful medium of the press. Its circulation is, predominantly urban because of the concentration of literacy and purchasing power in cities and towns.

The Indian press does not evince much interest in rural India. The press by and large does not take note of the problems of rural community such as poverty, credit and banking facilities, industries, roads, transport and communications, drinking water, health and nutrition, housing, marketing, sanitation, family welfare, electrification, etc. It is doing precious little to evoke national interest or arouse national consciousness on the plight of rural people.

The press in India is divided into English and language press. The former is metropolitan- and big city-based. It caters to the needs of a class of people who are unconcerned with the problems of villages. It devotes hardly any space to the happenings in the rural areas except providing coverage of natural calamities, sensational crimes, etc. The language press is limited to the States or regions. As such, it does not have any national impact. Because of limited resources, it confines its news coverage, reporting, etc. to local events. It thus serves the interests of only its local readers and advertisers.

The press does not provide any guidance to those who are engaged in rural development. It takes only casual interest in many vital problems affecting the life of the rural community. This is borne out by the complete lack of interest in such subjects as land reform or poverty of the rural masses. It has failed to create the necessary climate or to motivate people to take more interest in rural development. It has also not succeeded in educating, informing, motivating, or inculcating new attitude, awareness, and scientific temper among the rural community so as to enable them to get rid of their ignorance, superstitions, and resistance to changes.

The press pays only scant attention to bottlenecks to rural development or to rural statistics. It does not give periodical appraisal of the performance of developmental agencies working for the rural community. Nor does it adequately cover modern agricultural practices or availability of improved techniques and tools for the rural artisans or the research trials conducted by agricultural universities and other institutions for the benefit of farmers. The result is that there is a big gap between the available technology and its adoption by farmers.

The press has also not been able to adequately publicize the newly set up district industrial centres which make available necessary facilities to small entrepreneurs under one roof. It has also failed to expose the atrocities of landlords, money-lenders, and upper castes, or the injustices inflicted by one section of the society on another. As such, many of the evil deeds do not come to public gaze.

Broadcasting

All India Radio's 84 broadcasting stations with 157 transmitters cover nearly 90 per cent of the total population of India. AIR broadcasts daily for 1,045 hours in 35 languages and 137 dialects to listeners in India and abroad. The number of licensed receivers now exceed twenty million.

Despite the significant strides in broadcasting medium since independence, there is still only one radio receiving set for every 35 to 40 persons in India, whereas according to internationally accepted norms every household should have a radio receiver. Also, while 80 per cent of the country's population lives in villages, only one-fourth of the total radio sets are located there. There are also noticeable regional disparities in the ownership pattern, because of factors such as purchasing power of the people, the availability of locally manufactured and, therefore, cheaper sets and maintenance facilities. The effectiveness of rural broadcasting also depends on the extent of broadcasting service in rural areas, its frequency, contents, duration, professional presentation, use of local talent, decentralization of the production of media material by taking the media centres to the people, setting up of district-level radio stations, etc.

Radio programmes are, by and large, urban-biased and urban-oriented in both content and narration. Radio is at present largely used to cater to elite tastes or commercial values. It is, however, effective to some extent in the area of agricultural broadcasts with the result that high-yielding varieties of seeds and fertilizer-mixes are popularly called 'radio seeds' or 'radio *khad*' in villages in many parts of the country. In this field, radio is the initial and the important source of information. The fact, however, remains that our communication media including radio have not yet succeeded in carrying developments plans and programmes to every Indian home in the language and symbols of the people – an objective set in the First Five Year Plan.

Radio has yet to reach the rural masses. There is thus a clear need for the expansion of communication activities and also of institutionalizing of inter-media coordination to avoid multiplication or duplication of efforts. Communication through various media including radio can be effective for rural development only if the communicators identify themselves with rural poor and the under-privileged. The objective should be to create a new awakening among those for whom development plans are intended. They should be fully involved to ensure their active participation in development.

Audio-Visual Media

Television is a powerful medium, but its existing reach in India from centres originating programmes for rural viewers and from those established after SITE is severely limited.

Doordarshan covers at present nearly 8 per cent of the area and 15 per cent of the population. The positioning of India's own Satellite in 1981 is likely to improve the situation. The pressure of urban viewers, background and training of the communicators, recurring costs, heavy capital investment are some of the constraints in the expansion of TV in rural areas.

There are half a million TV receiving sets, but only less than 3,000 of them are for community viewers. The villagers have therefore very little access to TV viewing. At the same time, the urban people also feel unhappy with the rural interest programmes. It will take considerable time before the TV can serve the rural areas.

Like radio and TV, films also communicate with the people who are not literate. It is a very effective medium for entertainment, information, and instruction. It is a highly artistic and creative medium and can influence the captive audience. However, most of the 11,000 cinema houses are located in cities and towns. The news reels and documentaries have little relevance to rural audience. We need films for information and motivation which are relevant to rural conditions. Greater use of cassette tape recorders, small gauge cameras and photographic exhibition kits, film strips and graphic may prove useful in rural areas.

Inter-personal Communication & Traditional Media

The Directorate of Field Publicity of the Government of India, organizes film shows, photo exhibitions, seminars, symposia, group discussions, debates, etc. It seeks public support to national campaigns and development of the rural people including those living in remote and hilly areas.

The Song and Drama Division of the Government of India, disseminates information through folk art forms such as drama, composite programmes, folk recitals, puppet shows, ballets, religious discourses, etc. These efforts are supplemented by field publicity units of the State governments.

Traditional media are most effective in changing the unscientific attitudes, superstitions, etc. inherited as a part of tradition by the people in rural areas. The practitioners of traditional media can convert the message into local popular tunes. This can lead to pleasant and subtle persuasion. At this stage of India's development, the best results are perhaps possible by a clever mix of the traditional, inter-personal, and modern media. Electronic medium does not supplant the traditional media. It only supplements and supports them. Also, effective collaboration between change agents or extension workers and local practitioners of folk media can produce excellent results.

Spoken word, where the people see and hear the communicator, is still the decisive mode of communication.

Posters

Most of our rural people identify the problem through a visual symbol. This is so because of large masses of illiterate people in the country. But illiteracy in India is not synonymous with lack of culture or ignorance. This is proved by the rural people taking to new farming techniques and also actively participating in elections. If the message through the visual has to make any impact on rural people it must evoke a sense of identification in the viewers. For instance, a poster must portray a bearded sikh and a *kameez*-wearing wife if it is in Gurumukhi; a housewife with a red bordered sari, if the words are in Bengali.

Exhibitions & Demonstrations

Another medium which attracts rural people is fairs and exhibitions. Fairs are organized when a pilgrimage or a festival takes place. They have a great potential in rural areas.

A few case studies indicate that for the promotion of a product among rural people, a field trip is the most effective means of communication. Demonstration is the next best medium. Field trips, demonstrations, and exhibitions are highly effective in enhancing the knowledge of a particular product which PR intends to promote with farmers in the villages. These medium can be utilized in various situations irrespective of the socio-economic and psychological character of the farmers.

Promotion of Products

The first PR task in rural areas is to understand the factors affecting the adoption of a given process or product. Information about agricultural innovations and farm inputs is communicated to the farmers by various media through a variety of channels. But the effects of such a communication are not always well pronounced. However, it has been found that wherever the technology has been profitable, compatible, feasible, and communicated through extension methods and techniques, the farmers' response is encouraging. It is, therefore, necessary for the PR man to identify the farmers' attitudes and motives that stand in the way of adoption of new processes or products. We should recognize that the situation factor or the physical setting within which different categories of farmers work is not the same. The variables such as the size of farm, irrigation potentiality, fragmentation of holdings, geographical location, supply and availability of the given product, purchasing power, etc. make all the difference.

Also, the social make-up of an individual – including his level of education, extent of participation in social organizations, age, socio-economic status, and caste – as well as psychological factors such as aptitude, knowledge about the product, value orientation, level of aspiration, change-proneness, economic achievement, motivation, etc. affects adoption or otherwise of the product. The extent of adoption is also dependent on innovational factors – simplicity/complexity, cost, profitability, physical complexity, communicability, time and labour-saving, etc.

The rural communication process has five major elements – the communicator, the message, the media, the target public, and feedback. The PR effort should be directed to facilitate the adoption of the product by the farmers by creating the necessary awareness and interest in them about the product and also in influencing their minds at the stage of deliberations, trial, and evaluation of the product.

Multi-dimensional Approach

India is a vast country of over 620 million people with literacy percentage varying from 20 to 70 per cent. We have high density, sparsely populated, and remote areas. Social institutions, traditions and ethos of people also differ.

Communication problems of rural India cannot be solved through technology transfer. Indian reality is multi-dimensional and will not yield to a single-point approach. Whatever the medium used, the message will acquire relevance and effectiveness if the folk form prevalent in the region is judiciously used without violence to its purity and genuineness. Each of the major media available to reach the rural India has its own potentialities, skills, limitations, and possibilities. Since our information needs are diverse, no single medium can adequately meet the rural communication needs.

Rural Development and Communication Policies

The Seminar on Rural Development and Communication Policies, organized jointly by the Indian Institute of Mass Communication and the International Institute of Communications in February 1979 at Hyderabad, examined the interrelationship between communication and development, particularly with regard to rural development.

The following issues and problems which pointed to the inadequacies of current practices in regard to rural development communication were discussed:

- quantitative shortcomings with regard to the availability of and access to communication and information facilities in respect of origination, transmission, and perception of messages.
- qualitative shortcomings with regard to the content of information and messages.
- imbalances in communication between urban and rural areas, between regions, between groups in society, whether defined in terms of social classes, power, sex, or age.

These and other factors have led to a situation where development messages often do not reach those for whom they are intended. Even if they reach their target audiences they are often not used. Information losses are considerable both within the development agency systems and between these systems and the users.

Communication cannot be seen in isolation but as a part of the total development system. Thus, communication cannot be dealt with by itself but only in relation to the political and socio-economic structures and cultural patterns. It is, therefore, important to avoid a simplistic relation between communication and the development effort.

It is necessary to consider not only the various modern and traditional communication systems and means but also the communication functions performed by extension workers, and all other agencies active in rural development, including banks, credit institutions, etc.

This comprehensive approach also implies that consideration must be given to the total information environment of the rural population, that is, not only to the development messages mainly transmitted through the public agencies but also to the messages and value systems disseminated by other media such as the cinema, or other major knowledge systems such as education. Equally, in terms of this overall comprehensive approach, certain basic questions with regard to the functioning of various communication systems in developing societies require consideration.

There is a need for the formulation of communication policies on the basis of the adopted plans for rural development. The purpose of such communication should be:

- to promete change;
- to avoid alienation;
- to encourage participation; and
- to foster social justice and equity.

Communication policies should be based on clearly stated priorities in terms of investment, training, etc. for rural communication needs.

It is also necessary that these policies provide for correction of the inadequacies and imbalances which have been identified; greater decentralization for rural development purposes; and for efficient information systems for agricultural and other relevant information.

The seminar emphasized the importance of coordination between the development agencies and between them and the communication agencies. There is also need for including the communication and information dimension into all rural development planning at an early stage.

Equally, in framing a communication policy and planning, all communication and delivery systems should be considered with major emphasis on the need for development communicators to be in personal contact with the villagers.

Changes in structures of communication agencies, particularly those in the public sector, such as the grant of autonomy to the broadcasting service, should provide for access and participation by the disfavoured groups in the rural sector so as to promote communication 'from below'. Special strategies are required for this purpose as well as for reaching these groups with information.

Communication policies and planning should take into account the variety of messages required for a different audiences. Here again, decentralization and localization is necessary.

In terms of priorities for rural communication, it is desirable to make intensive use of telecommunication and broadcasting facilities in the rural areas. There is crucial need for adequate recruitment and training of rural communicators and also of rural development personnel.

A number of specific recommendations were put forward. These include the following:

- experiments in 'densification' of communication in order to

establish the role and impact of communication in rural development;
- more efforts towards establishing audience profiles;
- consideration of separate broadcasting channels for rural programmes, and broadcasts by agricultural universities and other institutions for development;
- consideration of all available technologies with regard to their adaptation and use in terms of the social and cultural circumstances in different societies and communities;
- the means of establishing an information system to aid rural development and industrialization.

Attention was also drawn to a number of factors and pitfalls:

- Incorrect or partial information plus the danger of loss of credibility which in turn implies a waste of major communication resources.
- More attention should be paid to the process of communication, implying, inter alia, that the task of the communicator extends to the adoption or acceptance of the information provided.

A diversity of views was expressed on the extent of the relevance and the effectiveness of the television medium for rural development. However, it was agreed that as a visual medium television has a specific role and potentiality to reveal and therefore to educate and stimulate action. In a country of India's size and dimensions in problems, the overall cost effectiveness has yet to be established and an entire system of installing and maintaining community television sets has to be evolved. Several Indian studies on SITE has brought out the inadequacies in the software. There appears to be some lack of clarity in the role of post-SITE terrestrial centres. A clearer policy definition of television's role in rural development should enable the organization to allocate the resources essential for its more effective contribution and to develop necessary expertise for that purpose. The use of domestic communication satellite to be launched in the next two years or so calls for an in-depth study.

CHAPTER X

Professionalization and Training for PR

We are in the age of specialization and professionalization in all walks of life. As in other fields, public relations can make an impact only if it develops as a professional discipline and professional service manned by qualified, trained, and experienced people. The role of public relations in the government, in the public and the private sectors is not only highly specialized but also complex and difficult. PR is gaining recognition as a profession in all sectors. It is increasingly realized that the PR man needs special aptitude and skills.

PR Qualities

Public relations in India is fast emerging as a separate discipline distinct from journalism. It is now a vocation. In the changed circumstances, there is a need for qualified and trained PR personnel in all sectors.

The PR man does require character, fertile imagination, and broad vision; integrity and courage; cultural and intellectual background; power of analysis and observation; flair for writing; pleasant manners; and the ability to understand the organization, its problems and intricacies, and also the nature of its publics. He should be a good 'mixer' but should also have the capacity to keep a secret when necessary. He cannot be a master in every field but he should have a total picture of the organization at his finger tips.

All these qualities are, however, not enough. In addition, he should have training in the mechanics of public relations and in the techniques of communication. Without PR skills, he would not be able to put across the message effectively. PR, if handled by amateurs, can do more harm than good to the organization.

It is difficult to define precisely what is meant by professional PR personnel. However, an inclusive, working definition can be given. Journalistic and public relations qualifications can be one criterion. Also, persons who have long and continued experience of PR work can be included in this category. However, persons who have done PR work only on ad hoc basis for short durations and who essentially belong to other disciplines cannot be considered professional PR personnel.

A person may be an excellent writer or a scholar but that alone cannot entitle him to professional PR category. Scholarship and ability to write are welcome qualities in PR profession. But more important than this is the mastery over the techniques of communication and an understanding and appreciation of the needs of the media. These qualities can be acquired only by professional training and long experience in PR work. It is too much to expect from a person, however brilliant he may be, to do well in PR work if he has no professional background or experience in public relations. Even for PR personnel who have journalistic or PR qualifications or who have long experience in the line, it is necessary to periodically expose them to refresher courses so that they acquire self-confidence in their work and also keep themselves abreast of the latest developments in the profession.

PR Set-up

Closely linked with the problem of professionalization of PR personnel is the functioning of PR set-up in an organization. No PR set-up can function effectively if it is treated as an adjunct to another department. If the PR set-up has to discharge its functions effectively it must have an independent entity and work directly under the head of the organization – the chairman or the managing director. The PR man should be given a proper designation and status so that he may be able to deal with other functionaries in the management effectively. The PR department should not be burdened with miscellaneous routine administrative functions.

The PR set-up in government departments and in public and private sectors in India has a history of its own. Mostly, the growth has been ad hoc and unplanned. It is not possible to make any radical changes to rectify the situation. However, a beginning can be made. The first step should be to enforce that the head of the PR set-up must be a professional person. The PR personnel down the line can be given suitable training at some professional institute. Also, in the future, care should be taken that persons with only journalistic and PR qualifications are recruited.

Courses in Public Relations – PRSI and IPRM

Training facilities in PR as a separate discipline in India hardly exist. This is a serious handicap towards professionalization of public relations. PR is included as one of the subjects in courses on journalism, marketing, or advertising. Only the Madras University runs a full-time three-year degree course in public relations. The course, first of its kind in the country, commenced in 1975.

The Public Relations Society of India (PRSI), the national association of PR practitioners, was established in 1958 to promote the recognition of public relations as a profession and to formulate and interpret to the public the objectives and the potentialities of public relations as an important, integral function of the management.

Four regional chapters were launched in Bombay, Delhi, Madras, and Calcutta during 1966 to 1969. Since then five more regional chapters have been formed: in Gujarat in 1971-72, in Bangalore and Andhra Pradesh in 1972-73, and in Kerala and U.P. in 1974-75.

The management of the PRSI is vested in a National Council consisting of representatives elected by all the regional chapters. The members of the Society are drawn from public relations practitioners and those generally interested in PR from all over the country.

The Society is recognized as the national PR organization by the International Public Relations Association, and is one of the founder-members of the Pan-Pacific Public Relations Federation.

The regional chapters of the Society periodically organize seminars, lectures, and discussions on various aspects and facets of public relations. In order to promote professional training, the chapters run, in collaboration with universities and colleges, courses on PR for students of advertising, mass communication, and journalism. From time to time, the chapters also hold, in collaboration with various management associations and government institutes, residential and non-residential training courses for PR practitioners, management personnel, and those who wish to take up PR as a profession.

The Society established a two-year research fellowship on public relations at the Indian Institute of Management, Ahmedabad. It also publishes a journal, *PRSI News*, which aims to keep the PR practitioners abreast of the developments in PR in India and abroad.

Every two years since 1968 the PRSI has held national conferences to highlight a topical or professional theme. The first All-India PR Conference was held in New Delhi in April 1968. One of the highlights of this conference was the adoption of the 'Code of Athens' (see Appendix), the internationally-accepted Code of Ethics for PR practitioners, presented by Albert Oeckl, President, IPRA. The subsequent All-India PR Conferences have been held at Madras, Calcutta, Bombay, New Delhi, and Cochin.

The Institute of Public Relations and Management, Madras, also organizes periodical training programmes for PR executives and others at different places in the country.

Another organization, the Press and Public Relations Organisation (PAPRA), based in Delhi, conducts seminars, workshops, round-table discussions, lectures, etc. It is a non-profit educational society for the promotion of journalism.

Training in Allied Fields

Students and fresh recruits who do not have journalistic or public relations qualifications can take advantage of the courses in journalism conducted at various universities and other institutions in India. Similarly, PR personnel working in the government, public sector undertakings, business houses, and other organizations can greatly benefit if they undertake refresher courses in journalism conducted by reputed organizations in the country.

A number of universities in India have Departments of Journalism. These departments conduct degree or diploma courses in journalism. A few universities also award a post-graduate degree. The universities offering courses in journalism are: (i) Banaras Hindu University, Varanasi; (ii) Calcutta University, Calcutta; (iii) Mysore University, Mysore; (iv) Panjab University, Chandigarh; (v) Osmania University, Hyderabad; (vi) Nagpur University, Nagpur; (vii) Madras University, Madras; (viii) Jabalpur University, Jabalpur; (ix) University of Pune, Pune; (x) Gauhati University, Gauhati; (xi) Punjab Agricultural University, Ludhiana (Agricultural Journalism); (xii) Bihar University, Muzaffarpur; (xiii) Gujarat University, Ahmedabad; (xiv) Bangalore University, Bangalore (Deptt. of Communication); (xv) Behram University, Behrampur; (xvi) Panjabi University, Patiala; (xvii) Kerala University, Trivandrum; (xviii) Marathwada University, Aurangabad; (xix) Ravi Shanker University, Raipur; (xx) Shivaji University, Kolhapur (certificate course).

The colleges that conduct courses in journalism are: (i) Horniman College of Journalism, Bombay; (ii) Sidhartha College of Mass Communication Media, Bombay; (iii) St. Xavier's College of Mass Communication Arts, Bombay; (iv) Birla Constituent College, Deptt. of Journalism, Garhwal University; (v) K.C. College of Management Studies, Bombay.

Nearly 25 agricultural universities also have Masters and Ph.D. programmes in agriculture extension with specialization in radio or TV or information diffusion and audio-visuals. Information about the syllabus, the duration of the courses, the eligibility, etc. can be obtained from the concerned departments.

Training is also provided for personnel manning public relations services. The government of India has set up the Indian Institute of Mass Communication (IIMC) at New Delhi and Film and TV Institute at Pune.

A number of organizations also conduct courses in Journalism. The most prominent among them is the Rajendra Prasad Institute of Communication Studies and its constituent colleges (Bhavan's Colleges of Mass Communication). These are located at Bombay, New Delhi, Bangalore, Ernakulam, Madras, Guntur, Hyderabad, Mangalore, and Ahmedabad and three affiliated colleges at Trivandrum, Trichur, and Kota. Other training institutions are: Dateline School of Journalism; Indian Institute of Journalism; Press Institute of India; Delhi Institute of Management and Services; Datamatics, etc. All these are located in Delhi.

The syllabus or the course content for diploma course in journalism at different colleges, universities, and other institutions in India varies a great deal. There is no uniformity in this respect. This is understandable in view of the linguistic and geographical diversity. The courses in journalism, however, do cover not only the print medium but also other communication media. A few important subjects covered in journalism courses are: sources of news including national and international agencies; news reporting and editing; editorial and feature writing; advertisements; photo journalism; press laws; information and publicity campaign; communication research; development journalism; history of press and other media; house journal; public and press relations; rural communication and role of traditional media; outdoor publicity; broadcasting; television; film appreciation, and other allied subjects.

CHAPTER XI

Planning PR Campaigns

Public relations is not merely a process of getting stories and pictures into newspapers. It is much more. It has to be properly planned, orderly executed, and a number of details carefully attended to. Public relations costs money, requires manpower, needs expertise, and consumes time and resources. It should be well planned like a military campaign, and executed in an orderly manner.

PR Objectives

The first step in planning a PR campaign is to fully know the organization for which the campaign is being planned. It is necessary to analyse the working of the organization, its successes, failures, plus and minus points. The publicist should examine the records and the relevant data on subjects that are to be projected. He needs to meet the key people and get the basic statistics and facts.

The second step is to set out clearly the PR objectives before any campaign is launched. The publicist must have a clear idea as to what is intended to be achieved. His approach should be positive and purposeful.

The next step is to decide the audience to be reached: local, regional, national, or international. Apart from geographical area, it should be considered if any specialized audience or a section of the community or professional people is also to be reached.

Selection of Media/Resources

Another point that requires a decision is about the media to be employed for the campaign: whether publicity is to be conducted with one medium or more than one or through multimedia.

The publicist has also to think about the resources in terms of money and staff available to him. The campaign has to be planned keeping in view the resources which the publicist would be able to mobilize. In the budget, provision will have to be made for the expenditure to be incurred on different media. The fee and honorarium to be paid for different types of work, expenditure on photographs, mats and blocks, advertisements, mailing, transport, and out-door publicity are to be worked out. A proper break-up of the budget is necessary.

The next point for consideration is the proper scheduling of publicity. It can be tied to important and special events of the organization. The decision about the commencement of campaign, duration, repetition, etc. is to be made well in time.

Advance Planning

For a meaningful PR campaign, the publicist is required to make arrangements well in advance. The arrangements include coverage instructions, supply of background material, and photographs. He would also be required to attend to the mechanical side of the publicity, setting up of a press room, provision of typewriters and telephones, arrangements for photo, television, and movie coverage, and provision of accommodation, transport, entertainment, and recreational facilities for those who cover the function.

Product Campaigns – Urban and Rural

The PR campaigns are organized to promote political, social, economic, or cultural purposes or to popularize a new product or service or the institution or an organization without any relations to specific item, or to influence public opinion on a matter of public interest.

Take, for instance, the case of a soft drink. Consequent on the termination of the contract by the government with the multi-national company, a few manufacturers in India have introduced new soft drinks. How should the publicist organize the campaign to make the new drinks acceptable to the people? The publicist in this particular case may not have much time at his disposal as the consumers' mind has to be motivated well in advance before the onset of summer.

The soft drink is used in both urban and semi-urban and even in adjoining rural areas. Almost all sections of the community have, therefore, to be motivated. The stress, however, has to be on children, students, and youth. The message of the campaign also must reach both the literate and the illiterate in the country.

The considerations set out in the preceding paragraphs indicate that almost the entire geographical area of the country has to be covered by the campaign. However, before making a decision about the target area, the publicist must find out the availability of the new drink in all areas. The campaign has to be tied down first to those areas which are to be reached by the new product.

The publicist should also have a clear idea of the resources available for the campaign. Since it is a new product intended to fill in the gap created by a popular drink, the funds should not come in the way of planning a meaningful campaign. However, an idea of the budget is necessary so as to decide the break-up of the expenses and to determine the priorities.

In a campaign of this nature, it will be necessary to have a multi-media approach rather than sticking to one medium. The campaign through print medium can be organized through colourful display advertisements in national newspapers and other newspapers of the region which are to be covered by the supply of the new drink. The display advertisement, particularly the illustrative part of it, should make the meaning clear to the illiterate. The message should be couched in such words that make a direct appeal.

Apart from advertisements, news, opinion pieces, and special columns of newspapers should be tapped. News items giving the beneficial aspects of the new drink, opinions of nutritional experts, and reactions of children, students, and others who have tasted the drink could be highlighted in the form of features and articles or through letters to the editor. The publicist can also send relevant data such as the extent of saving in foreign exchange, reduction in price of the new drink, and other features for the consideration of editorial and column writers of newspapers.

The oral briefing, i.e., press conference, should also be organized to have face-to-face discussions with the press correspondents so that doubts can be clarified and people could be approached directly through the press representatives.

The new drink is likely to be consumed in large quantities by well-to-do classes. The product, therefore, should also be publicised on television, through both spot and sponsored programmes. Since the final objective is to popularize the drink in all parts of the country and among all sections of the people, the national hook-up of the commercial services of All India Radio should also be utilized.

The publicist in a campaign of this kind should also resort to a large extent to outdoor publicity. Posters and hoardings can be very powerful tools in this type of campaign. Theatre screen advertising should offer the publicist an opportunity to reach the captive audience with the impact of sound and motion. Colour slides, advertisement shorts, and quickies can also be used. Painted signs and electric displays can be harnessed by the publicist.

The publicist can also send his message directly to the individuals through mail. The message may be in the form of letter, folder, booklet, brochure, postcard, catalogue, or coupons.

If funds permit, the publicist can requisition the services of an advertising agency to advise his organization and also to execute the publicity campaign. Such agencies plan for their clients marketing and advertising strategies, prepare copy and art work, arrange mechanical reproduction of printed advertisements, produce television commercials, contract space and time, select media, and advise on all public relations matters.

If the campaign is for a new product primarily for the use of farmers, the PR approach has to be different. Take, for instance, organizing a campaign to introduce and to popularize a new chemical imported from abroad by a multi-national company meant to kill weeds in wheat crop.

For conducting an effective campaign, it is necessary to spell out the objectives to be achieved, the main theme to be projected, the area to be covered, the targeted public, the duration of the campaign, the media to be chosen, the resources available in terms of money, manpower, equipment, and other related aspects.

The objective in this particular case would be to educate and motivate the farmers in regard to the weed problems in wheat crop, the damage caused to the crop, the resultant financial loss in specific terms, and the need for adopting an effective chemical to get over the problem. The monetary gains to the farmers from the larger yield in their crop by the use of the product is to be stressed. Apart from the farmers, the campaign has to be directed to influence the opinion leaders in the villages in favour of the chemical.

What should be the theme or thrust of such a PR campaign? It has to stress on the special qualities of the new product. Some of the themes in order of importance are: the only chemical of its kind to kill all major types of weed in wheat crop by only one application; no damage is caused to the crop in any way (safety aspect has to be emphasized); though it is being introduced in India for the first time, the chemical has been successfully tried and experimented at agricultural universities and other institutions (the findings of trial reports and recommendations to be highlighted); the product comes from a well-known industrial house which has already established its credibility in respect of quality of similar products; recognizing the usefulness of the product, the government has granted subsidy to farmers for its purchase; the chemical is imported from abroad, but it is now easily available in adequate quantities and in convenient packings; though there is no competitive product, yet cost-wise it is cheaper compared to other chemicals which kill only a particular type of weed.

In this campaign, the targeted public are the farmers, dealers, extension workers, government personnel connected with agriculture and allied operations, and the concerned teaching and other staff at the universities and extension farms. Since the campaign is to be confined to wheat-growing areas of Punjab and Haryana and the Terai belt of U.P., it has to be conducted mainly in two languages, namely, Punjabi and Hindi. As the chemical is only for the wheat crop, the duration of the campaign has to be only for three to four months, i.e. November to February. In the very nature of things, a campaign of this kind has to be a multi-media one.

It is also necessary to work out the financial implications of the campaign so that the PR man has a clear idea of the total cost. The best way to arrive at the campaign expenditure is to divide the total area into sectors, to determine the number of campaigning teams and their composition, etc. This can give a fair idea of the total requirements of manpower at supervisory and lower levels, of the vehicles and the equipment, and of publicity and technical literature, gifts, etc. An assessment is also necessary as to how much of these resources could be mobilized from within the organization. Once this is worked out, a realistic idea of the money required for the campaign would be possible. A part of the additional expenditure on the purchase of vehicles, equipment, etc. is of capital investment nature and cannot be debited to this campaign. Some of the items can be also used in future campaigns. Keeping in view all these factors, the approximate amount required can be determined. Having worked out the essential ingredients of the campaign, the next step is the actual conducting of the campaign including the preparation of publicity material.

In this particular campaign, the following publicity literature may be useful: a technical folder about the new product in English, Hindi, and Punjabi. This is meant for agriculture extension officers, university faculty members, etc. who are in a position to assess the technical aspects of the product. Only a limited quantity will be required. Publicity or sales booklet in Hindi and Punjabi giving information about the product, its special characteristics, uses, the doses, packing, availability, price, precautions to be taken in application, etc. and the handbills for mass distribution.

The product should be advertised in local papers and magazines, particularly in the agricultural university journals and over local TV and radio stations. Advertisements can be placed through recognized advertising agencies. Their services can also be utilized for preparing spots and sponsored programmes for radio and television and imaginative display advertisements for the newspapers.

A short documentary film and cinema slides can be prepared in Hindi and Punjabi.

Outdoor media such as banners (to display in *mandis* and public places); mailing cards (giving information to farmers about the product); posters, wall paintings, tin plates, stickers, etc. can be used for the campaign. Hoardings may not be of much use because the campaign is for a very limited period.

Demonstrations and field visits are extremely important. This is the surest way to convince the farmers about the efficacy of the new product. For this purpose, the campaigning teams will require spraying equipment, nozzles, measuring devices, demonstration boards, etc. During the field visits and demonstrations, the villagers can be also shown slides and documentaries. The PR man should also participate in *kisan melas*, exhibitions and fairs, if any are held during the period of the campaign.

PR campaign of this kind is incomplete without giving gifts, souvenirs, etc. to the farmers and others associated with the campaign. Gifts, however, should be selected with care and should not be very expensive. At the same time, they should be of some use to the farmers. Items such as torches, diaries, calendars with pictures of Hindu Gods/Sikh Gurus, soap strips, playing cards, measuring devices, key chains, etc. can be considered. In all cases, the names of the product and the company should find a place.

Projection of Institution

In the above examples, the publicity campaign is focused on the product and not so much on the manufacturer or the institution or the organization. At times, the campaign is directed to earn goodwill for the manufacturer or the organization rather than get popularity for a specific commodity. By this method, the organization's name gets accepted and this indirectly helps in popularizing its products. Such publicity campaigns are known as institutional campaigns. For instance, a private company such as Sandoz India Limited advertising 'Sandoz in the service of Indian agriculture', or 'Sandoz guarantees dependable medicines'. Here the stress is on the company without mentioning the particular pesticide or medicine produced by the company. The techniques of campaign are more or less the same, but such campaigns are not limited to particular areas if the products of the company have a countrywide market.

General Campaigns – Prohibition, Social Education

The PR campaign can also be for influencing public opinion for a particular cause such as enforcement of prohibition. In a campaign of this kind, if prohibition is to be carried out in particular areas, the campaign should motivate in advance the people of that area so as to prepare them for the acceptance of the reform. The oral communication supported by visuals can be very effective particularly in slum areas. The evil effects of drinking on health, family relations, economic conditions, etc. can be brought home to the people by quoting identifiable instances of the people of the area who have undergone sufferings because of alcohol drinking. The newspapers, particularly the regional papers, can be used for projecting the evils of drinking through articles, features, and advertisements.

People in our country resort to agitation over all kinds of issues, justified or unjustified. In the process of these agitations, they damage public property and obstruct running of essential services. The railways provide a classical example of how people, particularly the student community, interfere with the running of trains and damage railway property. This is done even when the agitations are in no way connected with the railways or when the agitators have no grievance against the railways.

What is the role of public relations in a situation of this kind? What kind of public relations campaign is necessary? The objective of the campaign in this particular case would be to educate the people, particularly the student community, that destruction of railway property or interference with the running of trains, particularly when they have no scores to settle with the railways, will only add to the difficulties of the people. The scarce resources available to the railways for equipment and rolling stock will get depleted and the railway services will also get further deteriorated causing a great deal of suffering and hardship to the travelling public.

This theme has to be projected against the background of the role of the railways in our economy, particularly in the context of railways carrying essential commodities to far-flung and remote areas and holding the price line. The enormity of railway operations, the part it plays towards the promotion of trade and industry has also to be highlighted.

A campaign of this kind has to be spread over the entire country, but it should be concentrated in the areas where the trouble persists, namely, northern and eastern India. Any such campaign to be effective has to be multi-media and more or less on a permanent basis till we get over the situation.

Radio and television should be harnessed to promote social education among the people. Through their programmes, talks, features, plays, skits, etc. the audio-visual media can highlight the dangers of this type of agitations against an important public utility service. A few quickies and short documentaries prepared by the Films Division of the Ministry of I & B or by approved film producers can also be very effective. Similarly, slides can be shown in cinema houses on the subject.

Imaginative display advertisements prepared with the help of advertising agencies can be inserted in the local and national newspapers. Similarly, posters on the subject can be prepared and displayed at prominent places including the railway premises.

To make the campaign effective and purposeful, the railways can organize conducted tours of students to railway stations and yards and show them the effort that goes into the running of a train and how anti-social activities can impede the normal work. Such tours can give them an idea of the intricacies involved in railway operations. Also, essay competitions can be organized with attractive prizes such as complimentary railway passes valid for a certain period. The subject for the essays to be selected for competition should have a close relationship to the campaign. Talks by railway personnel including retired railway officers can be organized in schools and colleges on the subject.

An illustrated booklet can be brought out in English, Hindi, and regional languages for distribution in universities, colleges, and schools. It can project the damage which such agitations can cause to the biggest public utility service in the country.

The campaign should stress on social education aspects through a well-thought-out publicity programme so that anti-social practices such as misuse of alarm chain, ticketless travel, theft and pilferage, and damage to railway property are effectively tackled.

To sum up, any publicity campaign to be meaningful must at the first instance clearly set out its objectives. It must also determine the areas to be covered and the people or the section of the community to be reached. A decision has also to be made in regard to particular media of mass communication to be employed. All this has to be fitted into the resources available to the publicist. The efforts should be to make the maximum use of the limited resources. Again, the publicity campaign should be properly timed so as to have the maximum impact on the public mind.

The ultimate success of any PR campaign is judged not so much on the preparation of publicity material, quality or quantitywise but in the publicist's ability to get the same projected in different media. The successful 'marketing' of the material necessitates good rapport with the media. The media relations, therefore, is an important PR function and it should be given due importance. 'Right contact' and 'knowing the right man' in the media is very important. The publicist's contacts with the editors, correspondents, reporters, etc. can certainly make his task easy and can contribute a great deal towards the success of PR campaign.

Entertainment and Gifts

Entertainment through social get-togethers in which media representative are invited in small groups is an essential public relations activity. This is a desirable thing, but it should be done in such a way that no particular representative(s) is patronised. Also, such social get-togethers should not be combined with functional or business sessions. On such occasions, no news is generally disseminated. The entertainment programme should be adjusted to the money available for the purpose. A big entertainment budget does not necessarily contribute to better public relations. The media people fully know that money spent on them is borne by the department/organization. Normally, courtesy extended to a media representative when he visits the publicist is more important than the formal get-togethers.

As a public relations activity some business houses and other organizations also give souvenirs or their products or some other gifts. It is wrong to expect something in return. In any case, lavish gifts should be avoided. The gifts must be on proper occasions and in a proper context so that they may not look cheap. Entertainment and gifts are therefore essential ingredients of PR campaign.

Professional Assistance

It is, however, a fallacy to think that excellent relationship can be developed on the basis of mere entertainment and gifts. What is more important is a good story, and professional assistance. The publicist should therefore do everything to provide information both on his own and when asked for by the correspondent. As far as possible, the publicist should answer all questions fully, promptly, and honestly. For him the newsmen and other media representatives are customers. They should be treated with due respect and courtesy. It will do more harm if any attempt is made by the PR man to bluff or misguide them.

Good public relations also means that the publicist should be able to give a story about his organization when the same is asked for. Even if provoked, the publicist should not get excited or abrupt in PR work. The publicist should be equally energetic to assist the media even in the coverage of an adverse story. Once the publicist establishes the reputation of sincerity, impartiality, and objectivity, it makes his task easy. He will be able to soften the criticism against his organization. Adequate and timely professional assistance is of crucial importance to any PR campaign.

Normal Courtesies

The publicist should make a point of periodically calling on the media representatives covering his subject field, even when he has no particular work with them. He should share in their sorrow and happiness. For instance, when the pressman is not well or hospitalized, the publicist must visit him. If there is a bereavement in the family, the publicist must pay a condolence visit. Similarly, on such occasions as marriage or birthdays or other celebrations, the publicist, if invited, can give appropriate presents. These visits not connected with official work are of great importance and will help a great deal in developing cordial and proper relationship on a long-term basis.

Publicity not Through Ads

The publicist who gives advertisements to a particular newspaper should avoid the temptation of getting into newspaper columns through the advertising manager. The editor or the news editor does not like to be pressurized in this way. It may work in one or two cases, but in the long run, the publicist is likely to become a persona non grata with the editor.

PR and Performance

Successful public relations helps a great deal towards projection of the image and in the removal of misconception and rebuttal of criticism about organizations. Public relations, however, has its limitations and these should be clearly understood by both the organization and the publicist. It is no substitute for good performance. PR can build even false image for a period of time, but disillusionment would soon follow. The image to be lasting has to have some relationship with performance and achievements. It cannot be based on stunts and gimmicks.

In a democratic set-up with a free press, it is not possible to insist on a newspaper publishing anything which the publicist would like to get into the newspaper columns. Again, the publicist cannot prevent a newspaper from publishing anything, true or false. He also cannot insist on a false statement being corrected. In view of these limitations, it is all the more necessary to cultivate the goodwill and cooperation of the media on a long-term basis.

PART II

PUBLIC RELATIONS MEDIA

CHAPTER XII

World Communication Media at a Glance*

News Agencies

News agencies are a major and, in most cases, the major source of supply and circulation of information within and among countries. Besides serving the press, they are increasingly serving broadcasting organizations, as well as a growing number and variety of other clients.

There are now national news agencies in more than one hundred countries. There are also many hundreds of specialized agencies for the collection and dissemination of news in restricted areas: business, stock exchange, tourist information, weather reports, scientific news, etc. The rapid development of the need for visual news gave rise to a new type of agencies specialized in the supply of photos, television programmes, documentary films, etc.

There are wide differences among news agencies in their nature, scale, scope, objectives, and operating methods. Regular worldwide collection and distribution of news is largely effected by and through the five world agencies, namely, Agency France, Associated Press of America, United Press International, Reuter, and Tass. Each of these has offices in more than one hundred countries and employs thousands of full-time staff and part-time correspondents.

Some of the problems faced are: need for the development of infrastructure and creation of national news agencies; the multiplication of sources and measures necessary to prevent

*Based on the *Interim Report on Communication Problems in Modern Society* by UNESCO's International Commission for the Study of Communication Problems, 1978, and *UNESCO Statistical Year Book, 1975*.

both restrictions on and imbalances in news circulation; ways and means to enlarge cooperation among the developing countries.

Some thirty-five countries have no news agency; these include eighteen countries with populations of more than one million. A recent development is the growth of regional cooperation among the Third-World news agencies and the setting up of a non-aligned news agency pool.

Daily and Periodical Press

The world-wide circulation of newspapers is more than 400 million copies daily – an increase of 20 per cent over the past ten years. The total number of dailies is over 8,000. The highest daily newspaper circulation per 1,000 inhabitants is in Sweden followed by Japan (nearly 600).

The developed countries share nearly 5,000 dailies including over 3,000 by the USA. The dailies published in Asian countries number a little over 2,000. Of the total circulation of dailies of about 400 million, as much as about 350 million copies are circulated in the developed countries. The share of Asia is about 177 million copies. There are 313 dailies per 1,000 inhabitants in the developed countries whereas the number is 59 for all Asian countries.

Newspaper circulation and readership are growing rather slowly compared to the growth in population, literacy, and educated public. There is a wide disparity in this respect between the developed and the developing countries. With almost two-thirds of the world's population, the developing countries publish less than half the world's dailies, and have a total circulation of only one-sixth that of the industrialized nations. In the developed world, there is one copy of a daily newspaper for approximately every three inhabitants, in the poorer regions there is one for every 30 persons. In 11 countries in Asia, the figure is one for every 50. India with 835 newspapers ranks third in the world. The circulation is only 16 copies per thousand people, and is almost exclusively limited to cities and large towns. Eight African countries and territories and three Arab states have no daily newspaper at all; 13 countries in Africa have only one.

The great majority of daily newspapers are privately owned.

In many countries, both developed and developing, there are dailies managed by political parties, social and religious groups, etc. In socialist countries, newspapers are either government-owned or published by public associations such as trade unions, sports' associations, youth organizations, factory groups, and cooperatives.

Around the world daily newspapers are confined mainly to urban centres. There is a trend, on the world scale, towards a reduction in the number of newspapers, towards press concentration. Concentration has not only affected the press, but other media as well, although sometimes in different forms.

Concentration also occurs in other directions: (i) concentration in the ownership not only of daily newspaper, but of various journals (dailies, weeklies, specialized papers, entertainment publications, etc.) by a single publishing house; (ii) merger of newspapers with distribution companies; (iii) control by industries and banks over the press; (iv) merger of press and other media (for example, in the U.S.A. groups and individual newspaper and magazine publishers also own some 650 radio and 190 television stations).

Press concentration is harmful and dangerous to the readers, to the journalists and to the owners of smaller units. The decrease in the number of dailies diminishes the variety of views in the press, narrows the readers' choice, and curtails pluralism. However, those favouring the view that press concentration is beneficial to the public claim that press concentration leads to more efficiency through rationalized organization and production; that modernization of the press may lead to increased sales and more efficient management; and that press concentration may permit the newspapers to get information more rapidly and from several sources.

Since economic reasons are often the main ones favouring press concentration, in a few countries (e.g. Sweden) the government attempts to alleviate financial pressures which limit diversified ownership by such schemes as launching support to newspapers, production grants to 'low coverage' newspapers, subsidies to joint distribution systems, and other direct or indirect assistance (low taxes, cost reductions, etc.)

The periodical press is such a diverse field that it is impossible to generalize about its structure, content, or even to estimate accurately its size, hence its influence. The International Federation of the Periodical Press claims that in 1975 there were approximately 410,000 periodical titles in existence.

Broadly speaking, periodical press can be divided into two main categories – general interest publications intended for mass circulation, and those addressed to specific audiences.

Newsprint

The total consumption of newsprint (in metric tonnes) in the USA is nearly one million, whereas it is 2,000 for the UK, 2,500 for Japan, and 1,100 for the USSR. The consumption in African, Asian, and other developing countries is very low. For instance, consumption in Egypt and India is about 50 and 175 metric tonnes respectively. The consumption of newsprint per inhabitant (in kilograms) is: USA, 45; UK, 29.5; Japan, 20.2; USSR, 4.3; Egypt, 1.3; and India, 0.3.

Books

Books were the first mass medium and despite increasing competition as newer forms of communication to vast audiences have developed, the book-reading public has steadily increased. Between 1955 and 1976, world book production has more than doubled, as regards the number of titles published annually, and tripled as to the number of copies printed. More than 590,000 titles and about eight billion copies per year are now on the market. The world average works out to be 186 titles per million inhabitants. The average, however, for Europe is 587, USSR – 317, North America – 284, and Asia – only 60. Similarly, the percentage of book production worked out to be: Europe – 48, USA – 16.8, USSR – 14, and Asia – 3.5.

In many countries publishing is essentially a private enterprise activity, but most also have extensive government publishing operations. In socialist countries, publishing is a part of the planned public economy. In many developing countries, the absence of adequate private supply forced the governments to undertake publishing themselves. The need for supplying educational textbooks also led to governments taking to book publishing work.

Radio and Television

Unlike the print medium, radio and television are operated or directly controlled by the state in most countries or by autonomous corporations in many countries. In some countries, mainly in America and to some extent in Asia, broadcasting is operated primarily by private commercial firms but subject to more or less encompassing regulatory legislation.

Broadcasting – radio and TV – because of its nature and coverage and actual and potential impact on individuals, societies, and nations is quite apart from other media. For this reason the governments are more concerned with its operations than with other mass media.

There are an estimated one billion receivers, i.e. an average of approximately one for every four persons, on earth. In developed countries, there is more than one receiver for every single person. In Africa, there is a radio set for every 18 inhibitants; in Asia, one for 13. The USA has more radio transmitters than all the developing countries put together.

Out of about 26,000 radio broadcasting transmitters, the developed countries have as many as 19,000. The number of transmitters in a few selected countries is as under: Egypt – 27; Canada – 531; USA – 7785; India – 150; Japan – 944.

No other medium than radio has the potential to reach so many people so efficiently for information, educational, cultural, and entertainment purposes. Radio can be used easily and economically to reach outlying regions and for communication in the many vernacular – often unwritten – languages existing in developing countries. In spite of this, radio messages still do not reach large portions of mankind in isolated areas and many of these messages when they reach mass audiences convey alien content and false images.

Television services now exist in 133 countries compared to 103 ten years ago. The number of television receivers doubled to 366 million, or 117 sets per thousand inhabitants. Out of this the developed countries have over 321 million sets. There is one receiver for every two persons in North America, one for every four in Europe and the USSR, one for 12 in Latin America, one for 40 in the Arab states and Asia, and one for every 500 persons in Africa. Out of the 25,000 TV transmitters, the developed countries have nearly 24,000.

The rapid growth of the medium has also brought with it a growing concern about some of its possible effects. Programmes are biased in favour of the needs and interests of urban populations and local elites, thereby giving a false picture of the society as a whole. Excessive control, either commercial or governmental, can lead to consumerism and indoctrination. Some fear that the TV medium almost inevitably tends (and does so in societies with different systems) to homogenize society, reinforce social stereotypes, promote-conformity and conservatism. Others are of the view that TV can effectively introduce new ideas and an awareness of diverse cultural patterns. Some contend that there is a causal relationship between violence on the screen and violence on the street. Many countries import 30 to 70 per cent of their TV programmes.

Films

With a total world production of 3,800 feature length films in 1975, Asia leads all other regions with 1,960 films; India is the world's top producer (510), followed by Japan (330). However, the volume of each country's film production is not the dominant factor in film circulation or in the impact it has on cultural patterns on the world scale.

The feature film industry is basically a private commercial enterprise, except in socialist countries and with few exceptions. However, public authorities find increasingly that common interests require some public involvement. Through various ways and awards, stimulus is being accorded to certain areas of film production and to particular themes.

Out of the 266,800 fixed cinema houses, the developed countries have as many as 235,500. Out of the total number of 76.6 million seats, the developed countries' share is 62.2 million. The world average of cinema houses for 1,000 inhabitants works out to 25. However, for the developed countries, the figure is as high as 56.

Apart from feature films, the industry has been notably involved in other productions – newsreels, animated films, cartoons, documentaries, educational films, etc.

Advertising

Advertising has become an enormous world-wide activity and exists in practically every country. In some countries, it has a minor role and is in the nature of public service. In other countries, advertising is itself a major industry and an important form of communication in its own right. Advertising is essentially a communication activity, part of the communication process and system, aiming to promote the sale of goods, commodity or service, to advance an idea, or to bring about some other effect desired by the advertiser. It represents a major source of revenue for mass media and thus influences to a greater or lesser extent their whole range of activity and orientation.

In many societies, advertising contributes efficiently to the generation of consumer demand and of a mass market, but its influence on the consumer and on the mass media may also be decisive and negative. Anywhere it can contribute to raising aspirations and can be a motivating force for an improved quality of life, but it can also contribute mightily to rising frustration and to consumerism.

Telecommunication

As defined by the international convention, telecommunication is 'any transmission, emission or reception of signs, signals, writings, images and sounds or intelligence of any nature by wire, radio, optical or other electromagnetic systems'. Thus, it includes, among other means, the telegraph, telephone, telex, and radio and television broadcasting. There are at present about 400 million telephones in the world and although 80 per cent of them are found in only ten countries, all nations are linked by direct dialling system.

Traditional Media

The performing arts, whose role has both a cultural and an entertainment value, can also serve as carriers of messages with social significance. Indeed, in some countries where mass media are not well developed, itinerant song, dance, and drama groups, puppet shows, and similar 'folk media' are a primary communication channel. In the course of traditional performance they transmit information and project ideas which may influence attitudes and behaviour, as well as entertain. The same is true of certain sports activities and games, of fairs, carnivals, and popular festivities.

In most developing countries, traditional communication has preserved its value and richness and plays an important role as a process of conservation and development linking the individual and the group. Almost all of the developing countries show a mixture of traditional and modern communication. There is a constant interplay and reciprocal influence between them. It seems very important to maintain their coexistence and mutual relationship.

While traditional ways of communication predominate in remote and rural areas, they are present in various forms in urban centres as well. One of the main problems and objectives is to consolidate the relationship between the two forms of communication without disrupting either the traditional roots or the necessary trend towards modernity. Outside its usual context, traditional means of communication have also been largely used during recent events occurring in the political and social life of many developing countries.

In the industrialized countries, vestiges of traditional communication survive in varying degrees. Theatre, and particularly the popular theatre, is a vehicle for preserving traces of traditional communication.

India – Communication Gaps

India has made significant progress in the field of mass communication since independence. India has today 82 radio stations against six in 1947. The radio network covers 87 per cent of the population compared to 20 per cent at that time. The number of radio licences has also stepped up to 1.78 crores from a mere three lakhs in 1947.

The TV, which was non-existent at that time, is now a major communication medium with 16 centres covering 8 per cent area and 15 per cent population of the country.

The Indian film industry with 550 feature films a year is at the top of producers of films in the world. It makes one and a half times more films now compared to 1947.

India has about 13,000 newspapers today against 1,000 in 1947. Book production has also considerably gone up.

The advertising business has increased twentyfour-fold from what it was at the time of independence. The commercial broadcasting and telecasting have made a significant difference in the field of advertising. However, only a very small percentage of the population is at present exposed to advertising compared to developed countries.

Despite these advances, the country is far away from the norms laid down by the UNESCO for adequate information services for the developing countries. Take, for instance, radio which reaches the largest number of people in India. The number of radio sets stands at 1.78 crores which works out 34 persons per set. This is far below the minimum laid down by the UNESCO, i.e. one set for every five persons. In this respect, India is also far behind of even several Asian countries such as Japan, Kuwait, Jordan, and Iran. The number of persons per radio set in these countries works out to 4, 5, 14, and 15 respectively.

The cost of the radio receiving set is a major constraint for the poorer section of our people living in rural areas and city slums. The solution, therefore, lies in either providing subsidized receiving sets to this vulnerable section of the society or expanding the community listening facilities with adequate arrangements for the maintenance of community sets. The people who live below the poverty line and who need information more than any other section of society should be reached by this powerful medium.

TV is still a largely urban-oriented medium in the country. A TV set is beyond the reach of an average middle-class family. The need, therefore, is to bring down its cost substantially. Even with the reduction in price, TV sets are still beyond the reach of the poorer section of the country. The supply of subsidized sets to a group of people or installation of community TV sets with proper maintenance facilities is a possible way out. These facilities can be provided in the areas which are already covered by the TV network at present and which are likely to be covered in the near future.

The circulation of 875 daily newspapers in India today is about 93.38 lakhs giving a ratio of about 1.5 newspaper for every 100 persons compared to the UNESCO norm of ten daily newspapers for 100 persons. Also, the daily circulation of newspapers is largely urban-oriented. Fifty per cent of the total circulation of daily newspapers is centred in the four metropolitan cities of Delhi, Calcutta, Bombay, and Madras. The daily newspapers, therefore, do not reach the bulk of our rural population.

With the spread of literacy in the rural areas, the small and medium regional newspapers can play a vital role in disseminating useful information to the people. Facilities to start such newspapers, therefore, need to be provided if the newspaper medium is to reach the people living in semi-urban and rural areas.

For the expansion of such newspapers there is a need for substantial increase of production of newsprint in the country. The limited annual availability of indigenous newsprint of about 50,000 tonnes against the requirement of over 200,000 tonnes is a serious bottleneck to the growth of newspapers. Simultaneously, these newspapers should be provided facilities such as supply of subsidized news, publicity material, printing machinery, etc.

Though there is a considerable expansion of feature and information films in the country, the exhibition facilities are poor. We have 0.8 seats for 100 persons compared to the UNESCO yardstick of two seats for 100 persons.

The Film Enquiry Committee recommended that the country should have at least one cinema house for 20,000 population. At present, we have only about 11,000 cinema houses against our requirement of 30,000.

The existing cinema houses are also unevenly distributed with the result that more than 55 per cent of our rural population have to travel in some cases 15 km to find a cinema house. There is, therefore, an urgent need for building more cinema houses, promote touring and open air theatres. The diversion of a part of entertainment tax, allocation of sites at concessional rates, and other forms of encouragement can help in building more cinema houses in the country.

India produced over 22,000 books in 1976. There has also been a qualitative improvement in book production. However, the print order has been very low, generally one or two thousand copies of a new title. This has resulted in higher cost of production and also considerable wastage of the effort on the part of the author, the publisher, and the printer. The small towns and villages at present remain outside the reach of the book world It is, therefore, necessary to produce better and more books and in large numbers. This can bring down the cost of book production and enable a larger number of people to buy books.

India needs substantial expansion of its existing communication facilities. At the same time, the country's resources are limited. There are also other higher priorities. It is, therefore, necessary to devise ways and means to utilize the limited communication facilities to the maximum use.

An intelligent and planned approach to the problem, the harnessing of all available resources, greater multi-media and Centre and State coordination, result-oriented strategy, innovation and improvisations, cooperation between the governmental and the non-governmental agencies, etc. are some of the areas that deserve the attention of the mass communicators in the country.

CHAPTER XIII

Press as a Public Relations Medium

The Press and Democracy

The press in a democratic country plays a vital role in creating, moulding, and reflecting the public opinion. It is a fundamental institution of our society. It contributes a great deal in shaping political, social, and economic development in the country. The press is also intimately concerned with the functioning of the state and the policy it follows. It touches almost every aspect of our public life.

The press in India functioned as a crusading agent for the freedom of the country prior to independence. Its contribution to our freedom struggle was substantial.

It is true that only a small percentage of people in India come under the reach of the press because of widespread illiteracy and limited circulation of newspapers. This percentage, however, is extremely important as it constitutes the intelligentia, the vocal section of community which not only creates and builds the public opinion, but also provides leadership to the society. The views of this section cannot be ignored. The influence of the press in any country on the people is admittedly a great deal more than circulation statistics.

Though press in India since independence has grown vastly in size and circulation, it suffers from many ills. It has yet to identify its true post-independence role so as to ensure against haphazard growth and directionless expansion.

The role of the press in India need not be that of adversary or of blind support to the government. The press should be the watch-dog and act as a catalyic agent to hasten the process of social and economic change and thus secure people's participation and involvement in the country's development.

The reasons for the present state of affairs in the press are not far to seek. There are a few in-built handicaps such as vast geographical area, illiteracy, poverty, multiplicity of languages, and absence of adequate communication facilities. The linking of ownership of newspapers with other industry or commercial enterprises, limited newspaper ownership with closely held share interest, urban-oriented expansion of newspapers leaving the vast country-side population untouched, inadequate and expensive availability of newsprint, and the lack of local advertisement support are some other bottlenecks.

The press in India today is too much obsessed with politics. The country needs creative reporting particularly on non-political themes such as unemployment, mal-nutrition, population growth, etc. The emphasis should be not on what the public 'wants' but what it 'needs'. The reporting should provide adequate local coverage and cover human activities in factories, farms, schools, and universities. All this can be accomplished if the press is able to evolve a philosophy of mass communication and code of ethics through consensus.

There is a great scope for regional, local, and small papers in India and they should receive all encouragement and support. In the present stage of country's development, there is also a need for economic and developmental journalism which is still in its infancy. The press to function efficiently also needs well-paid and well-trained journalists to report events particularly from small towns and rural areas.

Credibility is the life-blood of communication. Whatever given out by the media is believed only if dissent is permitted, otherwise any message received through oral communication would be accepted as the gospel truth.

It has been argued by eminent journalists that the system of present accreditation of journalists, government's allocation of newsprint, fixation of advertisement rates, favours to journalists in the form of perquisites such as subsidized housing, medical facilities, etc., and heavy dependence of the press on official releases, etc. stand in the way of making the press in India as an independent and impartial instrument of communication of news and views.

Finally, there is a need for a dialogue to consider an amendment to the Constitution to provide guarantees against suppression of the freedom of the press. This is necessary to ensure that the press functions without fear.

Indian Press at a Glance

The Indian press during recent years has grown in terms of publication, circulation, specialization, and linguistic and regional dispersion.*

The following are the highlights of the Indian press:

(i) The total number of newspapers (any printed including cyclostyled periodical work containing public news or comments on public news) are 13,320 with a circulation of 340.75 lakhs. This includes 875 total daily newspapers with a circulation of 93.38 lakhs.

(ii) The periodical publications in all languages excluding daily newspapers are: 12,371 – weeklies (3,801), fortnightlies (1,566), bi/tri weeklies (70), monthlies (4,993), and others (1,86[illegible]).

(iii) Nearly a third of newspapers (3,873) or 30.9 per cent are published from the four metropolitan cities – Bombay, Calcutta, Delhi, and Madras.

(iv) State-wise, Maharashtra tops the list with 1,948 newspapers followed by U.P. (1,597), Delhi (1,637), Tamil Nadu (869), Andhra Pradesh (802). Mizoram and Andaman & Nicobar Islands have only 8 and 4 papers respectively.

(v) Language-wise, the largest number of newspapers (3,289) are published in Hindi followed by English (2,765), Urdu (929), Bengali (855), Marathi (806), Gujarati (580) and Tamil (618).

(vi) The majority of newspapers (8,104 or 60.9 per cent) are owned by individuals with 27.7 per cent circulation. Firms, partnerships, joint-stock companies, societies and other associations and Central and State governments own 33 per cent of newspapers with 67.2 per cent of the total circulation.

(vii) The common ownership** units number 83. They own 331 papers (270 news interest and 61 non-news interest) and command a circulation of 109.10 lakhs or 32 per cent of the total

**Press in India, 1977*, Registrar of Newspapers for India, New Delhi. Information given is as on 31 December, 1976.

**A common owner is one who owns more than one 'new interest' paper including one daily paper.

circulation of newspapers.

(viii) The big, medium, and small newspapers (over 50,000; between 15,001 and 50,000; and up to 15,000 copies respectively) number 107, 240, and 7,188 with circulation of 38.1 per cent, 18.3 per cent, and 43.6 per cent respectively.

(ix) The political parties own 82 newspapers, including 9 dailies, with a total circulation of 2.40 lakhs.

(x) Twenty-six foreign and diplomatic missions in India own and publish 109 papers. The USSR tops the list (50) followed by the USA (8).

(xi) The highest circulation of daily newspapers – *Anand Bazar Patrika* (2,91,129); (Bengali); daily newspaper published from more than one centre – *Indian Express* (403,927); *Kumudam Weekly* (4,38,621); (Tamil); non-weekly periodicals – *The Reader's Digest* (1,95,117).

(xii) The number of centenaries – 23.

(xiii) Periodicals published by the Central and State government number 283 and 216 respectively.

(xiv) The total availability of newsprint in 1976-77 was about 2.35 lakh metric tonnes (imported 1.80 tonnes and indigenous from Nepa Mills 55,000 tonnes). Of the total allocation of newsprint during the year, the daily press received 84.2 per cent. Import of newsprint was from Canada, Czechoslovakia, USSR, Japan, Scandinavian countries, and Bangladesh.

(xv) The journalists working in the daily press number 17,102 including 164 photographers, 60 cartoonists, and 11 cartographers.

Second Press Commission

For a comprehensive and an in-depth examination of the state of the Indian press and the steps that need to be taken for its development on sound and healthy lines, the govermnent of India appointed the Second Press Commission on 18 May 1978. The Commission enquiring into the growth and status of the Indian press should suggest how best the press should develop with full vigour and strength in the future.

The appointment of the Second Press Commission became necessary since the Indian press had undergone several changes, had taken new strides, and acquired an added significance with the continuously expanding readership. The Commission is also to determine the role of the press in educating public opinion and to suggest ways and means to safeguard the freedom and independence of the press against pressures of all kinds. The Commission is expected to redefine the place, status, and functioning of the press in a democratic set-up.

The Commission is to inquire into the growth and status of the press since the first Press Commission submitted its report in 1954. It will, in particular, examine:

(i) The adequacy of the present constitutional provisions and laws with regard to the freedom of speech and expression.
(ii) Means of safeguarding the freedom and independence of the press against pressures of all kinds, including those from the government, trade unions, or others in a plural and democratic society.
(iii) The pattern of ownership and financial structure of organs of the press with a view to ensuring editorial independence and professional integrity and the readers' right to objective news.
(iv) The pattern of relationship between the government and the press, especially with regard to access to information.
(v) The structure and functioning of the existing news and feature agencies and measures necessary for their growth as strong and viable organizations.
(vi) The nature of relationship between different elements of the press, namely, publishers, managers, editors, journalists and so on.
(vii) Measures necessary to inculcate in the press a sense of social responsibility and public accountability.
(viii) Ways and means to promote the growth and development of the language press, the regional press, and a rural-oriented press.
(ix) The economics of the newspaper industry, including determination of the basis for a fair price for newspapers.
(x) Existing facilities for training in journalism and newspaper management and other areas of newspaper industry with special reference to the needs of the language press and to suggest measures to augment these facilities.

The Congress(I) government which came into power in January, 1980 has reconstituted the Press Commission with wide and more specific terms. It also appointed a new chairman and members of the Commission.

Role of PR Communicator

For effective public relations, publicity in the press, particularly through the daily newspapers, is the most effective and popular mode of projection compared to publicity through any other medium. Newspapers occupy a commanding position as a medium of mass communication. This is so, despite widespread illiteracy and limited circulation of newspapers in India. The reasons are both physical and psychological. A newspaper can be read at the reader's own convenience. It can also be referred to as and when required. Newspaper reading is more or less a habit with most people. It is also generally presumed that newspapers provide relatively impartial coverage of happenings compared to other media. Newspapers, therefore, make a greater impact on the public mind, particularly in urban and semi-urban areas.

The government at the Centre and in the States, business houses, local bodies, public sector undertakings, and other organizations and institutions in the country disseminate information to the people from time to time through the medium of the press. Information is given out on a variety of subjects and is canalized to the press in different ways – press releases, features and articles, backgrounders, advertisements, and orally through press briefings, press conferences etc.

The information given out by any organization has to compete with other news items. As such its getting into newspaper columns depend on a variety of factors – the news content, timing, availability of space, etc. The most important factor, however, is the technique of dissemination of information. In this context, the role of the PR communicator is extremely important as, to a large extent, the success depends on his skill and his rapport with the press.

The communicator's objective is to reach a sizable and diversified audience and to make the desired impact. The transmission of information, ideas, etc. through the press has to be done in such a manner as to make maximum effect. The communicator can succeed in this task if he has a clear idea of the objectives which he wishes to project or promote. He should have necessary vision and purpose before him. His task would be comparatively easy if the information he transmits is free from prejudice and influence and based on truth.

In a democratic set-up the communicator should not take the people for granted. The 'bullet theory' that a communicator can shoot any message into a person, and the person falls, is no longer valid. The receiver is as active as the sender. The audience is not passive. The communicator with the best of communication techniques cannot thrust his message against an unwilling mind. He will be successful only if his message is based on some solid foundation.

The public relations man has two distinct functions. These are basic roles irrespective of different designations, such as public relations officer, information officer, press relations officer, press relations manager, etc. He is both professional or technical expert and spokesman of the organization who gives advice on publicity matters to his organization and speaks on its behalf. He advises the organization as to the best manner in which the policies, activities, programmes are to be projected to the people through the medium of the press. Apart from proper presentation, he also decides the timing and other relevant matters.

The communicator can discharge his functions efficiently if he has not only easy access to the policy-makers but also is allowed participation in all important conferences and meetings. He would be an effective communicator only if he is taken into confidence in all matters and given proper background of subjects, particularly of those which are likely to arouse public controversy. He must have access to all office memoranda and important papers. In other words, he should be fully involved in the work of the organization. The communicator, to achieve success, must develop excellent rapport with the top officials. If necessary, he should be able to get the requisite information on telephone. He has to be polite but firm so as to make it clear to the organization that the functional facilities are absolutely necessary to discharge his duties.

The person communicating with the press apart from being adviser to the organization is also its spokesman. He disseminates information to the press which in many cases serves as a source material for other media such as radio, TV, etc. He has to have a thorough knowledge of his organization, its day-to-day activities, and other related matters. Only then he can speak with authority and confidence.

The dissemination of information to the press is not enough. He has to ensure that the same is published. For this he has to have a close liaison with the press correspondents covering his subject field, news editors, chief reporters of newspapers, and if possible with the editors also.

The communicator has yet another role. He not only disseminates information to the press but also feeds the management with the press reactions pertaining to his organization. This enables the organization to take necessary corrective action. The press communicator's role of public reactions evaluator is of no less significance. The information which he passes to the organization as reflected in the press, however, should not be mixed up with his personal observations or impressions.

News Releases

The term press release in its narrower sense is used for releases covering news. The press release contains worthwhile material which has some news value. It is not only unnecessary expenditure but also damages the reputation of the concerned publicity/information department if the release is on a very trivial matter.

The press release should be written in a journalistic style. It should provide facts or information of interest to the readers and should attempt to cover all aspects of a specific subject. There should not be any loose ends. It should be on a subject which is recent or in news. The release should not be generally lengthy. It should be concise and to the point. It has not much place for subsidiary or background material. The release is a piece of clear writing without any ambiguity, without any effort towards colour or ornamentation. The drafting should be done in a manner that if the last paragraphs in the release are deleted by the newspaper, no damage is done to the news story.

The introduction or lead should be in a summary format as it is in a news story. The relative value of the various ingredients of the subject in the press release is weighed and evaluated and the most pertinent of them are included in the lead.

The releases should have a consistent format. Generally, the name of the organization from where the release emanates is given on the top. The date and place are indicated on the top right side. The release should have a title and a sub-title also, if necessary. It should have a suitable introductory paragraph. In the case of releases from non-official organizations, it is desirable also to mention the designation of the person issuing the release and his telephone number.

The press releases covering news in the case of the government are mainly of four types – press communiques, press notes, hand-outs, and unofficial stories or unofficial hand-outs.

The press communiques are issued when some important government decisions or announcements are made such as cabinet appointments, conclusion of the foreign dignitaries' visits, international agreements, etc. The press communique is formal in character. It carries the name of the ministry or department and the place and date at the bottom left-hand corner of the release. Generally, the press is expected to reproduce the press communique without any substantial change. No heading or sub-heading is given on press communiques.

The second category of press releases are press notes. They are less formal in character. They are issued on important matters, e.g., raising or lowering of tariff rates, etc. The press note also carries the name of the ministry/department and the place and date at the bottom left-hand corner. Headings or sub-headings are given in press notes. Unlike the press communique, the press can edit or condense the press note. Both the press communique and the press note are the responsibility of the concerned government departments.

The third category are hand-outs. They are issued on a variety of subjects and on day-to-day activities of the ministry/department, VIP speeches, questions and answers in parliament, etc. The hand-out is a less formal type of release and not issued under the government's formal authority. It bears the name of the PIB or other releasing agency on the top without any mention of the ministry/department to which the release pertains. The place and date are indicated on top at right-hand side. One of the most important common categories of hand-outs relate to the speeches of ministers or other high officials. The hand-out is released only when the speech is connected with governmental activity. No official hand-out is issued if the minister has spoken in his personal capacity as a member of a political organization.

The speech when released to the press in the form of hand-out is summarized and properly edited. Formal introductory and concluding remarks are omitted and redundant and repetitive material taken out. A proper title and sub-title are given. The important aspects which are to be stressed are included in the beginning paragraph or in the lead. The full text of the speech is not released unless the subject is of very great importance.

While covering inaugural and other functions where VIPs make speeches, the press release should stress on the significance of the function and try to spell out in concrete terms the gains to the community rather than reproducing the speech. For instance, the opening of a new branch of a bank or of power house at a particular place should be an opportunity to the communicator to bring out in the press release the specific gains which would accrue to the people of that area rather than only spotlighting on the dignitary and his speech.

The speech of the Prime Minister or of a very important dignitary at formal occasions or at important gatherings is generally released in full to ensure correct reporting. The full text is also helpful to the editors and column writers. It is also utilized for reference purposes in the future. If the speech of the Prime Minister or the dignitary is extempore, advance arrangement will have to be made for reporters and for a tape-recorder.

Unofficial hand-outs are issued on a subject where the government would not like to assume official responsibility in the matter but feels that there may be positive advantages in making information public unofficially. These hand-outs are supplements to oral briefings. They are given across the table to press correspondents and no general release is made. The unofficial hand-outs do not have the imprint of the PIB or of other releasing agencies. The date and place are indicated at bottom left-hand corner.

Non-news Releases

There are many other forms of release which do not cover news but give information in an indirect way and help in building the image of the government. More widely-known releases of this type are backgrounders, biographical sketches, contradictions, articles and features, newsletters, releases on reports, broadcast talks, etc. In these releases, the releasing agency's name is given at the top. The place and date are indicated on top right-hand side while the exact type of release is mentioned in box on top left-hand side. Title and sub-title are also given.

Contradiction or denial of a news story is to be issued only when there is a serious mistake or the facts in the story are patently incorrect. Since denials give more publicity, it should be avoided as far as possible, particularly when the story is substantially correct. The best way for the publicist is to do a positive story after lapse of some time. The opportunity should be utilised to present correct statement of facts without referring to what has been incorrectly published in the past. Negative statements or refutation of a news story except in very exceptional circumstances is not good strategy.

Background material providing additional information and useful details is essential for journalists, newspapers, and periodicals. Events should be anticipated and necessary background material is prepared well in advance. It may also be supplied on request. The backgrounder should be, as far as possible, a self-contained release. It is useful for leaders and column writers. The backgrounder should give detailed rundown for a decision. It will go a long way in better appreciation of decisions, or activities.

Whenever the government or other reports are to be given to the press, it is necessary that a summary should also be released, which should be brief. The constructive side of the report is to be highlighted in the summary. Out of these reports, self-contained items can be taken out and released separately. Any report, if it is to be presented to the parliament, should not be given to the press before it has been distributed to the members of parliament, or laid on the table of either house of parliament.

The press releases from business houses also follow more or less the same format. It should also indicate the name of the organization, address, name of the concerned officer, telephone number, etc. to facilitate the work of the newspaper representative to get speedy clarification and additional information, if so required.

No payment is required to be made to newspapers if the releases discussed above are published in newspapers.

Timing of Press Releases

One important point to remember is about the timing of releases. If the publicist wants to reach both the dak ('dak' editions are meant for outstation and up-country centres and, therefore, printed earlier in the evening) and the city editions of the papers, the release must be in the hands of the news editor by noon latest. Even when the objective is to get into only the city edition, it is good policy to send the release before 1500 hours. In certain cases, the copy can be sent a day in advance with an embargo put at both the top and the bottom of the release.

Newspapers have a lot of prepared material for the magazine section of their Sunday editions. As such, it is not in the publicist's interest to send unimportant items on Saturday. Sunday and other holidays should be preferred for sending material for publication in newspapers on the next day. Through the technique of embargo, the publicist can release his story simultaneously from different centres in the country. While putting embargo, the requirements of radio should be also taken into consideration. For instance, when it is desired that the embargo story to appear in papers say on Saturday morning, the embargo should be only for the evening of Friday so that the news can be used in radio news bulletins on Friday evening. Embargo is to be indicated at both the beginning and the end of the release in either of the following two ways:

1. For Publication or Broadcast on or after.....hours on.... 19......
2. Not to be Published or Broadcast before......hours....on ......19......

CHAPTER XIV

PR and Oral Press Briefings

The purpose of oral briefing is to supplement and reinforce the conventional written publicity material. It is an opportunity to highlight certain events and also to clarify the complicated issues to the press representatives through questions and answers. Sometimes better results are achieved with face-to-face discussion with the correspondents rather than giving information to them through written publicity material. To get the best results out of oral briefings, it is necessary that these should be organized in a methodical manner. Every care has to be taken as to when and how to give oral briefing. The oral briefings are of several types.

Queries from Press Representatives

An accredited press correspondent can put a query on any aspect of the working of the government department or other organization. Such queries are treated as confidential and the replies are to be given only to the press representative concerned on exclusive basis. The confidence of the correspondent should be respected. The decision to treat the query exclusive or otherwise rests with the information man. He should exercise his discretion with care so that he is not charged with discrimination by other correspondents. At the same time, his action should not discourage the initiative of an individual correspondent and induce him to explore other sources of information for scoop or an exclusive story.

Generally, queries from only accredited representatives are answered. A city reporter's query can also be attended to if the matter is of local interest such as university, zoo, milk supply agencies, etc.

The query should be noted down and the official concerned should be approached for relevant and correct answer. The press correspondent should be replied without much delay and with as many details as possible.

The answering of queries from press representatives helps in checking correspondents relying on unofficial and unreliable sources or on gossip. Also, in the garb of query the public relations personnel can plant a story on exclusive basis in a paper. However, stories of general public interest should not be given to one correspondent.

Special Press Briefings

Press briefings are arranged for specially accredited correspondents taking interest in a particular subject field. The purpose is to explain the background of a happening, not necessarily for purpose of its being used as a news story. In press briefings all accredited correspondents are not invited. These briefings are in the nature of special briefings on a particular subject.

Besides the ministers and secretaries, these briefings are also organized for senior officials for giving detailed information and elucidation on complicated matters. The officials should not be too much reticent and guarded in replying inconvenient questions as that will defeat the very purpose of such briefings.

Separate press briefings are sometimes conducted for foreign correspondents on important aspects of national development since the foreign correspondents are not interested in many details or subjects which are of interest to Indian correspondents.

Press Conference – General and Special

Press conference provides an opportunity to communicate directly with representatives of the press. The latter, in turn, present the news to the public. The press conference is to be held only if the government or the organization has to give out some important news. It is wrong to hold a press conference when there is no worthwhile news to give.

The press conferences are usually held when actual news is to be given out. The purpose is to explain to press correspondents and selected editors the scope and purpose of an important report or a statement which is likely to be of public interest. It is also held to give a general view of the policy and activities of the government or other organizations. Sometimes press conferences are also held to explain to the press important developments of sufficient public interest.

The press conference should never be held on a routine affair or a trivial matter. On the other hand, the government press conferences can be utilized to announce all major policy decisions and important announcements when the parliament or the assembly is not in session. The conference should be conducted by those who are competent to explain the rationale and the implications of the issues. Only in this way the press conference acquires meaning and content and help in better relationship between the government and the press.

Press conferences are generally organiged for ministers and secretaries. For other officers also press conferences can be arranged on specific subjects if they are authorized to communicate with the press. In the case of public sector and private sector organizations, the chairman and the managing director and even other senior officers hold press conferences on specific subjects.

The invitees to the government press conference are normally all accredited correspondents including foreign correspondents, editors of local newspapers, accredited cameramen, and representatives from radio, TV, photo and films divisions depending on the importance of the subject and the dignitary who is holding the press conference. An up to date list is kept in the PIB and also in State public relations/information directorates for this purpose.

In the case of private organizations, all correspondents who normally cover the organization are invited to the press conference. For this purpose, a standard list of invitees should be kept and updated from time to time. Where the name of the special or the concerned correspondent is not correctly known, it is better to extend a blanket invitation to the news editor or the chief reporter who would assign a representative best qualified to handle the story.

Official invitees to the press conference should be reduced to the minimum. The information or the public relations officer should be present at the press conference. This holds good for non-official press conferences also. The chief executive and the head of the concerned department, should, however, be present at the conference.

Invitations to the press conference should be sent well in advance indicating the date, day, time, subject, and venue of the conference. Also, the name of the person who is to hold the press conference and his designation or status should be mentioned.

In regard to the timing of the press conference, it is advisable to hold it in the forenoon or early afternoon so as to catch also the dak edition of newspapers. The holding of press conferences late in the evening on unimportant subjects is of little use. If a press conference is over a cocktail party in the evening or over dinner on a subject not of immediate interest, it is advisable to ask the invitees to do the story the next day for publication on the third day. Generally, correspondents would agree to this suggestion, since it would mean that they would not have to rush to the office to file the story in the night. It will also be too late to get good display in the newspapers.

The duration of the press conference is generally from thirty minutes to one hour.

Tea, coffee, soft drinks, and snacks can be served at the press conference. It is better to give refreshments at the end of the conference and at a separate counter. It interferes with the work if refreshments are mixed up with the business session. In any case, it should not be made too lavish an affair.

For the press conference, the information or public relations officer should brief the speaker in advance about the correspondents and the nature of questions likely to be asked. Where business houses have public relations officers, they should fully brief the top executive and suggest the line of approach for the presentation of the subject-matter so that the executive can speak with informality and ease. Before the press conference begins, they should also give a proper but brief introduction of the speaker and the subject. This will help in making proper impression and impact on the press representatives.

The speaker holding the press conference should see that unrelated questions are not entertained and that no correspondent(s) monopolises the conference. Also, disproportionate time should not be given to any one question. Discussion on individual and personal cases should be avoided. Generally not more than half a dozen questions are to be allowed on any one aspect of the subject.

It is necessary to prepare a comprehensive note on the subject of the press conference. This note should be distributed a little before the press conference is scheduled to start. This will help in many ways, particularly in checking facts and statistics. Also, through this note, the department or organization can project its point of view. Such a note will also help absentee correspondents. The background note is not released to the newspapers but given to the correspondents who attend the press conference. If the press conference by the business concern is in regard to a new product, the prepared note on the subject is a 'must'. But if the press conference is in regard to the general policy, it is not absolutely necessary.

The press conference should be held at a centrally located and easily accessible place. There should be adequate space for the correspondents, and should have all necessary facilities such as mike, light points and writing desks if possible. The press conference should be held in the case of an urgent matter in the conference room of the business organization. If the accommodation is not suitable, it can be held at a centrally located hotel. If the conference is not on an urgent matter, it can be held in a leading club or in a hotel. In any case, the surroundings of a press conference should be congenial.

The press conference arrangements should be well thought out. Transport can be provided both ways if the press conference is held at some distance or out-of-the-way place. If the press conference is on an urgent matter, for instance, about a strike or labour trouble, there will not be any time for social niceties. However, if the conference is called for the introduction of some new product, etc., it can be over a lunch, dinner, or cocktails.

The person conducting the press conference should be advised to avoid 'off the record' remarks as far as possible. It is better to say at the press conference 'I cannot comment' rather than making some observations and asking the press to treat them confidential.

It is not necessary to have a verbatim record of the press conference, unless it is on a very important subject and by a very important dignitary. No press release is to be issued on the press conference.

It is a wrong policy not to give equal treatment to all newspaper representatives. Some of them may have been unfair in the interpretation of news or have embarrassed the organization in the past. Despite this, the publicist should treat them on equal basis. Under no circumstances should any press representative be excluded from the press conference on this account. In fact a dissenting or a critical correspondent should be called as a matter of policy. This may disabuse him of some of the wrong facts in his mind or false information planted in his mind by a rival.

The public relations officer should prepare himself for the follow-up of the press conference. There may be questions on which full answers could not be given at the press conference. He should immediately get the information and supply the same to those who ask for it.

A press conference by the Prime Minister or a VVIP, particularly a foreign dignitary, is somewhat different from the normal press conference discussed in the preceding paragraphs. The following are important points to remember:

1. The invitation to conferences in the case of the Government of India is normally sent under the signature of the Principal Information Officer. Invitation in the case of State governments is issued by the director of public relations. The head of the organization in public or private sector should send such invitations. The invitation should give a clear indication of the day, date, time, and venue but unlike other conferences, it is not necessary to mention the subject. The name and designation or status of the dignitary should be mentioned. In the case of press conference by chief ministers the subject of the press conference may also be given. Invitations should be sent to all accredited press correspondents including provisionally accredited, editors of local newspapers, accredited cameramen, including foreign news agencies and foreign newspapers. The invitations should also be extended to radio, TV, films division, photo division, accredited photographers, and TV,

newsreel cameramen including those representing foreign agencies and also to foreign broadcasting and television organizations.

Invitation to other officials should be given on specific request and after considering the request on merits. The information personnel who are not directly concerned are generally not expected to attend the conference. In any case, their number should be restricted to the minimum.

The invitation to the press should be marked 'NOT FOR PUBLICATION'. It should indicate that the invitees should be seated fifteen minutes before the start of the conference. The invitation should be made non-transferable and correspondents should be asked to bring the invitation letter or card along with them.

2. It is necessary to inform the Superintendent of Police (Security), Superintendent of Police (Traffic), Secretary to the VVIP, External Publicity Division, and the Foreign Regional Regulation Officer and other concerned officials.
3. The timing of the conference should be preferably in the forenoon or early afternoon so as to cover the dak edition of the newspapers. The timing would, however, depend on the VVIP's convenience.
4. The venue of the conference should be at a place which has the necessary facilities. The press representatives should be able to use mike without difficulty. In Delhi, the venue of such press conferences is Vigyan Bhawan. Outside of Delhi, it may be at the Raj Bhawan or the PIB office or at some other central place where adequate facilities are available. The venue should be got cleared from the security point of view.
5. The duration of the conference is normally of forty-five minutes.
6. Cameramen should operate from fixed positions without obstructing the view. They should not move from one position to another during the press conference. They should use noiseless or ruffled cameras. Cameramen are not expected to occupy seats which are meant for correspondents. Only accredited cameramen should be permitted for the coverage. They are given a few minutes in the beginning.

They should not click throughout the conference.

7. The correspondents should be asked to use the microphone if there is such facility while asking questions, to facilitate recording. Before asking a question, the correspondent should mention his name and the name of the newspaper or agency he represents. They should be advised that not more than two or three questions should be asked by any one correspondent. Monopolization of the proceedings by a few correspondents should not be allowed and the time should not be lost over minor and irrelevant questions or personal grievances.
8. The correspondent should not leave the press conference till it is over. The filing of the stories in between puts the other correspondents at a disadvantage.
9. The full text of the press conference should be released on the same day to all accredited correspondents and newspapers, for their use and also for reference and record purposes. If the conference is organized by the PIB, its regional and branch offices should also be provided with the text. For preparing the full text it is necessary to deploy an adequate number of reporters/stenographers to take verbatim record by rotation. Also, the transcript should be checked with the tape-recorder which should be used in such conferences.
10. The overseas communication service and the central telegraph office should be intimated in advance so that they make necessary arrangements to cope up with the rush of foreign press traffic on the day of the conference.
11. It is not necessary to give any background material – unless it is on specific subject.
12. No snacks or tea or coffee are served in such conferences. This makes the conference a functional affair.

Informal Meetings/Press Get-togethers

The purpose of informal meetings and press get-togethers is to develop and strengthen the relationship between the organization and the press. This gives an occasion to intimately know the correspondents at the personal level. These social gatherings are over lunch, dinner, or cocktail parties. Since these are not business sessions, no news is disseminated to the correspondents on such occasions.

It is not possible to call all the accredited correspondents at one time for such informal meetings. It is advisable to call them in groups by rotation. Care, however, has to be taken to ensure that all correspondents who are covering the particular subject field are invited during a reasonable period of time.

Press Conducting – Local and Outstation

Press correspondents are also invited to functions. If the function is of a local nature, reporters are invited, otherwise invitation is extended to all correspondents covering the subject field. If the function is at an out-of-the-way place, transport is provided both ways. The transport can start from a predetermined central place.

At the venue of the function, there should be proper press enclosure so that the press correspondents have a frontal view and can also easily listen to the speakers. No person other than the press representatives should be given entry in the press enclosure.

Background material should be prepared in advance. The same can be handed over to the press representatives at the time of the function. If there are prepared speeches, the text of the speeches should be kept ready and given to press representatives. The programme and other details of the function should also be provided to them. At such functions, refreshment, etc. are also provided to the correspondents. If audio-visual coverage of the function is to be required, radio, TV, and newsreel cameramen should be invited. Light points and other facilities required by them should be checked in advance.

When the press representatives are invited to the function, the organizers should not insist that they come in a particular dress. The dress may have been prescribed for others but to insist the press to conform to a formal dress is not a correct thing. They are invited to project the work of the organization and it is not fair to impose unnecessary restrictions. It is unfair to expect correspondents to keep a large set of clothes to suit particular occasions.

If desired, the press representatives should be allowed to leave the function before it is formally over. The correspondents sometimes have to leave earlier either for providing timely coverage to the function or to attend other engagements or assignments. Their leaving the function early should not be considered discourtesy.

Conducted tours of groups of correspondents are also organized to major development projects or manufacturing centres. These should not be rush visits and degenerate into holiday excursions. Such visits are of great benefit to small and medium newspapers. They should be invited on regional basis. The correspondents of medium and large newspapers can also be conducted to such projects. They should also be given facilities to cover the projects on their own. On such visits, sufficient time should be allowed to the press representatives to go round the project, meet concerned personnel, and see for themselves the progress.

The conducted tours should be organized with a great deal of care. This requires considerable expertise. The selection of correspondents, air/rail/road reservations, hotel bookings, messing and transport arrangements, recreational facilities, proper background material and other details should be carefully worked out before the tours are undertaken. These should not become counter-productive. They should result in greater harmony between the organizers and the press.

It is difficult to lay down any rigid rules or guidelines for conducted tours for journalists organized by the government, public sector undertakings, or other agencies. The size of the party and the duration of the tour would vary depending on several factors – resources, projects to be covered, and their importance in the national context. However, the upper limit of 20 persons and 15 days should not be normally exceeded.

The selection of the papers – national and regional – should be decided by the organization sponsoring the tour. Newspapers in Indian languages should get adequate representation. The nomination of the persons to be included in the party should be left to the editors. The organization can suggest names indicating the reason, if any, but the final decision should be that of the editor. Also, the selection of papers should be rotated for different tours to avoid any impression of patronage. This policy will also achieve wider and varied coverage.

Normally the travel of the party is by rail, road, or steamer. Travel by air, where considered necessary, should also be permitted. Expenses during the journey and on boarding and lodging vary depending on the places to be visited, but they should be kept within reasonable limits so as to make maximum use of the resources. For instance, members of the party who normally reside outside the place of commencement of the tour should be asked to join the party en route, if the programme permits of such an arrangement. Also, where any concession is admissible to an individual or to the party under the rules of airlines, railways, or shipping services, this should be availed of. No liquor should be served in prohibited areas or on dry days.

The organizations sponsoring the tour should prepare in advance background material about the projects to be visited by the party. Some knowledgeable person should be earmarked to brief the party on the spot. It helps the conducting officer accompanying the party to have assistance of a liaison officer from the organization to be visited by the party. The programme should be drawn up in such a manner that the members of the party have some time for leisure and also for sight seeing, for which suitable arrangements should be made.

It is not necessary for the conducting officer or others to 'vet' the story filed by the newspaper representatives except in the case of defence and of a few other projects. However, all assistance should be given to them to check facts and figures and to clarify doubts and misgivings.

Except in the case of spot news coverage, it is advisable to fix a future date on which the story would appear simultaneously in all the papers. This will give time to the members of the party to prepare the story. In the absence of such an arrangement, it will be rush work and would defeat the very purpose of the visit.

Meet the Press

'Meet the Press' is different from press conferences or press briefings in several respects. The latter are organized by the ministries, departments, business organizations, and other institutions to project their activities. All arrangements for the press conferences such as issue of invitations, background material, decision in regard to the venue, timing, subject, etc. are made by the organization concerned.

In the 'Meet the Press' programme, however, it is the other way round, i.e. the press clubs or press associations or press organizations invite the VIP to meet them. All arrangements for such 'Meet' are made by the press organizations. At such meetings, there is no fixed subject and no background material is given. Arrangements such as refreshments, etc. are all made by the press organization which is inviting the VIP to meet them.

CHAPTER XV

PR through Publications and Journals

Book Publishing in India

Despite phenomenal progress made recently by other mass media, books continue to remain the most effective means of education and mass communication. According to the UNESCO statistics, the world book production in 1974 was 571,000 titles compared to 269,000 in 1955. The year 1972 was also observed as International Book Year, to highlight the importance of book publication as an important medium of mass communication.

The six largest book producing countries in the world are the USA, the USSR, the Federal Republic of Germany, Japan, and the United Kingdom. The USA tops the list with 81,000 titles, closely followed by the USSR with 80,000 publications.

India has made significant strides in recent years in the publication of books not only in numbers but in quality and variety as well. India is now the seventh largest producer of books in the world. The country produces over 22,000 titles (15,000 according to the UNESCO standards) including 4,555 children's books. India is next only to the USA and the UK in respect of books in the English language.

Imported books significantly supplement the output of domestic book industry. The country imports books and journals of the value of about Rs.7 crores annually. The import of books is now placed under Open General Licence. Not only new firms, even individuals can import books without any import licence. Export of books is comparatively a recent phenomenon in India. Indian books including journals and periodicals are exported to nearly 100 countries. The value of exports amounts to about Rs.3 crores every year.

The main partners in the book industry are: the author, the publisher, the printer, and the distributor and bookseller. The author is the starting point in book production work. The publisher is the planner, the financier, and the entrepreneur. The distributor and the bookseller promote the sale of books and handle the actual selling operations.

The Author

The condition of the author who is the basis of all publishing activity is not very happy in India despite many steps taken since independence to improve his lot. The Government of India now grants the author tax exemption to the extent of 25 per cent of income from royalties/writings or Rs.5,000, whichever is less, per year, by way of expenses without the production of any documentary evidence. The author is also entitled to a 25 per cent deduction on his royalty income if his book has been prescribed as a textbook for a degree or post-graduate degree course of any university in India.

Under section 180 of the Income-Tax Act, the remuneration received by the author in lump sum as income from writings or royalties received during the first year of the publication of the work can be spread over to three years before the taxable income is calculated, provided the time taken in writing the work is more than twelve months. If the income is received from abroad by the author in exercise of his profession, a deduction of 25 per cent of such income is made while computing his taxable income.

To look after their professional and economic interests, an organized body of Indian authors – Authors Guild of India – was set up in 1974. There are more than 300 members representing the English and the Indian languages. The Guild has set up a Good Offices Committee of authors and publishers to settle disputes amicably. A litigation committee of the Guild assists authors to recover legitimate royalties from the publishers. The Guild has prepared a draft model agreement between the authors and the publishers. It also brings out a quarterly journal. The Guild has also set up Authors' Publishing House to bring out books on a cooperative basis.

The Indian Copyright Act of 1957 protects the literary works of Indian authors. According to the Act, the writer remains the owner of his writings during his lifetime and his successor can enjoy the benefits for 50 years after the death of the author. The author is always the proprietor of his writings and owns the copyright. He assigns or licenses his copyright to a publisher for exploiting his writings in consideration of royalty. The royalty usually ranges from 5 to 15 per cent depending on the type of the book. In some cases, the author gives his manuscript for lump sum payment. In this case, he foregoes his right on the manuscript. This practice is considered unfair as it amounts to distress sale by the author due to his economic plight. The lump sum payment, however, in the case of particular category of books (such as children's books, translations, where the remuneration is small) or where the author is keen to get the full benefit immediately falls in a different category.

A number of organizations award prizes to authors for outstanding works. The Bharatiya Jnanapith, a private trust, gives every year an award of Rs.1 lakh for the best creative writing in the Indian languages. The University Grants Commission gives fellowship worth Rs.10,000 for writing a quality book of university level in the English or in any Indian language. The Ministry of Education in cooperation with the State governments provides substantial financial assistance for production of university-level books in the Indian languages to facilitate smooth change-over of the medium of instruction in higher education from the English to the Indian languages. About 4,500 titles including 900 translations have so far been published in different Indian languages on a no-loss-no-profit basis. The Sahitya Akademi gives every year an award of Rs.5,000 each for outstanding works in the languages recognized by the Akademi.

The Publisher/Distributor/Bookseller

According to the *Directory of Indian Publishers* India has over 11,000 (large, medium and small) publishers. They publish books in all languages. A number of government and non-government institutions also bring out publications. There are more than 300 established publishers in the country.

The publisher transforms the written text into the printed word and puts it on the market for sale. To make his enterprise a success, the publisher needs the expertise and the experience of both the profession and the business. Before accepting any manuscript from the author, the publisher has not only to make a professional evaluation of the work but also a survey of sales prospects in India and abroad. The accepted work must fall within the editorial competence and specialized field of the publisher. Some publishers have their own printing presses while others get the work printed under their own supervision.

The role of the distributor and the bookseller is of no less significance. They generally handle the sales promotion and the actual sale of books. The trend now is that the publishers concentrate on the publication of books, and the distributors determine the market potential and take care of sales promotion and actual sales. The share of the distributor is roughly about 40 to 45 per cent of the price of the book. This includes expenses on the production of sales promotion literature, displays and exhibitions, stocking of books, and trade discount.

To promote sales of books within the country, the government has now reduced the registration fee from Rs.1.25 to Re.0.65 on V.P.P. packets of books costing up to Rs.10. This concession, however, does not apply to packets sent by registered post but not made value payable. In such cases, the usual registration charge is payable.

The different elements that go into the cost of publication of a work vary a great deal. According to a rough estimate, the cost of printing and paper comes to about 25 per cent of the total cost. The sales promotion roughly works out to about 5 to 10 per cent, while the distributor's commission is of the order of 45 per cent including about 33 per cent trade discount. The publisher is thus left with about 20 to 25 per cent and this amount is shared between the publisher and the author. It is estimated that about Rs.10,000 are required to publish an average size book of 250 pages (one thousand copies).

India has been organizing the National Book Fair under the auspices of the National Book Trust in different parts of the country to promote the interest of the people in the book world. The first World Book Fair was held in New Delhi in 1972, the International Book Year. The second and third World Book Fairs were also held in New Delhi in 1976 and 1978 respectively.

House and Trade Journals

A house journal is a medium of communication intended to project the image of the organization both within and outside of the organization. The purpose is to improve the morale of the employees, create favourable climate for the working of the organization and promote and provide opportunities for creative expression.

While internal house journals are meant for circulation within the organization, external journals are also circulated outside of the company or organization, such as dealers, consumers, shareholders, etc.

The trade journals disseminate information about the trade, equipment, or technical progress. Unlike house journals, they are not meant for image-building of the organization. There are a combination of the trade and house journals. They give technical information about the trade and also news about the employees and the organization.

The house journals are generally in the magazine format size of 8½"x 11". They deal with the welfare of the employees as well as other activities of the organization. The house journals in many cases accept advertisements. However, they should not be commercial in appearance since their primary purpose is to promote goodwill. Generally, house journals are also not priced.

Filing of Declaration and Clearance of Title

Under the Press and Registration of Books Act, 1867, for bringing out any newspaper (any printed periodical work containing public news or comments on public news), which covers also house journals, the printer and the publisher have to make a declaration before the District Magistrate or the Sub-Divisional Officer in whose jurisdiction such newspapers are printed/

published. The declaration is made in a prescribed form giving all relevant information such as title of the paper, language, periodicity, retail selling price, publisher's name, place of publication, printer's and editor's names, etc. It is necessary to file a fresh declaration whenever the place of publication or printing is changed or when the publication is temporarily suspended. Six copies of the declaration are filed. No declaration is, however, necessary in the case of government journals.

Before making the first declaration, it is necessary to ascertain from the Press Registrar, New Delhi, through the concerned District Magistrate or S.D.O., whether the title of the journal is permissible. This formality is necessary in the case of government journals also.

After the declaration is filed, the magistrate forwards one copy of the declaration to the Press Registrar, who then issues a certificate of registration to the publisher.

Every publisher is required to send a copy of the publication, if it is in English, Hindi, or Urdu to the Registrar of Newspapers for India, New Delhi. In the case of other languages, copies are required to be sent to the Press Information Bureau of the Government of India as given in Rule 5(2) of the Registration of Newspapers (Central) Rules, 1956. A certain number of copies are also to be sent to the addresses mentioned in the Rules made by the State governments under Act 25 of 1867.

Newsprint and Printing Machinery

The publicist has to apply for the allocation of newsprint to the Registrar of Newspapers for India in a prescribed form every year. The newsprint policy is revised every year and the quantum of allocation depends on the number of copies printed, frequency of the journal, number of pages, and other details. The Registrar of Newspapers should also be approached if the organization publishing such journals would like to import printing, composing, and allied machinery for bringing out the journals.

Sales Tax and Postal Concessions

The company publications distributed free to employees are

exempted from sales tax. House journals can be posted at the concessional rate provided they comply with the conditions laid down in Rule 122 of the Post Office Guide, Part I. The condition is that it should be registered with the Registrar of Newspapers for India and bear in print the R.N.I. Registration number on the journal.

For bringing out house journals and other publications, the publicist should know the different printing processes, types of paper, use of type faces, and art of proof-reading.

Printing Processes

The printing processes are mainly of three types – letter press, lithography and offset lithography, and gravure. The selection of a printing process depends on the type and the size of the publication, the quality aimed at, the number of colours involved, the print order, and the time and money available for the project.

Letter press is the most popular printing process. The printing is done through the relief method, where the raised printing surface of the type or the block is inked with rollers. The impression is then obtained on printable surface (paper, board, plastic sheet, etc.) by contact. This is a speedy and economical process, particularly for small runs. Newspapers, most of the books, magazines, and commercial printing jobs are done by letter press.

In lithography and offset lithography or photographic printing, the text or the image is transferred to a flat slab of stone or metal plate with greasy crayons or ink. The surface is then damped. Because of the mutual repulsion of water and oil, the greasy parts repel moisture but catch the ink when rolled on. The image is then transferred to paper. Gradually, the metal plate is replacing the stone slab and the printing matter is generally transferred to it photographically. Offset lithography is a further improvement on this process. This process is generally used for posters, calendars, and long-run colour jobs.

In gravure or intaglio printing or photogravure, the impression is made from ink deposited in engraved areas or 'depressions' in a plate. The matter on the image is transferred to a copper sheet or roller by photography and etched with acid, the desired depth of colour being determined by the depth of etching. The surface is covered with ink and the surplus ink is wiped off, leaving it in the 'depressions' which are impressed on paper. This process is increasingly used for illustrated magazines in multi-colour, requiring large runs.

Printing Paper

For the printing of house journals, there are generally two types of paper – coated or art paper, and uncoated paper. The quality of art paper depends on the type of finish (coating) given to the paper. The uncoated paper is mainly of two varieties – rough (antique) and smooth (calendered).

Printing paper is available in sheets of various standard sizes – foolscap (17″ × 27″), crown (15″ × 20″), demy (18″ × 23″), and royal (20″ × 25″). Different quality of papers are not available in all the sizes. For instance, art paper, maplitho, offset, and newsprint or poster paper are available only in crown and demy which are in fact most-used standard sizes in India.

Since the cost of paper normally accounts for as much as 50 per cent of the total expenses of the publication, it is economical to fit the publication into one of the standard sizes. This would avoid wastage when the paper is trimmed for printing. This is particularly important in the case of the publication with a large circulation.

While deciding the size of the page of a journal, it should be kept in mind that at least ¼″ is allowed on each outer edge for 'bleeding' or "trimming", after printing and binding the sheets.

Type Faces

An intelligent and clever use of different type faces not only helps readability, but also gives better 'look' to the publication.

Generally one type face is used for the text and more than two or three for headlines. The mixing of too many 'families' of types results in a chaotic situation.

Many type faces can be used at least in four different ways. Bold characters are used for headlines, subheads, and for giving emphasis to an important paragraph in the text while italic variety of type face is suitable for captions and subheads. The headlines can be varied by printing some of them in upper/ lower case and others entirely in capitals. Capital letters in the same type face as the text may also be used for subheads in articles and for other purposes.

The size of the type whether hand-set or machine-set is designated in units of points (A standard typographical measurement – 1/72 inch or point). The point size applies to the height of the type, as measured from the front to the back of the metal shaft bearing the letter. The width of the type line, column or page is expressed in terms of 'ems' (See Appendix for specimen of types).

Proof-reading

It greatly facilitates the publicist's work if he has some knowledge of the art of proof-reading. The use of standard marks of proof correction is of great help to printers. (See Appendix for proof-reading marks.)

The author's corrections should be kept to the minimum as the corrections cost money and cause delay. A few words added or deleted may mean the respacing of a large number of words by the compositor, or even resetting the entire paragraph. It may also affect a number of pages. All this can be avoided if the publicist carefully checks the type script before sending it for type-setting. As far as possible, all additions, deletions, and corrections should be carried out in the type script. This will save considerable time and money.

Projection Through Journals

The Central government, the State governments, and the public sector undertakings bring out nearly 1,000 magazines. The private sector also publishes a large number of magazines. They broadly fall in three categories, namely, general magazines, house journals, and trade journals. The frequency, size, contents, get-up, and other features in these magazines vary a great deal. No reliable statistics are available in regard to the publications of journals in the private sector or the total expenditure incurred in bringing out these publications.

Why do we bring out these magazines? Many a time we tend to follow a ritual and would not like to break the tradition. Sometimes it is considered a matter of prestige. At times a magazine is continued because it is considered self-supporting or a profit-making proposition. In other words, it has adequate advertisement support or guaranteed circulation. This viability may be real or illusory.

It is necessary to clearly spell out the objectives, the readership and other details so that the editorial staff can translate these objectives into concrete terms while selecting different types of material – advertisements, news stories, features, articles, etc. – for inclusion in the magazines.

The PR objective in nine out of ten cases is to disseminate information about the organization and project its image both within and without. Mostly it is an effort at image-building. The real question, therefore, is how this is to be done? What mechanics need be deployed to make the projection purposeful and meaningful. At the same time, it should help in establishing rapport and credibility with the readers. The best possible way to project governmental and other activity or 'performance' or 'achievements' is through human interest features. If skilfully done, the activities can be projected through features in a more powerful and effective manner than through straight news items, advertisements, or learned articles by specialists.

If the objective in the magazines is to establish credibility with the readers in regard to the organization, it is necessary to give a heavy dose of features in journals. The projection of an organization's activity through features has a greater and lasting impact on the readers.

If the aim of the publicist is to project the success of self-employment ventures with a view to encouraging potential entrepreneurs and instill in them the feeling of self-confidence, the publicist can interview a few successful entrepreneurs in different fields and portray their success. All such success stories through features about entrepreneurs who have taken up small-scale projects can motivate others to come forward and adopt self-employment as a means of their livelihood.

The publicist in the public sector undertakings, for instance a nationalized bank, can make a clever use of the feature technique in projecting the success of the bank. It will have a much greater impact if the publicist instead of talking in statistical terms about the expansion of branches of the bank in rural areas can spell out the gains to the rural people in concrete terms through a feature based on an interview of the people who have actually benefited. Again, instead of cataloguing the new schemes of credit for weaker sections of the community, the publicist can himself or through newspaper reporters, interview the beneficiaries – self-employed persons such as taxi drivers, artisans, small traders and entrepreneurs – and project their happiness and successes. This would be a more meaningful publicity.

It the publicist is called upon to defend the government decision about the hike in petrol price, he can certainly say in a news item that the intention is to restrict consumption of petrol and divert the supply for the production of 'Naptha' so as to to have more agriculture produce. A more effective publicity, however, would be to interview a few farmers who have received more supply of fertilizer made from 'Naptha'. The projection of farmers' happiness and linking this with greater agriculture production through a feature is perhaps the best defence of the government's decision on the rise of petrol price. However, if a free-lancer or a journalist working in a newspaper is called upon to criticize the price rise, he can interview car owners, taxi drivers, scooterists and portray their unhappiness by weaving their reactions into a feature.

Demolitions of slums and jhonpuris carried out in Delhi and other places can be supported or criticized depending on the publicist's situation through a feature. If he is to defend the action, he can interview a few affected persons and bring out the gains such as free ownership of land, prospects of better living conditions compared to the slums in which they had been living, cheap transport, banking, medical and schooling and other community facilities. However, if the purpose is to criticize the demolitions and new resettlement colonies, the publicist through a feature based on interviews can present the opposite point of view by projecting the hardships of the settlers such as exposure to cold and rain, non-availability of drinking water, ejection from their place of work, etc. The feature writer can also present a balanced picture by interviewing people holding different points of view on the subject.

At the time of railway or air or other strike, if the publicist's task is to support the government, he can interview the people adversely affected by the strike – porters, taxi drivers, and the passengers who wish to undertake a journey to see a dying friend or a relation, etc. – and can do a feature based on their reactions. This will evoke public sympathy against the strikers and to that extent provide effective defence for the governmental action against the strikers.

The power shedding and its adverse effects on production of essential items and consequent rise in prices, dislocation of work in offices, etc. can be forcefully brought out by interviewing the affected people, through a feature. However, if the publicist's intention is to defend the power shedding which is claimed to have been resorted to divert more power for agricultural operations, the feature writer can interview the beneficiaries, i.e. the farmers, and project their happiness and gains.

For criticism against the Life Insurance Corporation that it does not settle claims in time and this results in hardship to the families of the deceased, the public relations officer of the LIC can certainly give statistics and percentages to counter this criticism through a news item. The more effective and convincing way, however, is to interview a few persons in very distressing circumstances who have received the claim amount promptly. A feature based on the experience of these people can help a great deal in creating a better image of the LIC in the public mind. Similarly, the Indian Airlines Corporation's claim about regularity and punctuality of its flights and provision of other comforts such as non-smoking area, better catering facilities, and quick delivery of luggage can be projected more effectively through a feature based on interview of passengers who are regular users of IAC. A feature of this kind can be a supplementary effort to the news item giving statistics.

The Indian Airlines Corporation and a number of other public sector undertakings earmark money for the welfare of their employees. A personality feature giving a pen-picture of a sportsman who has won a national or an international award and linking this with the management's support to such activities would be a more effective publicity. Similarly, employees living in a colony can be interviewed in regard to schooling, medical, shopping, housing, and recreational facilities provided by the management and a feature can be built up on the basis of their reactions.

If the intention is to build up an image of honesty, for instance, of IAC employees, it is better to give some specific instances, identifying the names of the passengers who had left their belongings either in the plane or at the airport and the same has been returned to them by the IAC. A feature based on the reactions of the concerned passenger is a better way of publicising rather than giving out statistics of items returned to passengers during a particular period. Similarly, if the idea is to highlight the improved catering facilities in the railways or in the IAC, the reaction of passengers to these facilities is of importance. A news item from the management's side cataloguing the improvements effected does not cut much ice. It makes drab reading. It has no personal touch.

It is well known that remote areas in the country where the armed forces are stationed undergo rapid development and in the process the local people get certain advantages such as medical treatment, better roads, and drinking water supply. Instead of detailing these benefits through a news item, the defence publicist can interview the beneficiaries and bring out specific cases where armed forces personnel have given significant help. A human story with vivid details can enhance the image of the armed forces. This indirect publicity is more powerful than projecting the work of defence personnel in a direct manner.

Many of our socio-economic and welfare measures can be highlighted in magazines through a series of human features, clearly identifying persons and places.

CHAPTER XVI

Broadcasting as PR Medium

Broadcasting is the most powerful medium of dissemination of information in a country such as India where the large majority of the people are illiterate and the circulation of newspapers is almost negligible. Radio has a much greater reach compared to any other communication medium.

Through radio PR personnel can reach the people in any part of the country and in any language in the quickest possible time. For important national, regional, or local information of public interest, the PR man can try to get his message in the news bulletins of All India Radio. For other purposes he can use commercial service on payment.

It is, therefore, necessary for a PR man to have some idea of AIR's operations, programmes, etc. He should, in particular, know the working of the Commercial Broadcasting Service with which he is primarily concerned for PR work.

Broadcasting in India at a Glance

Broadcasting in India is a state monopoly. The Government of India took over two privately-owned transmitters at Bombay and Calcutta in 1930 and the Posts and Telegraphs Department started to operate them under the name of Indian Broadcasting Service. In 1936, the name of the service changed to All India Radio (also known as 'Akashvani', since 1957) and it was made a separate department under the Ministry of Information and Broadcasting.

Broadcasting in India with its network of 84 stations and 3 auxiliary studio centres covers all the important cultural and linguistic regions of the country. AIR's Home and External Services programmes including Vividh Bharati programme are transmitted for 1760 hours a day in seventeen foreign and eight Indian languages. The programmes which cover 77.60 per cent of the geographical area and 87.75 per cent of the population of the country are beamed from 157 transmitters including 123 medium wave transmitters with radiated power of 6210.50 kW. These programmes are heard through 1.78 crore receiving sets in the country.

New radio stations at Tura, Gangtok, Agra, Madurai, and Jamshedpur, and district level local radio stations at Kota, Diphu, Keonjhar, Adilabad, and Nagarcoil are likely to be set up during the Sixth Plan period (1978-83). Suratgarh radio station is also to be commissioned in 1980-81.

All India Radio not only informs and educates people but also provides healthy entertainment through music, plays, features, news, current affairs, etc. The composition of the programme in the Home Services is: Music – 41.4 per cent; News – 22.9 per cent; Talks and Discussions – 8 per cent; and Rural Programmes – 6.1 per cent.

News is broadcast directly through 244 bulletins in 19 Indian and 25 foreign languages and 34 local dialects. These include Home and External Services bulletins and 106 regional bulletins.

All India Radio broadcasts a number of national programmes on its all-India hook-up. These include a weekly national programme of music comprising both Hindustani and Carnatik systems of music; national programme of regional music; national orchestra – 'Vadya Vrinda' – consisting of Hindustani and Carnatik instrumentalists, and national programme of features.

A festival of music – 'Radio Sangeet Sammelan' – is organized every year by All India Radio. The Sammelan is preceded by an all-India music competition to discover new talent in both vocal and instrumental music.

Family Welfare and Farm and Home Units of AIR plan and produce family welfare programmes and programmes pertaining to agriculture, animal husbandry, cooperation, and allied subjects for broadcast.

Popular entertainment programmes in Hindi known as 'Vividh Bharati' programme – film music, humorous skits, short plays, and features – are broadcast from 31 centres.

The AIR Code on broadcast by individuals evolved in 1970

was suspended during the Emergency. The Code has been restored in March 1977. The details of the Code are given in the Appendix.

AIR broadcasts programmes for special audiences such as armed forces, women, youth, children, sportsmen, students, rural and urban people, and industrial workers.

The 'Yuva Vani' programme provides scope for self-expression by the youth and their involvement in AIR programmes. It comprises music, talks, features, plays, and interviews.

AIR publishes eight programme journals in English, Hindi and six regional languages. The External Division of All India Radio brings out a monthly programme journal, *India Calling*, and quarterly programme folders for overseas listeners in ten foreign languages.

The monitoring service of All India Radio monitors round the clock broadcasts of major radio stations of the world. The information is also fed to the news room.

AIR's Audience Research Unit undertakes regular surveys and analyses listeners' reaction and also reception quality of the stations.

The programme exchange and transcription service undertakes exchange of outstanding programmes of different stations, transcribes speeches of eminent personalities, and maintains library of sound archives.

The Central Staff Training Institute at Delhi and Regional Centres at Hyderabad and Shillong train the programmers and administrative staff of All India Radio. The Staff Training Institute (Technical) conducts training courses for the AIR technical staff.

The Research Department of All India Radio deals with problems of interest in both sound broadcasting and television. The work is handled by four sections – propagation, acoustics, research and development, prototype and production unit. Special stress is laid on import substitution of equipment required by All India Radio.

Because of the limited number of radio receiving sets, the broadcasting network does not reach more than 10 per cent of our population. The licence fee from radio and TV amounts to Rs.27 crores a year. (Rs.15 per annum for first radio set and Rs.3 each for more sets in one name and Rs.50 per year per TV licence. No fee is charged from the blind for radio licence.)

The AIR's external service broadcasts are beamed to 55 countries in 25 languages for about 56.30 hours a day.

For the first time since October 1977, all recognized opposition parties in India share radio and TV time on the basis of complete equality with the ruling party during the elections.

Commercial Broadcasting Service

The government introduced commercial advertisements on the Vividh Bharati medium wave channel at Bombay-Pune-Nagpur beam from 1 November, 1967. Encouraged by the initial success, AIR extended its commercial service to some other beams. The present network of commercial broadcasting centres consists of twenty-eight stations, out of which fifteen are main and the rest of the thirteen are link stations.

The aims and objectives of commercial broadcasting in India are:

(a) To provide a channel for additional revenue for the state exchequer.
(b) To help increase production, both agricultural and industrial, particularly of the commodities meant for mass consumption.
(c) To inform the consumers of the availability of their requirements.
(d) To encourage healthy competition among producers.

To ensure that the advertisements broadcast over the commercial service are in keeping with our national policies, a Code for Commercial Broadcasting was introduced. It spells out the general rules of conduct in advertising, discusses the procedure for the enforcement of the Code, gives excerpts from the Code of Ethics for advertising in India issued by the Advertising Council of India, and also incorporates the Code of Standards in relation to the advertisements of medicines and treatments. It also discusses the standards of practice for radio advertising as well as standards of practice for advertising agencies. Some of the salient features of the Code are:

1. Advertising should be so designed as to conform to the laws

of the country and should not offend against morality, decency, and religious susceptibilities of the people.

2. No advertisement should be permitted

   (a) which derides any race, caste, colour, creed, nationality except where such uses would be for the specific purpose of effective dramatization such as combating prejudice;
   (b) which is against any of the objectives, principles or provisions of the Constitution of India;
   (c) which will tend to incite people to crime or to promote disorder, violence, or breach of law;
   (d) which presents criminality as desirable or furnishes details of crime or imitation thereof;
   (e) which would adversely affect friendly relations with foreign states;
   (f) which exploits national emblems or any part of the Constitution, or the person or personality of a national leader or a state dignitary;
   (g) on cigarettes and tobacco products;
   (h) on real gold and jewellery (not artificial).

The Vividh Bharati Service of All India Radio was chosen as the vehicle for carrying the commercial advertisements for obvious reasons. This light service not only provided a popular medium for advertisements but also offered scope for the easy placement of advertisements between two programmes. Because of its national character, originally the Vividh Bharati programmes were mostly in Hindi. However, with the extension of commercials to other centres, certain local variations have been permitted. This happy blending of the national and the regional cultural colour has helped further popularization of the commercial service.

All the commercial advertisements going on the air can be broadly classified under two heads: Spots and Sponsored programmes. The spots are of seven-second, fifteen-second, thirty-second, and sixty-second duration. The seven-second spot is popularly known as 'Time Check', and is generally voiced by the announcer on duty. The 'Time Check' combines the announcement of the exact time as well as the broadcast of the commercial message. The other spots are varied in nature such as the spoken-word spots, the musical jingles, etc. All the spots and the sponsored programmes are screened before they are accepted for broadcast. For medicinal spots, there is a separate screening committee. Due care is taken to ensure that the spots are qualitative in nature from various angles and also in keeping with the Code for Commercial Broadcasting. The spots are inserted between two songs/programmes at suitable punctuation points. One capsule contains a maximum of three spots but in any case a capsule should not exceed 75 seconds in duration.

Sponsored programmes were a later addition and were first introduced in May 1970. As the name indicates, programmes are sponsored by the advertisers. Sponsored programmes are of varied complexions. These include skits, features of various types, quiz programmes, music items, sports commentary, etc. Most of the sponsored programmes are based on film music.

While a spot conveys a particular message to the prospective consumer in a brief and acceptable manner, the sponsored programme communicates that particular message through the medium of a programme. It also builds up the constitutional image and provides the business community an opportunity to serve a social purpose along with the business by presenting a programme of their liking.

The prices of products are broadcast along with advertisements except in the case of institutional advertisers. Also there is no insistence on price tags for goods which have a range in size and quality with different prices. But in the case of commodities where products are sold in one single pattern without variation in size or quality price is announced invariably.

The commercial service started commercial sponsorship of important games and test matches played in India and abroad from the year 1975-76. It sold all events of Olympic Games at Montreal. Earlier, India-West Indies cricket test series and test matches played between India and New Zealand and between India and MCC were sponsored by All India Radio. Subsequently a number of games/matches were also covered by the commercial service.

All India Radio conducts its commercial business mainly through advertising agencies of which 256 are at present on the rolls of the Commercial Broadcasting Service. The agencies have been categorized into three groups on the basis of their existence in the field of advertising and their financial soundness, etc. These are: (a) accredited, (b) recognized, and (c) registered.

Accredited and recognized agencies are allowed a commission of 15 per cent whereas the registered agencies are given a commission of 10 per cent on the business they place with AIR. Accredited agencies are also allowed a credit period to make their payments. Advertisers are free to approach AIR for the broadcast of their advertisements directly also on payment in advance.

Audience research is an integral part of the Commercial Broadcasting Service as in the case of the primary service. The advertiser would like to be informed of the number of radio sets in a particular service area, ratings and profile of the various programmes, listening habits of the people, and above all the effectiveness of radio as a medium for advertising. The audience research fulfils this need. It undertakes surveys periodically at different centres. These surveys reveal that the majority of the listeners has taken well to commercial broadcasting.

There has been a steady rise in the *gross* revenue earned by the commercial service. From Rs.2.96 crores in 1970-71, it has increased to Rs.7.75 crores approximately in 1977-78.

Verghese Committee

In 1977, the Government of India appointed a working group under the chairmanship of B.G. Verghese to examine the functioning of AIR and Doordarshan and make recommendations regarding their future set-up.

The group in its 504-page report (2 volumes) recommended that all the National Broadcasting Services should be vested exclusively in an independent, impartial, and autonomous organization – National Broadcast Trust named 'Akash Bharati'. It should be established by law by Parliament to act as a trustee for the national interest. The autonomy of the Corporation and its independence from government control should be entrenched in the Constitution itself and the idea of a trust woven into it. The group did not favour two separate corporations for Akashvani and Doordarshan.

The recommendation of the Verghese Committee, however, did not find favour with the government which came into power in January, 1980.

CHAPTER XVII

PR through Audio-visual Media

TV – Great Motivator

Television is an important PR medium for the projection of an organization's activities, programmes, services, etc. It combines sight, sound, motion, and immediacy with personal involvement of the audience. It brings directly into the home the personal identification with personalities and ideas. As such, it is an effective means of persuasion and motivation.

The close circuit TV provides dramatic opportunities to inform a large audience at a single showing about new products, services, events, techniques, and a variety of other subjects. It can cater to a widely dispersed but specialized audience. The wide availability of video tape enables the TV to show events with great flexibility. This has brought many new possibilities for using the TV for PR purposes.

The PR man utilizes commercial services of the TV which are paid for. On important occasions, he can also try to get through non-commercial channel – news and current affairs and other programmes.

Television in India

The first television centre was commissioned in Delhi on an experimental basis in 1959. Now the TV with 18 centres covers 8 per cent of the country's area and 15 per cent of the population. The transmission is for 38 hours a day in 12 languages. The TV coverages would be considerably expanded with the launching of the Satellite in 1981.

Today the television network in India consists of eight full-fledged TV centres, three relay centres and seven post-SITE transmission centres. Altogether this network covers an area of 212,100 sq. km. and a population of 877.68 lakhs. Plans for the expansion of the TV and the extension of its coverage envisage setting up of TV stations at three State capitals, viz., Ahmedabad, Bangalore and Trivandrum, and relay centres at nine places including Vijayawada, Jammu, Cuttack, Ajmer, Madurai, Varanasi, Asansol, Murshidabad, and Panaji and programme production centres at Gulbarga, Muzaffarpur, and Raipur during the Sixth Plan.

Television in India is still confined to a few cities. The TV centres including terrestrial transmitters function at Delhi, Bombay, Srinagar, Amritsar, Calcutta, Ahmedabad, Madras, Lucknow, Jaipur, Raipur, Gulbarga, Hyderabad, Muzaffarpur, and Sambalpur and relay centres at Mussoorie, Pune, and Kanpur. There are three base production centres at Delhi, Cuttack, and Hyderabad. The TV range varies from 70 to 100 km. There are no plans for multi-channel TV in the near future.

The initial growth and function of the television service in India was as a part of All India Radio. On 1 April, 1976, Television Broadcasting was delinked from AIR and was designated as Doordarshan. This has made possible fuller development of the distinctive features of television and the specialized skills peculiar to this medium.

From January 1976, TV has introduced commercial services. Both spots and sponsored programmes are telecast. About Rs.4 crore revenue is earned from commercial programmes and Rs.3 crore from TV licence fee.

The TV receiving licences are now estimated to be seven lakhs. About 1.5 lakh TV sets are produced every year in the country. Sixty per cent of the production is in the small-scale sector. About 70 companies manufacture TV receivers.

Satellite Instructional Television Experiment (SITE) using Application Technology Satellite-6 (ATS-6) was started in India in August, 1975. The programme covered 2,400 villages in Andhra Pradesh, Bihar, Karnataka, Madhya Pradesh, Orissa, and Rajasthan. Four hundred villages in Gujarat were also covered. The programme was transmitted to the satellite from the two earth stations at Ahmedabad and Delhi. Two thousand four hundred special TV sets received TV signals directly. Base production centres were opened at Cuttack, Delhi, and Hyderabad to produce special TV programmes in four languages. The one-year SITE ended on 31 July, 1976. Terrestrial transmitters now functioning at Jaipur, Raipur, Hyderabad, Gulbarga, Muzaffarpur, and Sambalpur cover 10,000 villages and disseminate information on such subjects as agriculture, health, hygiene, family and child welfare, adult education, etc.

The primary objective of television in India is to help the processes of socio-economic development of the country and to raise the quality of the life of the people. This is sought to be done through devising programmes that present the diversity and the richness of India's culture and intellectual attainment. Entertainment is combined with information and instruction. Doordarshan endeavours to plan its programmes in such a way that both the urban and the rural viewers benefit by the various services provided by the medium. Doordarshan in its programmes tries to project the problems facing our society and the common man. By telecasting such programmes, Doordarshan makes the people aware and conscious of their own power through which results can be achieved. To combat superstition, programmes on science in every-day life are telecast. Programmes on art and science, art and ancient culture are also telecast. Besides, wholesome entertainment is provided to the viewers by showing feature films, etc.

Special programmes to meet the needs and aspirations of special categories of viewers, such as farmers, industrial workers, women, youth, and children are also telecast from different stations of Doordarshan. Programmes on family planning and welfare and adult literacy are also a part of this endeavour. Wherever possible, particularly on issues which concern the common man, participation of ordinary people in programmes is sought.

A beginning has also been made in the application of TV to formal and informal education. Formal curriculum-based programmes are telecast by Delhi and Bombay TV stations. Fourteen lessons in a week of 20 minutes' duration each are telecast by the Delhi TV station and 6 lessons in a week of 20 minutes' duration each are telecast from the Bombay TV station. Non-formal educational programmes for school children are telecast from Delhi, Madras, and Srinagar TV stations.

For the day-to-day work PR man in India particularly in non-governmental sector is more concerned with Doordarshan's commercial services. He should, therefore, be fully acquainted with the Code for Commercial Advertising over radio and television; Code of Ethics for advertising in India; standard of practices for radio and TV advertising, and advertising agencies.

Some useful information on commercial broadcasting is given in the Appendix. Technical information on films, spot, static caption advertisements and rates of sponsored programmes produced by the TV centre or by advertisers is also given in the Appendix.

Film – A Powerful PR Medium

The film is an effective medium of communication, instruction, education, and entertainment. It brings the audience in direct contact with facts and ideas through sight, hearing, and emotions. It thus makes a direct impact on the captive audience.

The motion picture offers a number of advantages as PR medium. These are: greater impact because of its powerful appeal to eye, ear, and senses; effective learning aid on account of auditory and visual qualities; accurate reproduction of objects and events; clarity; long life-span; measurability of circulation and effectiveness statistically; etc.

Film is a versatile means of expression. It establishes a dramatic and articulate bridge between the organization and its publics. There are many types of films – full length feature films, narrative or voice-over picture type, direct dialogue or newsreel type and cartoon, educational, musical, technical, animation, training, and travelogue films.

Film Making

One of the important PR functions is to advise the organization on film-making. It is not necessary for the PR personnel to be trained film-makers. They should, however, have competence enough to give expert advice in regard to the objectives of the film, the target audience, the cost involved, distribution, and other allied matters. The PR men in several departments and organizations act as consultants or links between the organization and the film producers.

The PR man at the outset should clearly spell out the objectives of the proposed film. It is for either imparting information or putting across a certain point of view. Also, it must be aimed at specific audience which should be clearly identified and the possibility of reaching it should also be examined. The audience can be general public (theatrical) or selected or classified audience (non-theatrical). The two types of audience generally require different approaches and different techniques in film production.

The film-making for the government and to some extent of the public sector undertakings in India is undertaken by the Films Division of the Ministry of I & B or through its approved film producers. The PR directorates provide the necessary link between the organization and the producers.

The film producer should be selected with care after examining his experience and standing. The work should be given only to a professional and not to an amateur. The PR man has to have close contacts with the film production team – the producer, the screen play writer, the director, the cameraman, the editor, etc. The producer finalizes the contract with the sponsor; the screen play writer prepares the 'treatment' (working draft) and also the 'shooting' script or complete script which gives shots, dialogues, commentary, etc.; the director interprets the script into film form; the lighting cameraman and camera operator create pictures in light and shade; and the editor turns isolated sequences into a finished film.

The PR man has to provide a 'brief' or 'the line of approach' or a statement of policy for the guidance of the producer. This should include the objectives of the film, types of audience to be reached, contents, length, assistance to be provided by the organization's staff, shooting facilities, the time of completion, distribution instructions, cost, the name of the consultant, background material, etc. A contract or agreement has to be signed between the organization and the producer incorporating all these points including penalty clauses.

The producer after study, investigations, visits on the spot, etc. prepares the 'treatment' or rough draft. He should be given a free hand and intelligent cooperation by the organization so as to allow him to use his creative talent without any hindrance.

The PR man examines in consultation with the concerned people in the organization, the contents, approach, presentation, etc. in the rough draft of the film. After the general approval, the producer prepares the final or 'shooting' script or the blueprint of the film. The shooting schedule has then to be decided, keeping the locations to the minimum so as to keep down the costs. The editor arranges the shots in their correct sequence, according to the script, and produces the rough cut or the first version of the film. At this stage, opticals, commentary, etc. are not provided. The sponsor can suggest deletions, additions, alterations, changes in sequences and emphasis, etc. The final cut is then prepared by incorporating the changes, where necessary, and by adding opticals, dialogue, commentary, music, sound effects, etc. The PR man must ensure that the message to be conveyed is put across effectively.

A film in colour costs a lot more than the one in black and white. The colour film should be made only if it is absolutely necessary. All films shown in public are on 35 mm stock irrespective of their being in black and white or in colour or with sound or silent. The film in 35 mm is more expensive but it can be reduced optically to 16 mm. Films for non-theatrical audiences are generally in 16 mm.

It is necessary to decide in advance the number of copies or prints required for distribution to theatrical or non-theatrical audiences. Arrangements have to be worked out with distributors and with cinema houses for showing it to theatrical audience. For non-theatrical audience, the PR man has to ensure that the authorities concerned have projection equipment. Special shows for invited audiences or at public places, special mobile units, film shows at exhibitions, etc. can be organized. The PR man should see that the shows are properly publicised to the section of community interested in the subject through film columns in general newspapers and in trade and technical press and by organizing special film shows for the press.

Uses of Films

Films can be used for a variety of purposes – for internal PR communication to inform or motivate the employees about the concern's activities, programmes, philosophy, outlook, etc., for training or for promotion of morale or safety or employer-employee relationship. The film to be exhibited should be well produced, interesting, and shown preferably during working hours. An organization can also sponsor films for external audience or general public. The documentary, if intended to promote a national objective or educational and cultural values, can be given to the Films Division of the Ministry of I & B for distribution on its all-India circuit. Any commercial or image-building film, however, is not acceptable to the Films Division. An organization or a concern can also produce a documentary to promote its activities or its products. For exhibition of such commercial films, the organization has to buy time in the cinema halls.

To sum up, the film is an appropriate medium of PR, but the organization has to have necessary resources for this expensive medium. Also, the decision to use film as PR medium should be made in relation to costs and relative effect of other media available to PR.

Slide films or film strips usually consist of series of still pictures, with or without captions, photographed on a strip of 35 mm film and projected in a sequence. They can also be used in conjunction with recorded sound. Film strips provide a half-way house between colour slides and fully animated cinema films. Slide films are cheaper to produce than films. Film strips accompanied with automatic sound are known as talkie-strips. When no captions appear on the film, a narration to explain the pictures can be provided in printed form or recorded on tape or disc with music or sound effects.

Films in India

India tops among the film producing countries in the world. Over 550 feature and over 2,000 short films are produced annually including about 200 in colour. Besides, 140 short films and weekly national and regional newsreels in English and regional languages are brought out by the Films Division of the Ministry of I & B.

The capital investment in film industry is to the tune of Rs.500 crores. The industry provides employment to about two lakh people. The annual entertainment tax revenue amounts to about Rs.100 crores. The main producing centres are Bombay, Calcutta, and Madras. The gross annual earnings from production, distribution, and exhibition of films amounts to over Rs.225 crores.

Despite the growth in exhibition in recent years only 20 per cent population is exposed to cinema medium in India. The country has 5,650 permanent and 3,367 touring cinema houses. The total seating capacity in these cinema houses is a little over 50 lakhs. The average daily attendance of people going to cinema houses is about one crore.

Indian films are exported to nearly 100 countries, including countries in East and South East Asia, East Africa and also to the UK, the USA and the USSR. The export earnings amount to about Rs.8 crores. Cinematographic films – raw and exposed – and other equipment are imported to meet the requirements of the film industry. The imports in terms of value amount to Rs.6.50 crores every year.

Guidelines on Film Censorship

The Ministry of Information and Broadcasting has simplified and rationalized the Film Censorship Directions and has issued guidelines (January, 1978) to help the Board of Film Censors in clearing films for public exhibition.

The new guidelines replaced the 18-year-old censorship guidelines in the form of directions under Section 5(B)(2) of the Cinematograph Act, 1952, to the Board of Film Censors.

The revised guidelines give greater scope to the serious minded and sensitive creators of aesthetic films and ensure that restrictions on artistic expression are truly reasonable and reflective only of the requirements of the law.

The earlier guidelines have not worked satisfactorily and their objectives also have not been fully achieved. They have also, with the passage of time, become outmoded and are not in tune with contemporary standards or requirements of society. Some of the directions were unduly restrictive of the freedom of expression guaranteed under the Constitution and thus open to question in courts of law.

The revised guidelines have been evolved after taking note of the recommendations of the Enquiry Committee on Film Censorship and the views expressed by the film industry, as also the Central Board of Film Censors.

The new guidelines are simply stated and so worded as to avoid an exhaustive set of instructions for the censors as it was considered that too detailed a catalogue of instructions would inhibit a proper and independent interpretation by them. At the same time, it has been ensured that the censors are appropriately informed of the basic criteria which must govern their approach to film censorship.

The following are the new guidelines:

1. The objectives of film censorship will be to ensure that

   (a) the medium of film remains responsible and sensitive to the values and standards of society;
   (b) artistic expression and creative freedom are not unduly curbed; and
   (c) censorship is responsive to social change.

2. In pursuance of the above objectives, the Board of Film Censors shall ensure that

   (a) anti-social activities such as violence are not glorified or justified;
   (b) the modus operandi of criminals or other visuals or words likely to incite the commission of any offence are not depicted;
   (c) pointless or avoidable scenes of violence, cruelty and horror are not shown;
   (d) human sensibilities are not offended by vulgarity, obscenity and depravity;
   (e) visuals or words contemptuous of racial, religious or other groups are not presented;
   (f) the sovereignty and integrity of India is not called in question;
   (g) the security of the state is not jeopardized or endangered;
   (h) friendly relations with foreign states are not strained;
   (i) public order is not endangered; and
   (j) visuals or words involving defamation or contempt of court are not presented.

3. The Board of Film Censors shall also ensure that the film

   (a) is judged in its entirety from the point of view of its

overall impact; and

(b) is examined in the light of contemporary standards of the country and the people to which the film relates.

4. Films that meet the above mentioned criteria but are considered unsuitable for exhibition to non-adults shall be certified for exhibition to adult audiences only.
5. The notification of the Government of India in the Ministry of Information and Broadcasting (No. G.S.R. 168), dated 6 February, 1960 has been superseded.

Under the new guidelines on film censorship, it is claimed that there is no substantive change in the government's approach towards the depiction of vulgarity, obscenity, lasciviousness, violence and the like. Only undue restrictions, rigidities and contradictions of the previous guidelines have been removed. Films are now to be judged as a whole and in the light of the overall impact that they make. This gives free reign to artistic expression and creative freedom. The new guidelines nevertheless ensure that this freedom is kept within the bounds of our social values and moral standards. There is no shift in favour of permissiveness.

The guidelines are being again reviewed by the government which came into power at the Centre in January, 1980.

CHAPTER XVIII

Photographs - an Aid to Public Relations

The Use of Photographs

Photographs and illustrations are an important aid to public relations. Good and quality photographs are required for a variety of purposes – to illustrate stories in newspapers, magazines, technical press; for house journals, booklets, and reports; for advertisements, posters, and exhibitions; and for training, research, and record purposes.

Photographs are generally accepted as authentic proof of facts, ideas and events. They add to interest in the story, and at times have a compelling appeal. To be useful for PR purposes, the photographs should not only tell the story, but should also be striking, interesting, topical, natural, action-oriented, adequately captioned, and pleasing aesthetically. The tendency to feature a VIP or top executive on all occasions should be discouraged. The picture of an ordinary worker engaged in the organization's productive activity can enliven a house journal. It also gives a sense of belonging to the employees.

To achieve the best results, the PR man should engage a competent photographer. He should be given proper briefing about the coverage but thereafter left fairly free to make use of his skill and talent.

The PR man need not be a professional photographer. He should, however, have some knowledge of the various aspects of work – coverage instructions, functional facilities, general idea of the photographic equipment, cropping, retouching of prints to remove blemishes (accidental and unwanted extras); photo agencies and accredited photographers; release of photographs on exclusive basis; photo libraries; the captioning of photographs to include vital facts and additional information;

and making of blocks, etc.

Illustrations include photographs, cartoons, maps, drawings, graphs, diagrams, charts, sketches, etc. The publicist can make a skilful use of illustrative material while sending news releases, features, and articles to the newspapers and periodicals.

Advantages over Printed Word

Photographs have many advantages over the written word. A picture can be worth a thousand words. It enhances the meaning of a news story or a feature or an article. It is more effective. The hurried reader may miss a news story but he would hardly miss a picture. Through pictures, the reader absorbs the message at a glance. Also, unlike news releases, the photos can seldom be altered by editing at newspaper offices.

Most of the pictures clarify, support, and explain feature stories. The reader learns faster and remembers longer through pictures. The publicist can make his subject-matter more lively and realistic, if he supports it with photographs. With the help of pictures, he can even cut down the length of his story.

The Guidelines

The planning of the news story and also of the photo coverage is to be done simultaneously. There has to be perfect coordination between the publicist and the photographer. Since illustrated material is an important tool in the hands of the publicist, it requires very careful planning and advance preparation. The publicist should extend all help to the photographer including writing of captions. He should, however, allow the photographer full freedom in taking photographs. He can certainly suggest the broad angle but the details of execution should be left to the photographer. The publicist should not hamper in any way the photographer's work and he should be allowed all initiative.

The publicist can himself take the photograph or use his photographer, if any, or hire a photographer either for specific assignment or on a long-term basis. There are advantages if the publicist can himself take the picture. In that case, he is not dependent on the photographer. Also, during the travel, he can take pictures of unusual subjects, crafts, etc. which can be used for illustrating features. The lack of professional skill and proper equipment and preoccupation with his own work will, however, make the publicist's task very difficult if he combines the two assignments. In any case, in large organizations, the two functions should not be combined.

The technical quality of a photograph should be of a high order. The picture should not be over- or under-exposed, and there should be no spottings. The publicist can compose a photograph and include what he wants and exclude what is not desired. The best pictures are those that can be either used in full or cropped – with part of the picture cut off without hurting the remainder.

There are different types of pictures: (i) news event, prize distribution, train accident, etc.; (ii) portrait pictures; (iii) cheese cake – sex, women, romance; (iv) action shots – mechanic working on an engine; (v) pattern shots – views of inanimate objects used for industrial publicity; (vi) product shots – show off a product.

For press publicity, posed photographs are of little use. Similarly, VIP-oriented pictures should be avoided in features. The picture should be sharp and have one dominating and central point of interest. It should tell the story, and tell it at a glance. It should not tell many stories. In the case of features, the photograph should explain the theme of the feature. It should be clear in its details which the publicist would like to project.

The picture which the publicist sends to the newspapers should be as large as he expects it to appear. Blown-up pictures reduce clarity. Since editors generally have space only for small pictures, it is good strategy to send pictures to fill up small space. Most publicity pictures are printed on glossy 8″ × 10″ paper.

Caption is a must for a photograph. It should be effective and striking. It identifies all the persons in the picture with full name and initials in the order of left to right with sufficient background. It is better to tell too much than too little. A caption can be pasted under the print so that the editor can look at the photograph and caption without turning the photograph. This method is convenient. But the slip is liable to be torn off in handling. As such, the slip can be pasted on the back of the photograph. In no case should the caption be written on the reverse side of the picture.

It is better to give a choice of pictures, i.e. horizontal and vertical. Also, give more than one picture on the subject so that the editor can make his own selection. Always keep copies of pictures which are sent to the newspapers. Negatives are not sent to the newspapers.

While despatching and mailing photographs, a 'Manila' envelope with cardboard inserts is used to prevent cracks and breaking in transit. The image side is kept towards the back of the envelope so that the post office stamps may not damage the print. The envelope is marked 'Photographs – Don't Bend'.

Photographs can be placed on exclusive basis in the case of both news photographs and photographs of features and articles. It should be clearly indicated whether the photograph is exclusive for a particular paper or papers in a particular language or papers in a particular region.

A freelancer can illustrate his material with photographs. For this purpose, he can contact photo agencies, the government departments, embassies, business houses, etc.

There are a number of photo agencies operating in metropolitan cities and towns in the country. They supply photographs to newspapers and periodicals and also to others including freelancers on payment.

A number of embassies and high commissions located in Delhi have photographers to cover assignments. They also send photographs to the newspapers for publication. This is yet another source for a freelancer to obtain photographs to illustrate his publicity material.

CHAPTER XIX

PR through Exhibitions and Fairs

Exhibition is an important medium to project an organization's materials, processes, products, or its activities, services, ideas to the public.

The aim is to either boost up sales or to project the activities or the corporate image of the organization or to develop contacts with similar other bodies in the country and abroad in the specialized field or to earn the goodwill of the people or of a section of the community.

Types

Some exhibitions are sales-oriented, while others are intended only to inform, educate, or instruct, or to motivate people towards a particular idea, policy, programme, or cause. The exhibitions can be on such subjects as family planning, adult education, prohibition, cleanliness, etc.

Exhibitions are also organized to promote a class of industries, for instance, small-scale or village industries, or to focus attention on some category of people – children, women, tribal people, etc., or to depict the progress and the development in a specific field or of a particular area.

While exhibitions are organized for a variety of purposes, trade fairs are specifically held for the purpose of selling or demonstrating products, new ideas, or techniques.

It is of crucial importance that the sponsor should be clear in his mind in regard to the objectives, the scope, and the limits of the exhibition. This is important, since all the subsequent steps revolve round the central idea or the main theme.

Exhibitions in India are organized by industrial and voluntary organizations, Central and State governments, local bodies, etc. Their coverage can be national or confined to a State or a district or a village or a group of villages. The organization may be required to put up a pavilion in an exhibition, or only a stall or a stand, or a complete exhibition.

Participation

The public relations department normally acts as a professional adviser to the organization in regard to the participation in an exhibition. It has also a role to play in preparing and servicing of displays in the organization's permanent showrooms, museums, etc.

The PR man has not only to tender advice in regard to participation, but also to indicate the extent of support for a particular exhibition. The organization has also to undertake construction of the pavilion, preparation of display items, internal decoration, publicity, dismantling, etc. It is, therefore, necessary to prepare a time schedule for the completion of different stages of work. The deadlines must be adhered to.

A number of requests come to an organization in regard to participation in an exhibition, big or small, sponsored by the government departments, Trade Fair Authority of India, semi-government and other bodies. Before arriving at a decision about participation, it is necessary for the public relations department to find out the credentials of the sponsor, the objectives and the scope of the exhibition, the size and type of the visitors to be attracted, the extent of sales likely to result, the venue and timings of the exhibition, the likely participation by similar organizations or competitors, and the prospects of earning goodwill of the people or of the targeted sections of the community.

Since exhibition is a very expensive medium, the cost-benefit ratio is to be carefully worked out before the decision is reached. The PR man should resist all pressures and decide the issue on merits after mature consideration of all pros and cons. A firm decision, however, must be made by the organization well in time in regard to participation keeping in view the objectives to be achieved, the main theme, availability of funds, etc.

Budget

A break-up of the total amount available for participation in the exhibition is necessary to include items such as rent of the space, cost of construction, expenses on making models and other display material, fees for the architect and the interior decorator, expenses on staff, transportation, telephones, furniture, insurance, publicity material, hospitality, dismantling, etc.

Space

The next step would be to decide about the extent of space or area required for the pavilion. While the expenses have to be limited to the minimum on this account, the space should be adequate enough for proper display of the organization's products and services. The participation should be commensurate with the organization's standing. The extent of the space to be taken, however, also depends on the rent charged by the exhibition authorities and the total funds available with the organization for the purpose.

Design

The exterior design of the pavilion can be done by the organization's own architect, if any. Otherwise, the work can be entrusted to an agency which has the requisite expertise. For this purpose, it may be necessary to invite general or limited tenders and to enter into an agreement. It has to be ensured that the exterior design corresponds to the main theme and objectives of participation. The models of a few designs can be seen before selecting one.

Exhibits

Simultaneously, action should be taken in regard to the items to be displayed. A small committee can be constituted to prepare a list of models and other display items and the work assigned to the concerned wings in the organization. The display items, where necessary, can also be got prepared from competent agencies.

Whatever the type of exhibition, the exhibits to be displayed are of great importance. Solid objects, or ideas which lend themselves to three-dimensional representation, should be portrayed. Photographs, diagrams, illustrations, and text can be used effectively to support the presentation. Animated models, coloured photographs, graphs, recorded sounds, murals, sculptures, and other novelties can be used to give the exhibition a projection of its own. The pavilion or stall must tell its story three-dimensionally. The text should be kept to the minimum.

Interior Decoration

In bigger exhibitions, it may be necessary to employ the services of an interior decorator to advise about the display of material. The interior decorator can provide consultancy or consultancy and supervision or consultancy and execution services. The decorator should have the expertise in the kind of exhibition the organization is participating in. The terms and conditions of hiring the decorator and the rate of payment should be settled and an agreement entered into with penalty clauses, in case he fails to adhere to the agreement.

The interior decorator should not only have professional competence and experience, but also be locally available. He should be properly briefed about the objectives to be achieved. The objective may be building the image of the organization or informing the concerned publics about the activities and capabilities or highlighting the organization's outlook, philosophy, technology, quality exports, welfare of employees, etc.

Staffing and Administration

The PR department is also responsible for the day-to-day running of the pavilion. Suitable staff, preferably from within the organization, should be selected and assigned specific duties. The pavilion should be under the overall charge of an experienced functionary, who should see that the staff employed behave well and properly guide the visitors and attend to their enquiries. The observance of punctuality and courtesy is absolutely necessary. Cleanliness, smartness, and devotion to work on the part of the staff will make all the difference.

Other points that deserve attention are: fixing different timings of visit for business visitors and the general public – two types of public – one genuinely interested in assessing the organization's capabilities, and the vast multitude of people; fire fighting equipment; insurance of the exhibits and third-party cover; space for storage of unpacked material and other miscellaneous items; security arrangements; provision of telephones; proper illumination and availability of an electrician; free entry passes, badges, car park passes for the staff, etc.

Publicity

The PR department has also to take care of the publicity. Suitable literature – illustrated folders, souvenirs, leaflets, etc. – for free distribution to general visitors and other publications for restricted use for special category of visitors in English, Hindi, and concerned regional languages are to be brought out. Publicity can be organized in a variety of ways – advertisements in press, radio, TV; press releases, press conference and press preview; newspaper supplements; films, cinema slides: and by organizing inaugural and other special functions.

Evaluation

The feedback of the exhibition is extremely important for the management. It is necessary to keep a visitors' book or devise some other method to have the visitors' reactions in a systematic manner. A proper assessment or evaluation of the accomplishment of the aims and objectives should be made. The lessons learnt and the deficiencies noticed can help in taking corrective action in the future.

Complete Exhibition

Where an organization has to put up a complete exhibition in which other parties also participate, it is necessary for the sponsor to make decisions on a number of points. Some of these are:

1. The venue – acquiring and developing or hiring of the site,

site drawings, outline plans, etc.

2. Defining different categories of exhibitors eligible for participation.
3. Terms and conditions of allocation of space including the licence fee for open space, open display platforms and covered space, mode of payment, deposits, etc.
4. Framing rules and regulations for the erection of pavilion, approval of the construction plan, supervision of construction, etc.
5. Decision about the dates of opening and closing of the exhibition and the timings of opening for business visitors and the general public on week days and holidays.
6. Entry of vehicles and car park.
7. Provision of services – fire prevention and fire brigade; electric installations, sewerage and sanitary facilities, public conveniences, water supply, telephones etc.
8. Security – guarding against pilferage, liaison with police.
9. Recreational facilities – cinema, projection of cultural, trade, and promotional films, open air theatre, fashion parades, etc.
10. Medical facilities – first-aid, ambulance.
11. Air, rail booking office – international and domestic.
12. Tourist services – conducted sight seeing, excursions.
13. Post and telegraph services.
14. Commercial complex – restaurants.
15. Insurance of displays, models, exhibits, stands, and third-party risk cover.
16. Liaison with the railways – railway priority for the movement of exhibits, return railway freight concession, exhibition railway siding, terminal tax exemption, etc.
17. Publicity – exhibition catalogue; advertisements in different media and supplements; posters, brochures, leaflets; press conferences and press releases; publicity through radio, TV, films, cinema slides; press preview; formal opening by a newsworthy personality, and special functions.
18. Dismantling of pavilion – removal of models and exhibits and procedure of settlement of claims, etc.

Stalls/Stands

If only a stand or a stall or a limited space is to be taken in a pavilion the task is relatively easy. The stand can be put up by the organizer or the work can be entrusted to a contractor. If it is desired to limit the expenses, the contractor can be asked to lend construction and other material for the duration of the exhibition. However, models, photographs, transparencies, etc., which can be used by the organization for future exhibitions, can be retained after making payment to the contractor.

The PR man can also finalize a standard design of the organization's stall for exhibitions. This can be used over and over again. Some difficulty may arise if the design is not suitable for the shape and size of a particular exhibition. In that case, a new stand can be designed to fit the actual requirements.

Mobile Exhibitions

Mobile exhibitions, which are simple to erect and easy to man, are becoming popular. The material should be of light weight to avoid heavy transportation and labour costs but sufficiently strong to stand the rigours of frequent transport. It should also survive the removal to other sites without extensive repair and renovation.

Foreign Exhibitors – Special Facilities

If the exhibition is a big one or of a specialized nature and where the organizers expect foreign exhibitors' participation, it is necessary to provide special facilities to foreign exhibitors. The following points deserve consideration:

1. Import of exhibits – exhibitors are to be allowed to import exhibits in reasonable quantities free of duty for exhibition and display against customs clearance permits, subject to the condition that the goods will be re-exported within a period of six months of the date of the closing of the fair or exhibition.
2. Customs clearance – customs office can set up a warehouse at the exhibition or fair grounds. Boxes and crates can be opened and customs clearance permits granted on the spot. Similar procedure can be followed at the time of repacking of the exhibits for re-export after the close of the fair.

3. Disposal of exhibits and allotment of 'fair quota' to foreign exhibitors.
4. Import and disposal of construction material.
5. Import of publicity material including samples without payment of customs duty under certain conditions.
6. Assistance for visa.
7. Special arrangement for observance of National Days to attract attention to particular pavilions.
8. Payment to organization to be made by foreign exhibitors in foreign exchange.

Trade Fair Authority of India

The Government of India set up on 1 March, 1977 an organization, the Trade Fair Authority of India, to promote the country's trade through fairs and exhibitions. It participates in exhibitions and trade fairs abroad and organizes Indian exhibitions abroad and national fairs and exhibitions in India.

The Authority also maintains a list of approved architects and designers and interior decorators, etc. who are grouped in different categories on the basis of the quantum of work. Exhibitors putting up pavilions can take advantage of these lists.

A number of ministries in the Government of India, the State governments and public and private sector organizations have separate exhibition wings. However, in many cases they form a part of PR directorates. Even where they have separate existence, they work in close liaison and coordination with the PR directorates. As such, the PR personnel should develop necessary expertise and experience in exhibition work, right from the planning to the execution and evaluation stage.

CHAPTER XX

Other PR Media

Traditional Media and Their Role

The modern communication media in India coexist with traditional media such as music, particularly the folk and tribal music, dance, drama, and puppetry. There are two main schools of classical music – Hindustani and Carnatic. The folk and tribal music and light music are becoming extremely popular. The leading forms of classical Indian dance are: Bharat Natyam (Tamil Nadu); Kathak (North India); Kathakali (Kerala); Manipuri (eastern region); Odissi (Orissa); and Kuchipudi (Andhra Pradesh). The folk and tribal dances vary from region to region. The classical theatre now exists only in a few parts of the country. The folk theatre, however, can be seen in its regional variants in almost every linguistic region of the country. The puppetry theatre in many forms – string puppets, rod puppets, glove puppets, leather puppets – are found in different parts of the country.

The traditional media have played a very important role in solving several emotional problems and channelizing the destructive forces into constructive ones. In India, too, music, dance, and drama have always played an important role in combating destructive elements and in harmonizing emotional outbursts relating to caste, creed, religion, and language issues. Several folk forms of entertainment, prevalent in different parts of India, were powerful media of public instruction and a unifying force for emotional integrity. They brought the poor and the rich together. Thousands of people, suffering from domestic and psychological problems, used to witness them as a relief to their perplexed life. Such healthy entertainment did dissuade the human beings from destructive activities.

Folk Drama

The network of folk dramas, as envisaged in the 'Tamasha' of Maharashtra, the 'Khyals' of Rajasthan, the 'Noutankees' and 'Rasleelas' of Uttar Pradesh, the 'Swangs' of Haryana and Punjab, the 'Jatra' of Bengal and Assam, and the 'Yaksha-natya' and 'Kuchipudi' of South India and the 'Bhavai' of Gujarat have always been providing healthy entertainment to rural and urban masses. The drama, being a product of the masses and having undergone an unconscious process of evolution through the creative genius of the people, represented different trends of the society in their true colour. It was, at first, in its community form and was performed by the villagers themselves. Such enthusiasm was witnessed among the people that they would collectively construct and decorate the stage, spend their own money for costumes and ornaments for the play. The artists gave their voluntary services as a part of their national duty. The organization of a drama in the village was a great event accompanied with festivities, community singing, dancing, and ceremonial feasts. The guest artists from other villages used to receive the highest honour at their hands. A network of such folk dramas was spread all over India. The regions full of artistic activities were less infected by behaviour problems and litigation cases.

A folk drama is liked by people not because of its production value, but because of its communicability and the relationship between the audience and the performer. The informal way of presentation, the simplicity and freedom from all boredom of technicalities are the very life of a folk drama. The audience should have the feeling of oneness with the performer and should be in tune with his emotions and aspirations. If these factors are lost the whole drama is lost. The traditional folk drama, in India, has its deep roots in the society, only because it strictly adheres to the tradition. Themes have always been changing. Nobody ever sticks to one theme, but, never was there any departure from tradition.

There are several other semi-drama type of traditional media of communication such as the Bahurupia art, the Mask procession, the Nahan, and Chouk Chandni of Rajasthan. The Bahurupia, for example, is one of th[illegible]t ancient forms of entertainment prevalent in almost all parts of India. They are most witty people, well versed in the art of costuming, mimicry, and imitation. They stay at one place for days together and perform jhankis and mono dramas of several types before their patrons. These Bahurupias can be very effectively used for mass communication.

Community Songs and Dances

India had a band of religious teachers and gurus, leading people to the path of pious living and high thinking. Their teachings were made palatable through artistic renderings, such as community singing, dancing, and devotional songs. These artistic activities and ways of living were a very healthy substitute for destructive and immoral ways of living. But, due to several disintegrating forces, the art and the artistic ways are now confined only to professionals and professional ways of earnings. The stage shows, cinemas, and musical recitals are capable of providing only casual joy and have no permanent bearing on life.

Our country, some time back, was not so accessible and communicable as it is today. Even then Indian people were much nearer emotionally and culturally than what they are today. The four pilgrim places – Badrinath in the north, Dwaraka in the west, Jagannathpuri in the east, and Rameswaram in the south were a cross-section of our culture and were visited equally by Indians coming from all parts of the country. Community singing, such as kirtans, bhajans, and hari kathas were great potential factors in bringing people nearer, irrespective of their class, creed, and colour. The numerous folk entertainments such as 'Bahrupi Kala', 'Snake charming', 'Terahtal', 'Dummy horse dancing', 'Nat acrobatics', etc. were so popular that no Indian home, in both rural and urban areas, was left without a performance of these at least once a year. All Indian ceremonies, festivals, marriages, and festivities were full of dances and songs. All religious and community centres were associated with some sort of artistic expression as a means of spiritual development and understanding of the complex human nature. These art forms were practised in relationship with life and for the achievement of *Artha*, *Dharma*, *Kama* and *Mokshah* – that is for the growth of a complete human being. They helped us love each other, and live and let others live peacefully and harmoniously.

These joyful activities were also useful in developing a relaxed mental attitude for a healthy body and a happy mind.

Puppetry

Puppetry is perhaps the most outstanding traditional medium which requires patronage and trial. The Indian traditional puppet art, as envisaged in Bommallatom of Kumbhakonam and Tanjore, the Tholu Bommalata of Andhra, the Rajasthan Kathputli, and the Orissi puppets, was principally meant to highlight the achievements of our ancestors and all those distinguished personalities who had contributed to the growth of the human society. The puppets were carved in most fantastic and interesting figures. Their limitations and deficiencies in the sizes, action, movements, and anatomy have a science of their own and are governed by principles based on experience and study on the part of the Indian traditional puppeteer. They may look obscure and primitive to a modern mind, but they have inspired the modern puppeteer to conduct revolutionary experiments in this field.

The heavy stress on stylization and symbolization in Indian puppetry is to make the emotional appeal of the puppet powerful and lasting. That is why a puppet character, while in action, has more impact on the audience than a human character. Another factor that contributes to the effectiveness of the puppet is its independent personality unlike a human actor. The puppet character is exclusively made and designed for a particular role, but in the case of a human actor he has only to be dressed and made up to play that role. The anatomy of his body, his throbbing heart, and active mind, cannot undergo any change to suit the particular character. His personality and individuality invariably become a disturbing factor in doing his role effectively. But in the case of a puppet character, this problem is eliminated. A puppet, therefore, always has a powerful impact and is used not only for entertainment but for all educational work in the schools and for the society.

Puppetry, therefore, is a very powerful medium of education as well as entertainment and provides tremendous opportunities to those who wish to use the same as an independent art form. A puppetry is quite different from a human drama. It has its own dramaturgy, its own technique of play production and play writing.

Folk Art in Modern Context

The influence of art, music, dance, and drama, if rightly presented and practised, can be of immense help in developing creative genius. The use of art forms for the cultural development of the masses and training of emotions have lately been experimented upon, but they are lacking in imagination, planning, and foresight. The art that used to be patronized by the aristocrats and the individuals has now transcended to the common man, but there too the aristocracy of the professional artist and the professional group has replaced the old feudal aristocracy. The technique-overpowered art has gone beyond the reach of the common man. There is a distinct gulf between the art of the aristocrat and that of the common man. The art which one day carried the highest emotion of a devotee and was the main stream beneath the great religious movements has become a monopoly of a few illustrious rich men. The common form of art which is in use for the masses too has not shown much promise. The drawbacks in the present use of the traditional media for emotional education of the masses are:

1. The cultural groups used for such purposes lack in the spirit of social service and social welfare.
2. The folk items presented for the healthy entertainment of the people lack in authenticity and depth.
3. The new themes given to these traditional forms such as dance, drama, and song do not suit the purpose for which they are meant and the technique in which they are used. They are either very unsuitable or too direct for assimilation and moral impact.
4. The traditional forms used for mass communication are not properly assessed for their suitability. Proper documentation work is not conducted before their use.
5. The various art groups working in the field of publicity under some governmental projects too are of low calibre. The contents of their performances aim at publicising the govern-

mental achievements and not at developing the personality of men.

The use of a traditional medium for communication according to modern needs is a very delicate affair and only expert choreographers, educationists, and artists can undertake this work. The PR man can make clever use of traditional media for his campaigns, particularly in the rural areas.

Oral Communication

India has a rich tradition of oral communication. It takes many forms such as sermon, speech, verse, song, folk music, drama, etc. Information is disseminated through hari kathas, qawalis, public meetings, and group discussions. The daily group prayer meetings in towns and villages, travellers' tales, fairs and festivals, religious concourses held periodically at major pilgrimage centres such as Kumbh Mela at Allahabad have been popular media of oral communication. Gandhiji's daily prayer meetings provide an excellent example as to how his message travelled by word of mouth.

Face-to-face communication is the oldest form of communication but it is still most effective. The expansion of newspapers and electronic media has in no way diminished the role of oral communication. Even today a lot of information is disseminated orally by travellers who travel in different modes of transport, from slow-moving bullock-cart and bicycle to automobile, rail, and aircraft (about ten million people travel daily by rail alone in India).

Oral communication has proved to be most effective for political purposes in India particularly for electioneering by political parties. It is a common sight to see audience ranging from thousands to a million and more assembling in large towns to listen to their leaders. The political parties particularly the opposition rely heavily on face-to-face communication as it does make greater impact on the vast audience than any other media – press, radio, TV or film. The instant dialogue between the communicator and the audience puts across the message definitely more effectively than other media, though they have greater reach.

Role of Outdoor Media

The message through media such as press, radio, TV, etc. reach us at home or circulate around us. In the case of outdoor media, on the other hand, people circulate around the message.

Outdoor publicity is the oldest form of publicity in India. Emperor Asoka's rock edicts are monumental evidence of publicity of this kind. It is carried through a variety of items – panels, hoardings, kiosks, posters including metallic posters and strips, display boards including enamel boards, wall paintings, neon signs, glow signs, cinema slides and colour transparency slides, short films or quickies, audio-visual vans, scotch lite, matchbox and other labels, stickers, sky-writings, etc.

In view of the widespread illiteracy in the country and limited circulation of newspapers, outdoor publicity has special significance for India. Outdoor publicity appeals to both the literate and the illiterate – illustrations as symbol of the product or service to the illiterate and the message to the literate. Outdoor publicity compels attention by its very size, strategic location and colourful and pleasant design. It has also an impact of frequency – 'a salesman round the clock'. Outdoor publicity can be subtle, effective, strong, and powerful as any other medium.

For a variety of reasons, the outdoor publicity medium in India has not developed to the extent it has assumed importance in other countries. The medium is still in its infancy. There is no professionalization. There is no effective outdoor publicity association to take care of a number of requirements. The outdoor publicist finds difficulty in getting sites and material such as steel sheets, etc. required for fabrication of the display. The orderly development of essential facilities has suffered a great deal in the absence of any uniform national policy on the subject. There is no 'code of ethics'. The medium is afflicted with unhealthy competition from non-professional people.

Cinema Slides and Quickies

Cinema which combines the element of sound, sight, motion, and colour is the most effective and popular medium of publicity. The message is put across to the captive audience. There are, however, not enough cinema houses in the country particularly in rural areas. The cinema slides can be displayed for five to seven seconds at a time. The message on the slide has therefore to be bold and brief. The colour transparency slide is also used for advertisement but it is expensive. The slides can be exhibited in cinema houses, free of charge, if they pertain to campaigns of educative nature and of national importance and without commercial value. The 'quickies' are also most effective for communicating the message. There are advertising agencies which can produce such films and also exhibit them through cinema houses. The audio-visual vans with screen, movies, projector, and public address system play music, give free show, and distribute publicity literature, samples, etc. It is a very powerful medium particularly for rural areas.

Posters, Boards, Panels, and Hoardings

Most commonly used posters are paper posters. They are cheap, easily changeable, and convenient to handle. Metallic posters or 'tablets' are made of aluminium. They can stand the rigours of weather and as such are economical in the long run. Rear illuminated plastic posters are made out of acrylic plastic sheet. Individually cut-out plastic letters are superimposed on them to display the message. The colour of sheets for the background is contrasted with the colour used for lettering. Such displays are colourful and attractive. Posters can be displayed at prominent places including the points of sale and purchase.

Large size boards or spot news boards (6′ × 20′ or 9′ × 20′) are used for communication of spot news. The boards are put up at newspaper offices and at prominent locations during special occasions such as elections to give headline news. They are operated manually. Enamel boards are produced through the process of vitreous enamelling. The colour finish lasts for several years. This type of display is useful for messages of permanent or semi-permanent nature. The disadvantage of these boards is that they cannot be repainted. The freshness of display is therefore not possible. Panels are put up on the sides of buses, trams, and on trains. The panels put inside long distance buses and trains directly communicate the message to a captive audience. The railways and State transport authorities are to be contacted for this purpose.

Hoardings are made of steel sheets mounted on a wooden frame. The standard sizes are 10′ × 20′, 8′ × 12′, and 12′ × 14′. The making, painting as per approved design, displaying at selected site, maintenance, etc. are generally given to contractors or agencies in the field, normally on yearly basis. The ownership rests with the agency, the client pays the agreed rental for all the services. Highway hoardings from airports to cities known as 'head on view sites' or 'long view sites' are becoming popular in India. The design on hoarding is dependent on the location of each site, particularly the height from the ground and sociological background of different regions. It can be also made more attractive by three-dimensional cut-out effect.

Neon Signs, Sky-writings, and Labels

In foreign countries, scotch lite (adhesive tape) is cut according to the size and shape of lettering and used in messages. When headlights of vehicles fall in the night on such message, it gets brightly luminous. The message is clearly readable as if it is illuminated. In India, it is not used on a large scale as the scotch lite was an imported item till recently. Neon signs mainly in red and blue colours are most powerful and popular media of outdoor publicity, particularly for commercial advertising. Neon signs are made of glass tubes through which neon gas is passed to obtain red colour. A similar gas is passed through a clear tube to obtain a blue colour. The medium is very expensive. The difficulty of installation in remote areas, maintenance, replacement, etc. are some of the problems. Sky-writing is yet another medium – the trail of colour gas left behind the plane in the shape of a message. It is a costly medium. The scope of its use in India is very limited at present. Labels printed with a message and pasted on the back of match boxes is yet another device extensively used to transmit the message to every housewife and every smoker.

The Message

Outdoor publicity as a rule caters to the audience which is on the move or in motion. The message to be effective should have the following characteristics: (1) simplicity of the idea;

(2) brief, simple, and straight message; (3) boldly written and clearly visible; (4) pleasing and effective colour scheme; (5) should appeal to the consumer, help him in understanding and building up his desire for the product; (6) preferably include picture of the product, reproduction of package, name of product, trade-mark and slogan in bold letters in straight lines (not in zig-zag way of writing); (7) design should depend on location of each site – if it is at ground level, the lettering need not be very bold, but if it is on the top of a multi-storey building, the lettering and picture should be clearly visible; (8) the design including the picture should suit the sociological background of different regions in the country; (9) simple or complicated design – depending on the rural or urban area.

CHAPTER XXI

Advertising in Public Relations

PR and Advertising

There is no general agreement whether advertising is a part of public relations. Like PR, advertising also effects relationship between an organization and its publics. Advertising has, therefore, a close relationship with PR.

Since advertising supports different media of communication, it is important to both the media and the public that are exposed to it. Advertisement is a direct form of communication from the interested party to its concerned publics. Largely directed to sell the organization's products, advertising is also used for PR purposes. The relationship between the PR and advertising has been described thus:

> PR and advertising are not parties to a forced marriage or even a marriage of convenience. Nor are they identical twins who merely wear different clothes. They are more like college room-mates, wearing each other's coats and ties on occasions, dating the same girls once in a while, but alike in their loyalty to alma mater.*

Advertising, being one of the effective and predominant forms of communication, is undoubtedly an important PR activity. In India, it is the PR departments that are generally responsible for the organizations' advertising. At times, public relations, or institutional advertising is distinguished from product advertising. The former is included in PR, while the latter is considered as a part of sales or marketing operations.

*Howard Stephenson (ed.), *Handbook of Public Relation*, Mc-Graw Hill Book Company, pp. 15-16.

No public relations campaign is complete without 'prestige' or 'institutional' type of advertising, which is aimed at building the corporate image of the organization in the context of its contribution to national welfare or directly seeking to educate or inform the community on behalf of the organization on subjects of public interest such as road safety, family welfare, etc. Advertising is also resorted to to clear certain misconceptions or to disseminate information through public relations announcements.

It is necessary for the PR man to understand and appreciate the intricacies of advertising, though he himself need not design or place advertisements. He can work through advertising agencies which provide advisory service on a wide range of problems. The PR man, however, must spell out the objectives, the target publics, and ensure that the advertising message is simple, clear, direct, and appealing in content, style and presentation.

The *Encyclopedia Britannica* defines advertisement as 'a form of paid announcement intended to promote the sale of commodity or service, to advance an idea or to bring about some other effect, desired by the advertiser'.

The American Marketing Association has defined advertisement as 'any paid form of non-personal presentation and promotion of ideas, goods or services by an identified sponsor'. In other words, advertisement is paid use of any channel of communication – radio, television, film, press, etc. – to identify, explain, or to urge the use or adoption of a product, service, or idea.

The Role of Advertising

Advertising has developed in all industrial countries as a major adjunct to industry and commerce. It is the life-breath of the modern society. Advertisement differs from publicity because it is paid for directly and its sponsorship is almost always clearly identified. It is also not personal selling because it is non-personal presentation. Again, advertisement and sales promotion are not one and the same thing. Sales promotion in a wider sense includes advertisement, personal selling, and other selling activities such as exhibitions, displays, demonstrations, etc. Advertisement is thus only one part of sales promotion activity.

Types

Advertisements can be classified in several broad categories. Product advertisement is intended to present and promote goods and services. For example, a particular brand or model of a car. The objective of institutional advertisement is to sell the idea or the firm itself. Here the stress is not on the merits of a specific product but the effort is to build up the image of the manufacturer or the institution. In such advertisements, no specific merchandise is mentioned but an attempt is made to build patronage for the institution. Institutional advertisement is designed to step up profits by increasing the prestige of the institution through means other than selling the merits of its product.

Public relations institutional advertisement is used to forestall public ill-will against a firm. For instance, presenting the management's side of a labour dispute. In a way, it is an adjunct to the overall public relations programme of the organization. Through service institutional advertisement, many firms promote public service such as observance of traffic rules. The motive is altruistic though it helps them in building good public relations in a subtle way.

Advertisement can also be divided into commercial and non-commercial. Commercial advertisement may be consumer advertisement or business advertisement. Consumer advertisement can be national or retail. If advertisement is by the producer, it is national though it need not be national in scope. If it is by the retailer, it is known as retail advertisement irrespective of the geographical scope of the advertisement.

Business advertisement is industrial advertisement, if it is directed at industrial production. It is trade advertisement, if the target is the middle man. It is professional advertisement, if it is directed at a group of people such as doctors, lawyers, chartered accountants, etc.

Commercial advertisement can stimulate two types of demand – primary and selective. The primary demand is for the generic product of an entire industry. For instance, drink milk rather than beverage or demand for TV. Selective advertisement is for a special brand of milk or TV produced by a particular firm.

Non-commercial advertisement is undertaken by the governmental bodies, charitable institutions, religious organizations, or by political groups. These advertisements have objectives such as support to civic ventures, asking for donations, vote for candidate, etc. The government and other organizations also in some cases engage themselves in commercial advertisement.

The advertising activity is generally carried by the following three agencies:

(a) Advertisers including advertising departments of the government, public sector undertakings, business houses, manufacturers, retailers, etc. (They determine advertising policy, supervise advertising programmes, and maintain liaison with the advertising agencies and advertising media.)
(b) The advertising agencies.
(c) The media that carry advertisements – press, radio, film, and TV.

Advertising Agencies/Associations

In India there are 142 IENS accredited advertising agencies having many offices and branches. Many of the larger agencies maintain offices in the principal cities. Some of the Indian advertising agencies extend their activities to foreign countries.

The advertising agencies develop, prepare, and place advertisements in the advertisement media. They also do public relations work, chalk out marketing strategy, and offer counselling assistance such as marketing research, sales promotion activity, etc.

Advertising agencies' income comes mostly from commissions not from the clients but from the advertising media in which the advertisements are placed. The advertising media bill the advertising agency according to their rates, less commission, which is generally 15 per cent. The advertising agency in turn bills the client at the gross rate. Some advertising agencies make no charges for making copy and preparing lay-outs.

The advertising media pay commission only to advertising agencies recognized by the Indian and Eastern Newspaper Society. To receive such recognition, the agency should be completely independent without control or ownership of the medium or client; it should not rebate commission received from advertising media to its client; and must have financial capacity to meet its obligations.

The IENS accredited advertising agencies have over 6,400 clients and they employ 6,300 people. These agencies are entitled to 15 per cent commission from the advertising media. There are a large number of non-accredited advertising agencies. They claim to serve 10,000 clients with 2,000 staff.

Advertising agencies are the backbone of the advertising business. The agencies vary in size, organizational structure, and services offered but they provide media planning and creation of advertisements. It costs less for an advertiser to use an agency than to bypass it. The agency receives commission from the media whereas the advertiser normally does not get any commission.

The advertising agencies perform a number of functions. These are:

(i) *Research:* For a purposeful advertisement campaign, it is necessary to gather information and facts to build up an effective advertising strategy. Advertising research includes marketing research – information about consumer markets, products, or services to be advertised. The agencies set out both short- and long-term objectives for selling goods and services.

(ii) *Selection of media:* The advertising agencies select media – print, audio-visual or a combination of more than one. The decision about individual publications in the print medium has also to be made. It carries out statistical study to determine which medium would suit the advertising message at the lowest cost to the advertiser. In print medium, the advertising agency is a space buyer while in broadcasting and TV media, it buys time.

(iii) *Preparing the copy:* It involves creation and execution of advertisements – preparing the copy, art work, print, radio or TV production, pictorial work, lay-out, etc.

The advertising agency with its expertise can put the advertisements to more effective use. It can prepare more creative advertisements and can thus make a greater contribution to the publicity efforts. There is no easy way to select a particular advertising agency. The advertiser can ask the agency to prepare a tentative advertisement campaign. This method is, however, not in the best interests of either the agency or the advertiser.

In the absence of a thorough knowledge of the needs of the advertiser or the advertising objectives of the client, it is not possible for the advertising agency to do full justice to the job.

A few guidelines for the selection of advertising agencies are given below:

(i) The record of advertising agencies with some related products.

(ii) The agency should be as large as is necessary to handle the work of the client. However, the mere size of an agency is not the index of its ability.

(iii) The agency should have necessary facilities to execute the task assigned to it. That is, whether it deals only in the preparation of advertisements or also handles marketing research or public relations functions.

(iv) The organizational structure and the reputation of personnel manning the agency need also to be considered. It is to be found out whether the advertising agency is dealing in one medium or in multi-media. If the advertiser's need is limited to the medium in which the agency has the expertise, it is of little consequence if the agency's operations are confined to one medium.

(v) The philosophy and advertising policy of the agency has also some relevance to selection. For instance, the publicist would like to know whether the agency subordinates advertisement work to marketing or handles advertisements as an independent affair. Its reputation for good client relationship is also to be taken into consideration. Some agencies give stress on copy while others on visualization. There are agencies which are reserved and conservative in approach while others are all for innovations. This aspect has also to be taken into consideration while selecting the agency.

The advertisers and the advertising media generally depend on advertising agency associations for relevant information on advertising agencies. In India there are the following advertising agency associations:

1. Advertising Agency Association of India (1948), Bombay.
2. National Council of Advertising Agencies (1967), New Delhi.
3. Indian Society of Advertisers, Bombay.

Advertising Media

The basic objective of all advertisements is that the message should reach the desired target. The message needs some communication carrier. These carriers or vehicles of communication are called advertising media. The commercial mass media available to the advertisers are newspapers, magazines, radio and TV (both spots and sponsored programmes), films, and outdoor advertisements, etc. The advertiser can also produce his own medium of advertisement such as direct mailing advertising (post-card, brochure, leaflets, folders, catalogues, handbills, etc.). Many other new media are coming into being such as fairs and festivals, exhibitions, dramatic performances, kavi sammelans, mushairas, etc.

The print advertising media generally have their own advertising departments. They sell space, and in some cases also offer advice and assistance in the preparation of advertisements for those who desire or need such help.

Supplements/Sponsored Features

Many a time, the publicist working in a business house or public sector undertaking is approached by newspapers for advertisements for commercial supplements brought out on an industry as a whole or in respect of some particular firm or undertaking on the occasion of anniversary of starting of an industry or of opening of an undertaking. In the case of such supplements, the advertisements are also sought from contractors, architects, merchants, and others concerned with the industry. The reading material in these supplements is generally of not much interest to the readers. The advertisements in such supplements do not offer publicity commensurate with expenditure incurred on advertisements. The commercial supplements are, therefore, not a suitable mode of publicity.

Non-commercial supplements brought out by the newspapers on occasions such as Independence Day or Republic Day or on national projects, however, fall in a different category. These supplements carry useful information material on certain topics. The publicist can certainly consider release of advertisement for such supplements.

The publicist can also suggest to a newspaper or newspapers to bring out a supplement/sponsored feature on a particular occasion, for instance the Armed Forces Flag Day. These supplements are of two varieties – the one in which the advertisements are secured by the publicist through his own efforts and the other where the newspaper takes initiative to get advertisements of its own with some help from the publicist. In both cases, however, the publicity/background material, photographs, etc. are to be supplied by the publicist. In this way, the publicist can not only push his publicity material but also, depending on the occasion, request the newspaper to donate a part of advertisement revenue of the supplement to the welfare fund.

Advertising in India

Though advertisement business in India is not very large compared to the USA and other developed countries, it has recently grown into an independent industry with its own techniques, business practices and code of ethics. About 40 per cent of the total space in big newspapers in India is occupied by advertisements.

The volume of advertising in different media has been steadily growing in India. Advertisements worth Rs.120 crores a year are given and about 25 per cent of the country's adult population is exposed to advertising.

Despite these advances, there is no organization, official or non-official, to regulate undesirable practices in the field of advertising. Also, there is no special law to guide the advertisers, the advertising agencies, and the advertising media. Anything considered offensive or objectionable has to come under the provisions of the Indian Penal Code or under the legislation relating to harmful drugs and magic remedies. The consumer has no legal protection against spurious and quack remedies publicised in the advertisements.

There is thus a definite need for a statutory advertising council with the support or under the aegis of the government not only to improve the standards of advertising but also to effectively regulate and enforce discipline in this field. The council can deal with complaints from consumers in regard to false, exaggerated, misleading, and untenable claims in respect of products and services. Its role can be of particular significance in regard to advertisements relating to pharmaceutical remedies and appliances, prize gimmicks, maii order business, sex appeal, vulgarity, public morals, decency, etc. The proposed advertising council can also create and distribute advertisements pertaining to social service and community welfare as it is done by such councils in the UK, the USA, and other countries.

ABC/ADV Council/INFA Year Book

The Audit Bureau of Circulation set up in 1948 with its headquarters in Bombay certifies the net paid circulation of newspapers and periodicals. It is a non-profiteering venture of advertising agencies and advertisers and newspapers and publishers. It covers more than 50 major towns in India and 14 languages.

The Advertising Council of India, a voluntary association of advertisers, advertising agents, printers, and newspapers, was set up in 1959, to uphold the cause of advertisers, to improve advertising standards, and to protect the interest of consumers. Its headquarters is located in Bombay.

The INFA *Press and Advertising Year Book* gives comprehensive information on various aspects of advertising in India. The following data are of particular use to advertisers and others interested in the subject:

(i) List of national advertisers giving names and designations of executives, principal products, advertising agents, and advertising year.
(ii) Advertising agencies and their clients (advertisers with Rs.5 lakh advertising budget and over are listed).
(iii) Non-accredited advertising agencies (list given regionwise).
(iv) Classified list of advertisers and agents – those who advertise on all-India basis. They are divided in groups – agriculture and industry, banking, insurance, investment, food articles, hotel and travel, household goods, office equipment, pharmaceuticals, public undertakings, textiles, toilets, vehicles, miscellaneous.
(v) Advertising film producers.
(vi) Outdoor hoarding contractors.

(vii) Neon-sign makers and contractors.
(viii) Radio spot makers.
(ix) Trade and professional advertising associations.
(x) Advertising agencies accredited to IENS along with business secured in different media – press, radio, film, and TV.

The Advertising Policy

The Government of India announced an advertisement policy on 16 November, 1977. Under the policy, the Directorate of Advertising and Visual Publicity, the centralized publicity organization of the Government of India, has been authorized to place advertisements in newspapers and periodicals with the primary objective to secure the widest possible publicity coverage. Political affiliations are not to be taken into account while placing advertisements.

Advertisements would not, however, be issued to newspapers and periodicals which incite communal passions or preach violence or offend socially accepted conventions of public decency and morals. A balanced and equitable placing of advertisements is aimed at by the new policy. The policy also makes it clear that government advertisements are not intended to be a measure of financial assistance. In pursuance of broader social objectives of the government, weightage or consideration will be given to:

(a) Small and medium newspapers and periodicals;
(b) Language newspapers and periodicals;
(c) Specialized, scientific and technical journals;
(d) Papers and periodicals being published especially in backward, remote, or border areas; and
(e) Any other category which the government may consider appropriate for special and bona fide reasons. Small, medium, and big newspapers/periodicals shall be categorised as under:
   (i) Small: up to 15,000 of circulation.
   (ii) Medium: between 15,000 and 50,000 of circulation; and
   (iii) Big: above 50,000 of circulation.

The advertising policy is again being reviewed by the new Government which came into power at the centre in January, 1980.

In selecting newspapers for placing Government advertisements, the following considerations are taken into account:

(i) To aim at coverage of readers from different walks of life, particularly in the case of national campaigns.

(ii) To reach specific sections of people depending upon the message of advertisements.

(iii) To use only newspapers/periodicals with a minimum paid circulation of not less than 2,000. Relaxation is to be made in the case of Urdu and Sindhi language papers and specialized, scientific and technical journals, where the minimum paid circulation of 1,000 will qualify for government advertisements, and in the case of Sanskrit papers and papers published especially in the backward, border, and remote areas or in tribal regions, the minimum paid circulation of 500 will qualify for government advertisements.

(iv) The newspapers/periodicals should have uninterrupted and regular publication for a period of not less than one year.

(v) To use only genuine newspapers which circulate news or writings on current affairs; likewise to use only standard journals/periodicals on science, art, literature, sports, films, cultural affairs, etc.

(vi) House magazines and souvenirs shall be excluded.

(vii) Pulling-power, production standards and the language and areas that are intended to be covered.

Code of Ethics

Some excerpts from the Code of Ethics for the advertising media in India are given in the Appendix.

CHAPTER XXII

Projection through Features

The work of government departments, public and private sector organizations, and other institutions is projected to the people through different media and in a variety of ways. The dissemination of information in the form of news stories is one way. The success and achievements and other information can also be high lighted through paid publicity in the form of advertisements, etc.

Role of Features

A more difficult, though more effective, way of publicising the work is through features. Features require more space or time depending on the media. Also, newspapers have their own staff to prepare features. As such, it is rather difficult for publicity personnel to get their features into newspaper columns. However, if the publicist finds some way of getting his features, not necessarily written by him, into newspaper columns, it would result in more effective and meaningful publicity compared to news stories or paid advertisements.

Features have two important roles. They supplement news stories. Also, if the news is not of much importance, particularly from the point of view of national newspapers, the papers will not take notice or adequate notice of a particular item in their news columns. In all such cases, the publicist can adopt a different strategy – that is to turn this type of soft news into human interest features. In this way, the publicist can get into newspaper columns and in a much bigger way.

Characteristics

The term 'feature' is most common among newsmen but one does not know what it exactly means. There is no consensus among journalists in regard to its scope, types, nomenclature, and other related matters.

Brian Nicholas in his book *Features with Flair* has described features as the 'soul' of newspapers. A few important definitions are given below :

1. The news story stops after it has presented facts or ideas. The feature story goes further. It explores the background, the birth and growth of the idea or event, provides a glance at future too. It conveys to the reader what the writer, or some one else, think about the idea or event. It has greater appeal to the reader's imagination.
2. Feature story is not just recitation of facts but rather an adroit presentation of facts and associated ideas so as to spotlight that which is significant but not apparent to the casual observer.
3. A feature has its impact outside or beyond the realm of the straight news story's unvarnished who, what, where, why, and how.
4. The justification, strength, and the very identity of the feature lie in its presentation of the imagination, not in departing from or stretching truth but in piercing the peculiar and particular truths that strike people's curiosity, sympathy, scepticism, humour, consternation, or amazement.
5. Feature is similar to a news story in that it gives the reader facts in an interesting form and is adapted to rapid reading. But it goes beyond those facts by amplifying them with study, research, and interviews and to instruct, guide, or entertain the readers who know about the subject as well as those who do not.
6. A detailed presentation of some interesting subject in a popular form. It deals with the day's news, a timely or seasonal subject, or any topic that appeals to a number of readers. Its purpose is to entertain, inform, or to give practical guidance, i.e. to show to readers as to how to do something.
7. The news story and feature articles are no doubt different but they are not two widely separate types of writing.
8. Longer bits in newspapers – a piece of writing which explains, amplifies, and interprets issues with study, research and interview.

9. The exploration of facts – the purpose is to guide, instruct, or entertain.
10. In its broadest meaning, it is material selected for presentation by a mass medium primarily because of some element other than the timeliness of its materials. The recency of the material is not the dominant characteristic. The peak of interest comes from one or other elements.

Feature and News Story

To understand the role of features, we should distinguish between interpretative or coloured news and features. A word of caution here. The two, however, cannot be divided into watertight compartments. At times, one overlaps the other. However, feature has some distinct characteristics which make it a class by itself.

News is an objective and factual account of events where the reporter sticks to facts and tries to answer, as far as possible, the six basic questions which make a news story. He gives answers to who, what, where, when, why, and how. The reporter weighs and evaluates the relative value of different ingredients in the story and the most important of them are included in the lead. His purpose is to give facts or information of interest to the people.

The feature on the other hand goes much beyond news story. It gives a new dimension to the news. It examines and dissects news and throws new light on different aspects. It tries to explore the background, probes in depth an idea or the event. It is not just narration of facts. The purpose is to both inform and entertain, and also arouse curiosity, sympathy, humour, and other feelings among the readers. The feature writer reacts to the people, situations, events, and places and provides colourful background and explanatory matter to his feature story. His scope is much wider than news writing.

Take for example an air accident. A news item generally gives when, where, how, and why of the accident and other facts and details. The job of the feature writer is to probe deeper into some aspects which are not taken care of in the news. For instance, the reaction of survivors and their relations to the accident, background of similar accidents, the technical inspection of the plane before it took off, and the loopholes in the inspection procedures, comparative statistical study of accidents with other airliners, loss of articles and behaviour of the community, etc. are interesting themes of a feature. Similarly, in the case of the hijacking of a plane, the news story deals with the hard facts. A feature writer can project the experience and feelings of passengers, relations of passengers, and the pilot.

While news coverage of elections is concerned with the size of the electorate, candidates, constituencies, performance of the candidate, etc., the feature writer portrays the mood of the voters and a vivid picture of the election scene.

If there is a hike in the petrol price, the news item gives the extent of increase, the need for it, and the possible consequences. A feature writer on the other hand tries to find out the reaction of the car users, taxi drivers, transporters, so as to find out how they have been affected in their day-to-day life. The car users switching over to scooters, scooterists taking to cycles, the reaction of petrol dealers, etc. can be probed by a feature writer. Even social effects of increases in cost of transportation can be an interesting subject for a feature writer.

At the time of air or railway strike, while news items give details in regard to people on strike, the number of services in operation, etc., the feature writer gets the reactions of porters, taxi drivers and others whose livelihood have been affected. Similarly, people travelling on important missions – marriage, death, illness, business, etc. – can be interviewed to find out their reactions to the strike. This type of probe results in excellent features.

Features not only differ from news items in regard to their scope but also in several other respects such as timeliness, length, style, etc. The news story deals with recent and current events. It is like a dairy product, a perishable commodity. The speed is of great importance. It has to meet certain deadlines. This is not so necessary in the case of features. A feature need not be only on a recent subject. The event might have taken place some time ago but it can still be a subject of a feature, if it is of interest to the readers. For instance, a feature on hijacking of a plane in Lahore in 1970 became readable when an IAC plane was hijacked to Pakistan in 1976.

Brevity is the soul of news writing. A news story has not much place for subsidiary or background material. Every word counts in news writing. There is relatively more freedom to a feature writer in this matter. He can to some extent adjust the length to his requirements. A feature certainly occupies more space than an average news story.

Events taking place near the place of publication of a newspaper are of great importance. For instance, an accident near at home has a much greater relevance than an accident taking place in some far-off place. It is not necessarily so in the case of a feature. The feature writer can take the reader to a far-off place if he can keep the reader's interest alive. For instance, a feature on how judges – men and women – are adorned in different countries can still be a readable piece irrespective of the geographical area covered by the feature writer.

A feature and a news item differ a great deal in the style of writing. The news story's basic purpose is to give a glimpse of an event, a factual account of the happening. The news might have been written in excellent literary style but its success depends on how effectively it recreates facts. Since this is a hurriedly written piece to meet certain deadlines, the scholarly style is neither possible nor very necessary. The style followed in news writing is generally inverted pyramid or summary format. It is concise, terse, and matter-of-fact. The lead or introduction in the news story attempts to present as far as possible all important facts. News writing has a set format and pattern. There is not much room for colour or ornamentation.

The feature, on the other hand, follows an altogether different style. The feature writer has more freedom. He can freely react to situations, events, and people with emotion and imagination. The feature can be written in a colourful and fiction style depending on the subject and circumstances. The feature writer communicates his thoughts in an effective, interesting, and entertaining manner. He can develop his own style. Through informal style he can make readers his partners. He need not put himself in a strait jacket like a news writer.

A reporter doing a news story does not give title, heading, or sub-title. This is the function of the sub-editor. However, in news releases issued by the government or other organizations, the title and the sub-title where necessary are indicated.

The title tries to project the main thrust of the news story or the new or predominant angle in the news item. The selection of a title and sub-title is definitely of greater importance in a feature. The title should 'sell' the feature. It should capture the attention and arouse interest of the readers. Dull, weary and lengthy, commonplace titles do not click with the readers. The title should carry off the feature, catch the reader's attention, and the reader's eye. However, care should be taken that it should not mislead the readers. It should rather convey in an interesting manner some important aspects of the subject-matter of the feature.

The sub-title need not be used in all cases. Its function is to supplement and strengthen the title and to provide further attraction to the readers. It is in a way the connecting link between the title and the lead or introduction. A title such as 'Family Planning' for a feature cuts no ice. Instead 'Baby-Boom' is more catchy. It can be followed with a sub-title such as 'Sixty-thousand babies a second – can we prevent this catastrophe ?' The title and the sub-title also depend to some extent on the type of newspapers for which the feature is written. For instance, snappy titles for sober papers will be out of tune.

The beginning or the lead in a feature need not be in a summary format as in the news reporting. It can be simple, direct, creating interest of the readers in the subject. The introduction can convey the central idea and also indicate the boundaries or limitations of the scope of the subject. One can start a feature with an anecdote, dialogue, interesting conversation, striking, startling, or interesting statement but this should have a direct bearing on the subject-matter. In any case, the introduction in a feature should not be a bald statement. It must give a lead and create a congenial atmosphere. Some feature writers plunge straight into the subject and simultaneously introduce the special angle which they have in mind. The success of the introduction lies in whether the feature writer has been able to set the necessary tone for the reader so as to get him in proper receptive frame of mind.

The style and the length of the feature also depend on the newspapers and periodicals for which the feature is written. The style will have to vary depending on the type of the paper. Simple and clear writing without too many statistics or documentation will add to the value of the feature. Only well-known abbreviations should be used. A feature writer can make use of wider vocabulary than what is used in news writing. Similarly, paragraphs can also be longer than in the news story. The style can be literary, ornamental, colourful in a feature.

There are some other significant differences between news items and features. For instance, the news story is limited to a single time and place. It is not always a complete story in itself. The presumption is that the reader is aware of the earlier happenings on the subject. The feature, on the other hand, is a self-sufficient and self-contained piece.

News is more or less common in all papers since the sources of news, i.e. agency, broadcasts, etc. are the same. The difference in news coverage in different papers lies in emphasis, extent of space, and slant. This is not necessarily so in the case of features. In fact, features give an individuality or distinctiveness to the newspapers.

The purpose of the news story is to inform, educate, and enlighten the readers about certain happenings. The feature, on the other hand, entertains, guides, and instructs the readers.

A reporter or a correspondent doing a news story does not generally put his name. The name is given only when the story is of some significance. The feature, on the other hand, can be signed.

While the news stories are generally written in third person, the features which are more in the nature of personal chat can be written in first, second, and third person.

Most of the news go without illustrations or without any visual aid. In the case of features, illustrations are more or less a 'must'.

Feature and Article

There are many things common between a feature and an article, and yet each has a character and personality of its own.

Both articles and features are non-news form of writing. They thrive on the quality of good prose. An article often acquires the character of a feature and a feature sometimes takes to the characteristics of an article. It is not easy to draw a line between the two. Each encroaches on the other's territory.

An article is generally written on a broad subject, covering more than one aspect. In features, the subject-matter is specific, minute, and narrow. Only one or two aspects are dealt with at a time. It deals with a single mood. The approach to the subject in an article is general, while it is specific in a feature.

An article is an elaborate piece of composition, a product of mind, based on study and research. It is more scholarly and more serious in tone. It is generally well documented. There are facts, figures, and a lot of statistics. The feature, on the other hand, is a product of heart-based emotions, the feelings, and of reactions of the writer to the people, places, and events and written in a much lighter vein. In features, facts and figures are not so essential.

In terms of length, an article can be lengthier than a feature. Again, besides information and educative material, an element of entertainment is generally there in a feature. It is not necessary for an article to provide entertainment or instruction.

While photographs, etc. are very essential in features, it is not so in the case of articles.

The style of writing an article is generally formal, more learned, heavy, and sober. It can even survive dullness. The style in features is more informal, more colourful. Dullness is fatal to a feature. Features can dramatize, humanize an event or idea and provide joy and delight so as to make a greater appeal to the readers.

In articles, an element of personal opinion is always there, as they are generally written by experts. The expert gives his views and conclusions after making a comprehensive study of the subject. In features, personal opinion is generally projected through others. The features can be written on a variety of subjects by the same person.

While an article has a conventional beginning, middle, and end, the feature can begin and end even abruptly.

The feature is a sort of lyric in prose, 'a momentary mood garnered in words'. An article, on the other hand, deals with several moods, from the grave to the gay, and from the sublime to the ridiculous. If the article is like a many-roomed mansion with several storeys, the feature is a neat little beautiful one-room cottage.

An example makes the difference between an article and

a feature clear. If one has to write an article on the 'Beggar problem in India', the writer surveys the entire situation, gives relevant statistics, and throws light on what has been done on the subject by the government and voluntary organizations. It deals with many aspects of the problem. But if a feature is to be done on the same subject, the writer portrays the actual life of the beggar and his family. He presents a vivid picture of the conditions. The documentation in the feature, if any, is subservient to the human aspects.

A single news item, event or situation can provide a varied approach and result in different types of stories. Take, for instance, the announcement that the US President is to visit India. There will be a straight news story giving the dates of visit, programme, etc. There will be editorials weighing the relative value of the visit, editors giving their opinion about the visit. A column writer gives his individual opinion about the visit. An expert can write an article surveying the Indo-American relations in all its aspects – political, economic, social, and cultural – giving lots of facts and figures.

The feature writer is not interested in the aspects mentioned above. He would like to do a personality feature on Jimmy Carter as to how a relatively unknown man has become the President of the USA. He can do a background feature in regard to the former US President's visit to India or the Indian PM's visit to the USA. The feature writer can do features on the projects which the US President would be visiting in India. He can also interview experts on Indo-American relations so as to find out about the success or failure of the visit. The feature writer can do a feature on the press and broadcasting team accompanying the President. Features can also be written on the visiting First-Lady's social engagements, shopping, etc. in India.

CHAPTER XXIII

Projection through Features - Variety and Preparation

The 'sky is the limit' as far as the scope of feature writing is concerned. Features can be written on every possible subject provided the writer has imagination and skill. These qualities can be acquired and developed in course of time, if the writer has the necessary aptitude for such writing.

Types

Just as it is difficult to define precisely a feature and also to distinguish it from an interpretative news or article, so also it is extremely difficult to classify features into types. There is no consensus among the writers about the classification of features or their exact nomenclature. One type of feature blends into another, and at times different types are indistinguishable. In any case, features cannot be divided into water-tight compartments. However, a rough classification of features by types indicates the scope of wide range of subjects, and helps in the location and collection of material.

One way to classify features is on the basis of the technique of writing. A feature is 'interview feature', if the major portion of the feature is in the form of interview. An interview feature can be a personality or a narrative feature.

Features can be classified according to purpose - expository, explaining things or timely topics; descriptive, giving verbal pictures of persons, things and places of interest; and narrative which narrates events with plot, setting, and characters.

News and Background

The most common type of features are 'news features' which are also called 'news follow-ups' or 'news in depth' or 'news behind news'. These features are tied to current events and one gets ideas of these features from the newspapers. A few instances are: Prime Minister's forthcoming visit to the USSR can give an idea of features on the pen pictures of the people the PM would meet in the USSR. The idea of a feature on detailed cultivation practices and impressions of farmers can come from a news item that a farmer has won a prize for producing the best crop; an advertisement about making a new car can prompt a feature writer to write a feature pointing out the defects in the existing models of cars; a personality feature can be on a politician who has been shot at; an official handout giving family planning facilities can be the starting point for a feature writer, he can interview eligible couples in regard to the facilities that actually exist in the hospitals; a news item that some blind people see for the first time after years of blindness can lend itself into an excellent feature if a few such people are interviewed and their experiences projected; an advertisement 'Best way to prevent lung cancer is to stop smoking' can be probed through a feature by interviewing smokers, doctors, and cancer patients.

Features which are not directly connected with news but deal with subjects of continuing interest such as smoke pollution, road safety, slums, etc. are known as background features. These features can be also on anniversaries of battles or birth or death of a person or on hijacking of a plane or [illegible] earthquakes, which can be linked with the current events. Features written on religious festivals or on the memory of G[illegible] fall in the category of mythological background features.

Statistics can be turned into interesting features. Such features add to public understanding. Statistics in regard to radio licences, State-wise collection of Flag Day Fund, crime, etc. can be used for writing features.

Personality

Another important type of features are – biographical or personality features. Personality features are on well-known persons and their achievements. In such features, the emphasis is on what has made the man great rather than cataloguing his achievements.

Personality features can be written not only on newsworthy personalities or on great men who capture the imagination of people but also on little-known persons such as a beggar who has become a millionaire. These are rags-to-rich stories which hold the readers' interest. These features are not biographical sketches. It is not necessary to tell the story from birth to death. It is sufficient to give just enough background of the person and his recent achievements. A feature writer need not give all details or deal with all aspects. The objective is to tell the readers about the qualities of the man and how he has achieved the position of eminence.

Human interest and Utility

Human interest features are now becoming more popular in India. One can get ideas of such features in a number of ways. Human interest features can be written on a day in the life of a common man such as a constable, a gardener, a sweeper, a beggar, or a 90-year-old man marrying a fifth time or a blind teacher taking a class. Then there is the story of a man who passes matriculation at the age of 50 or so, on his fifteenth attempt. The emphasis in these features is on the unique views of life or on unusual occupations. A feature writer can probe on a subject such as 'Hippies' – why they behave as they do, and from where they get the money, or why dogs form a part of the Republic Day parade, and many other interesting and unusual subjects.

How-to-do or utility or process features give direction and guidance on doing something, such as repairing or assembling radio or TV sets, gardening, child care, health and hygiene, etiquette, preparation of a new dish, making of dolls. Such features should be on a definite and concrete piece of work. The directions should be simple, clear, and in logical sequence, so that they can be followed by readers without specialized knowledge or skill.

Experience and Enquiry

Experience features are of three types : based on own and others' experience; experience of groups of people; and experience amounting to confession.

Personal experience features are based on actual testimony of a person who has undergone the experience. In such features, no attempt is made to preach or sermonize the beneficial effects of new practices. The readers are allowed to draw their own conclusions from other persons' experience. Features based on personal experience of a space traveller or a pilot whose plane has been hijacked or survivor in a plane or train crash fall in this category. The experience should be unusual. It should entertain or provide additional information to the readers. Where a number of persons are interviewed and a feature is prepared on their experience such as the harrowing experience undergone by hijacked passengers is known as group experience features. Confession features are more personal. In such features, the person narrates his intimate experience – success, omission, and failure. The confession of a priest who recited death ceremony *mantras* at the marriage because he remembered only those *mantras* would yield an excellent confessional feature.

Enquiry or investigating features go into the depth of the matter and assess the accuracy or otherwise of the allegations. Such features can be on subjects such as shortage of drugs, housing problem, road death-traps, manholes, and the plight of jhuggi dwellers where probe is necessary to elicit the truth.

Places, Pets, Hobbies, and Scientific Subjects

In features on places, the feature writer gives concrete details of the place with an observant eye. Features on places which have undergone remarkable transformation or places of tourist interest or of scenic beauty can be fit subjects for feature treatment.

Features can also be written on animals and pets such as the arrival of a rare animal in the zoo, the death of an old favourite, feeding of a cranky, operation of a sick one, tribulations of keepers, pets of unusual breeds, training of pets, and fighting among pets living together.

Technical and scientific features explain in the layman's language advances in science and medicines, technology, or electronics. Such subjects are projected through features in a simple language so that even a layman can understand the significance of these changes.

Features on hobbies, particularly unusual hobbies, others' hobbies and how one has got interested in a particular hobby is yet another field for a feature writer. The hobbies of well-known retired people in different walks of life can be interesting subjects of features.

Photo, Institutional and Narrative Features

Photo features are pictorial features. In such features, a series of photographs arranged according to a particular pattern 'tell' the story, in an effective manner. There is very little writeup in such features.

Features on organizations and institutions such as an artificial limb centre, a blind school, a bird sanctuary, or informative features, where the writer tells the readers something of interest and significance such as the fastest aeroplane, the newest ship, and the biggest rocket are yet another variety of features.

In institutional features, the good or bad work of the institution should be projected through the beneficiaries themselves. It makes little impact if the head of the institution alone tells of the progress or the facilities or the feature writer only conveys his own impressions.

Narrative features present facts vividly. They can be travel experience or eye witness accounts from the battle-front. The emphasis in these features is on action and adventure. The writer shares with the readers what he has seen, felt, or witnessed.

Selection of Subject

The preparation of a feature or article by the publicist or a freelancer has to be carefully planned and methodically executed. He has to take a number of steps before the finished product is ready for marketing or placement.

The selection of the subject, collection of material, visiting of places, conducting of interview with people, drawing up a blueprint or the skeleton, decision in regard to the title, subtitle, and the lead, style, revision, physical appearance of the manuscript, illustrations, and marketing or placement, etc. are some of the necessary stages to be gone through meticulously.

In regard to the selection of the subject for a feature, there can be two situations – the freelancer, writing on a variety of selected subjects for general newspapers or for a particular category of papers or the employee writing for his employer which may be the government, the public sector organization, the business house, or any other organization or institution including the newspaper.

Whatever may be the situation, there are certain common criteria for the selection of the subject of a feature article. The subject should be definite and specific and not of a general nature. It should be further limited to one or two aspects of the problem. Also, a special angle is to be given depending on the purpose for which the feature is written and the category of papers in which it is likely to be published. The subject should be of general interest to the readers, if it is to be placed with the daily newspapers. In that case, it should also be topical or made topical by relating it to some current happening. While selecting the subject, one has also to weigh carefully the availability of material, written or otherwise.

For instance a feature writer decides to write a feature on animals. This is too general a subject. It should be limited to one class of animals, say, dogs. This is relatively a narrower subject. At the same time, it is also a definite subject. The feature should deal with only one or two aspects of the subject. For instance, the relationship between the dog and men/women can be a subject of feature. A special angle or slant can be given to this subject depending on the journal for which the feature is written. For instance, if the feature is for a women's weekly, the subject can be 'Do women make good masters?', or 'Women are not fit to own dogs'. However, if one is writing for a popular weekly, one can have subjects such as 'A million a year goes to the dogs', or 'More on dogs than on public health', or 'Big money in dogs'.

If the writer is writing for the company, the broad subject field is more or less decided for him. However, care should be taken to deal with some specific aspects of the subject at a time. Special slant can be given depending on the journal for which the feature is written and the purpose the publicist has in view.

How to get ideas of subjects for writing features? There is hardly any newspaper that does not cry out with a feature idea.

A number of news items give ideas not only for follow-up stories but also for a variety of features. One has only to look at the news items and apply one's mind to get a number of novel ideas on which features can be written.

One can also get ideas of subjects for features by associating two or more subjects. By associating children and money, a new idea emerges such as 'Children have too much pocket money' or 'What do children do with pocket money?'.

To sum up, the most important point in regard to the selection of the subject for a feature is that the subject-matter should be very specific and narrow and should not be of a general nature. Take, for instance, a subject such as transport problem in Delhi. It is too general a subject. It is still relatively a general subject if it is limited to DTC buses in the capital. However, a number of human interest features can be written on different aspects of DTC buses in the capital. Some of the subjects can be 'Buses in Delhi now and in the past', 'Buses in Delhi and other cities in India', 'DTC bus and women', 'DTC bus and the old', 'DTC bus and the children', 'DTC bus and the office-goers', 'Smoking in DTC buses', 'DTC buses and patients'. one can also write features on special aspects such as frequency, over-crowding, behaviour of conductors and drivers, failure to stop the bus at bus stops, physical conditions of the buses, non-coverage of routes, travelling without tickets, the missing trips, the accidents, the non-numbering of buses, double-deckers, behaviour of passengers, and so on. In all the above situations, the subject is narrow and limited and only one or two aspects are covered. The treatment of the subject would depend upon the purpose the publicist or the freelancer has in view and the papers for which he is writing.

Collection of Material

The second stage of preparing a feature is collection of suitable material. The feature writer's anxiety should be to say something different which has not already been said. For this purpose, he needs access to relevant material such as reference books, encyclopedias, directories, year-books, and government publications and reports for getting the latest information and also for checking the facts and figures.

Newspaper clippings and indexed articles from journals on the subject on which a feature is to be written can be of immense help to the feature writer. One can refer to press clipping files and indexed articles in some library. The feature writer can build up his own reference collection over a period of time on special subjects or in areas of his interest. He can also record ideas occurring in his mind now and then which can be used later for writing features. Unusual piece of information, interesting personal observation, memorable conversation, etc. can be added to his personal reference collection. The collection, however, should be organized in a methodical way and in some logical order so that retrieval of information is easy and handy.

The next stage for the feature writer is to decide about the places to be visited and persons to be interviewed for his feature. The art of interview has developed into a fine technique and is extremely important for feature writing.

After the selection of the subject, collection of material, and interview of people, the feature writer has to sit down for writing the piece. It will be a good idea to make a blueprint or plan to serve as a guide. The 'skeleton' will indicate the broad scope as well as the boundaries of the feature.

Title and Lead

It is also advisable, at this stage, to decide a tentative or working title. This can be changed later, if necessary. The title of the feature is of crucial importance. It should 'sell' the idea of the feature and it will sell and capture the attention of readers only if it is catchy, attractive, clever, effective, and impressive. The title can be of a few chosen words put together in an unusual and effective manner. In any case, a commonplace, dull or weary, lengthy or misleading title should be avoided. The title has to be in accordance with the paper for which the feature is written. A feature writer has, therefore, to give considerable thought about the title.

There can be a sub-title but it is not always necessary. It can be longer than the title. The sub-title supplements and strengthens the title. It is the connecting link between the title and the lead or the introduction. For instance, a feature on family welfare programme titled 'Baby-Boom' can have a sub-title 'Sixty-thousand babies a second? Can we prevent a catastrophe?', or a feature on Armed Forces Flag Day can be titled 'A noble cause' with a sub-title 'Are we doing enough?'

The purpose of the lead is to arouse further interest of the readers in the feature. The lead also tells the readers about the central idea of the feature and its boundaries or limitations. Its main function is to put the reader in a receptive mood. The lead in the feature can be simple or direct and need not be in a style which is followed in reporting news. The introduction can be made interesting either by interesting material or by presenting the material in an interesting form. For this purpose, one can use anecdote, dialogue, interesting conversation, striking or startling statement, but all this should be related to the feature and must have some bearing on the subject. In any case, an introduction should not be a mere general statement. It should lead directly to the subject and create a congenial atmosphere for the readers.

The lead is the most difficult part of feature writing, as a good lead can make all the difference. For instance, a lead such as 'Everyone loves dogs' is a bald statement. Instead, one can state 'Because we love dogs, the industry with a turn-over of fifteen million flourishes.' Here, the feature writer is plunging straight into the subject. A feature on diseases of dogs can begin 'Diseases among dogs are common in our country. In spite of good care in feeding, they get diseases!' A more effective lead, however, can be 'Dogs have a habit no one has ever liked. You feed them well, look after their housing and upkeep and yet they get diseases and, what is still worse, a few of them die of it.'

Style

The style of the feature depends on a number of factors, such as the paper for which a feature is written and how the feature writer reacts to situations, people, and places. As far as possible, the feature writer should develop his own style. Unlike news writing, the style of feature writing need not be terse and matter of fact. It can be more colourful, narrative, and imaginative. It is better not to interrupt thoughts in the first instance.

The length of the feature depends on the paper for which the feature is written. The paragraphs can be longer than in a news story. More literary style than what is used in news reporting can be deployed including the use of flashback technique.

Obscurity and dullness are fatal to the feature. Involved sentences should be avoided. There should be more use of active voice. Too much use of punctuation marks or of abbreviations only irritates the readers. The aim should be clear and simple writing, making the reader your partner. The end of the feature should not only round off or review the subject, it should make a lasting impression on the reader and support the theme of the feature.

Revision and Physical Appearance

The feature writer should keep in mind that he has to compete with other skilled writers. It is, therefore, necessary that the finished product should not have any loose ends. To ensure this, it is not enough only to revise the draft in a routine fashion but to give it a critical look after putting it under cold storage for some time. The feature writer should not become complacent with his draft. He should be tough with it, and if necessary re-write and re-arrange the whole thing till he is fully satisfied. Self-criticism while revising the draft is of crucial importance, so also the checking of facts and figures and quotations and correcting grammatical, spelling, and punctuation slips.

The physical appearance or the 'look' of the feature is also of no less importance. The use of standard paper, neat typing, wide margins on top, bottom and sides, suitable headings and sub-headings, clean copy – are some of the points which should receive careful attention of the feature writer.

The finished product is of no use if it is not properly marketed or placed with some newspaper or journal or with other media. Getting the feature into newspaper columns should be the ultimate objective of any public relations effort.

PART III

RELATED SUBJECTS

CHAPTER XXIV

PR and Media Men

Press Rooms

Press rooms are set up on important occasions. The size of the facilities to be provided naturally depends on the importance and the needs of the occasion. In any case, the press room should have all functional facilities such as adequate space to move about, proper furniture, typewriters, stationery, telephones, telex lines, press lounge, press conference room fiited with mikes for both the speaker and the correspondents, and canteen facilities. In the press room, postal and tele-communication facilities are also provided to accredited representatives of news agencies, other media and cameramen.

For transmission of press messages abroad, permanent press rooms of Overseas Communication Service (OCS) are available at Delhi, Calcutta, Bombay, and Madras. International telegrams can be filed at the counter in the press rooms on pre-payment or collect basis. For 'collect' basis facilities, the credit card, national or international, is required. Photo telegrams service is available to most countries. The maximum size of the picture accepted is 25×22.5 cm.

Commercial telephones can also be leased out for 24 hours on exclusive basis. In these cases, the telephones can be used for originating, on a fully automatic basis, local and long distance calls within India and also international calls. Fully automatic service is available only to certain important cities in India and to the whole of the UK. In all other cases, the call requests have to be placed with inland or international trunk operators. International telephone service is available to almost all countries round the clock. In a few cases, however, the service is restricted to specified hours. The 'collect' facility is available to a few countries on an unrestricted basis to any caller.

International or inland telex calls can be made from telex

public call offices on pre-payment or collect basis. Assistance is also available for the preparation of perforated tapes in Roman alphabets. In other cases, the correspondents make their own arrangements to produce a tape. The service is available round the clock, practically to all the countries.

Programme transmissions (voice casts) can be arranged if requests are received from the connecting foreign administrations. At least 24 hours' notice is needed. Correspondents can contact the OCS to fix up studios and broadcast circuits. Studio facilities are available at the OCS centre at Parliament Street, New Delhi.

On special occasions, a fully equipped special press room with arrangements for transacting all telegraph, telephone, and postal business is set up by the Posts & Telegraphs Department in coordination with the OCS. The special press rooms provide all the facilities mentioned above.

If a special press room or a press centre is to cater to a large team of correspondents accompanying a VIP it should have facilities for international live voice casts. For this purpose, studios are set up by the Overseas Communication Service. Such press rooms have a number of telex lines and direct telephone links connecting New Delhi to the country of the VIP so as to enable the press correspondents accompanying the VIP to cover the visit. Such press centres also have channels for transmitting radio photographs. If possible, satellite can be used for conveying radio and TV programmes. The press centre is also equipped with machines for punching tapes. On very special occasions, such press rooms have also arrangements to pipe live all the speeches of the VIP made at different public functions into the press room for the benefit of the reporters working there and who are unable to keep pace with the VIP's hectic schedule.

Facilities to Accredited Media Representatives

In India, press relations wings of the Press Information Bureau and the State governments' directorates of public relations and information and PR set-ups in the public and the private sectors provide several facilities to the press corps. These include grant of accreditation and invitations for functions and social get-togethers including press briefings and press conferences.

Press facilities in their wider context also include conducting of press representatives for local or outstation coverages and making necessary arrangements for this purpose. These include provision of accommodation and messing, air, rail, road bookings, supply of transport, setting up of press rooms and press enclosures, extending facilities for photo, movie, and TV coverage, supply of background material and provision of entertainment and recreational facilities.

To facilitate coverage of events in the capital and in the country accreditation at the headquarters of the government of India is granted by the Principal Information Officer to representatives of newspapers, news agencies, radio, TV, films, and photo organizations. Similar accreditation is given at State capitals by the State governments.

The accreditation requests at the Government of India level are considered in consultation with the Central Press Accreditation Committee, a body composed of journalists. While applying for accreditation, the applicants are required, among other things, to give particulars of professional career and also three prints of latest photographs. A press identity card bearing a photograph of the journalist is issued. Accreditation entitles the journalist to the following facilities :

1. Supply of publicity material.
2. Invitation to press conferences and press get-togethers.
3. Concessional travel facilities on bona fide professional work within the country.
4. Invitation for conducted tours.
5. Speedy dispatch of exposed films.
6. Meeting with PIB officers attached to the ministries including officers in the Directorate of Public Relations, Defence Ministry, and in the External Publicity Division.
7. Entry to Government of India offices in Delhi which are under the security control of the Ministry of Home Affairs.
8. Allotment of telephone connections for office and residence on priority basis.
9. Membership of Central Government Health Service Scheme.
10. Allotment of accommodation from Press Housing Pool.
11. Press Gallery Card for entry to the press gallery of the Lok

Sabha and the Rajya Sabha.

12. Allotment of residential plots/built houses from reserved quota for journalists at certain places.

Accredited photographers are provided all facilities for the coverage of functions. Photography is not allowed inside of the Parliament House, at airports, and in certain restricted areas. However, on special occasions, permits for photography are issued by the authorities concerned. Non-accredited photographers are generally not allowed to cover official functions.

Foreign correspondents are given accreditation on request from their principals and are provided facilities enumerated above. They can obtain press collect authority for filing messages and radio photos after presenting their international cable authority card to the International Telegraph Office, New Delhi. They are exempted from payment of customs duty on professional equipment, import of raw film, and recording tape and export of exposed film and recording tape. They are free to travel across the country, meet and talk to people from all walks of life, and send out verbal and pictorial dispatches. There are very few restrictions on travel to certain border areas for which permits are required.

CHAPTER XXV

News and News Reporting

Definition of News

News constitutes about 60 per cent of the space in a newspaper. It pertains to some recent event which is a matter of interest to readers or listeners. News implies new thing or latest information.

A few definitions of 'news' are :

'News is anything timely that is interesting and significant to readers in respect of their personal affairs or their relation to society, and the best news is that which possesses the greatest degree of this interest and significance for the greatest number.'

'News may be defined as any accurate fact or idea that will interest a large number of readers.'

'News may be defined as an accurate, unbiased account of the significant facts of a timely happening that is of interest to the readers of the newspapers that print the account.'

'News is the first report of significant events which have interest for the public.'

'News is an account of a current idea, event or problem that interests people.'*

'News is the record of the most interesting, important and accurate information obtainable about the things man thinks and says, sees, describes, plans and does.'**

According to B.G. Verghese, former Editor-in-Chief, *The Hindustan Times*, 'The standard definition that only "man bites dogs" is news is obsolete and inaccurate. In view of the "communication gap" in a democratic society that which is reported

*Roland E. Wolseley (ed.) *Journalism in Modern India*, Asia Publishing House, Bombay, 1964.

**Bostian, Casi and Baskilli, *Editing the Day's News*, Macmillan, New York.

becomes news and that which is not reported remains non-news. Sensationalization, disaster, fraud and the like is news but it is not sole news or the highest news.' He advocates reporting of more constructive developments and trends in great social, economic, and political changes, technological advances, modernization processes rather than concentrating only on political news.

News stories are particularly of two types – straight news and interpretative or explanatory or opinionated writing. A straight news story gives a factual account of what has happened in simple, clear, and accurate way. This type of story never distorts, misrepresents, or gives wrong facts. It draws no conclusions, makes no accusations, offers no opinions, and does not indulge in any speculation. Interpretative news story, on the other hand, reports happenings in depth, gives all sides of the picture, provides background, and puts some meaning into the news so that the reader can better understand and appreciate the event.

Most of the definitions of news agree that news is of interest to the public. The interest, however, differs from person to person and place to place. Some other characteristics of news are immediacy, proximity, oddity, conflict, suspense, curiosity, and consequences.

Elements of News

The following are the important elements of news:

(a) Immediacy or timeliness is of great importance. The new thing or latest information makes all the difference. As news ages, it loses its potency. The nearness of an event in time is vital to daily newspapers.

(b) Truth and objectivity is another quality of news. The balanced picture of an event or a happening or accuracy in reporting event enhances the value of news.

(c) Nearness or propinquity, i.e. closeness in space is yet another element of news. The newsworthiness of an event is in direct ratio to its physical nearness to the public served by the newspaper appraising it. An accident or crime nearer home has a much greater news value than a bigger accident or a crime abroad.

(d) News should be of interest or concern or significance to readers. The interest, however, differs. It may be of interest to a section of the community or of local, regional, national, or international interest.

(e) Names of individuals also make news. The person may be widely known because of his position, wealth, or status. Even an unknown person can make news because of some oddity, eccentricity, or unusual occupation or some other factor.

(f) Timing and place of occurrence of an event are also important elements of news. The hour of an event may decide its news importance, so also where a thing happens is important. Suicide in a city may not be big news but in a small place such news may hit the headlines.

(g) Number and size make news. An accident in which a large number of people have been killed or injured makes news. If very few people are involved and nobody has been killed, the news value is of less importance.

(h) Suspense and mystery adds to the value of news. It holds readers' interest in the news. The more the suspense, the greater is the curiosity of the readers in the news.

The other elements which are dominant in news stories are action, movement, and mobility; combat, struggle, contrast, rivalry; sex and scandal; beauty and romance; adventure and pathos including exploration, discovery, excavation, invention; novelty and humour; and stories about children and animals.

In brief, news is associated with something new or something novel or relates to famous persons or of importance to a large number of people or pertains to conflict, mystery, crime, or reveals something confidential or forecasts the future or deals with funny situations or romance or sex, suicide, murder, etc.

The Reporter

To be a successful reporter, one must have news sense or flair or nose for news. He should have the ability to recognize the news value in ordinary things. The qualities necessary in a reporter are: patience and perseverance to get the story; eye for details; capacity for hard work; gift of imagination; skill for clear and concise presentation of news and views; and spirit of enterprise and adventure.

The reporter has to work with great speed and under pressure. He will succeed only if he has an understanding of time value and necessary flexibility and adaptability to change himself to the changing situation.

The reporter must report the news accurately and fairly without prejudice and personal opinion. The following remarks of the late Frank Moraes, Editor-in-Chief of *The Indian Express*, about the qualities necessary in a news reporter are very pertinent: 'What do I regard as the most important quality in a news reporter? I would unhesitatingly say – accuracy. This, and the ability to express himself clearly and concisely. The average newspaper reader is a man in a hurry. He should never be required to read a sentence twice to get its meaning.'

To sum up, the essentials of good reporting are – accuracy, balance, brevity, and speed. Loose writing and unverified details create difficulties and should be avoided.

The Coverage Guidelines

The reporters cover a variety of assignments – accidents, court cases, crime, proceedings of legislatures, communal incidents, demonstrations, deaths, etc., besides political, social, economic, and cultural events, and sports.

In covering accidents, the competent authority, an identifiable official spokesman, should be quoted. The time, place, and cause of the accident and if possible an eye-witness account is to be given. The reporter should give the names of casualties only if he can verify their accuracy. He should show respect for the dead and avoid horrid details. Legal complications would arise if a person who is alive is 'killed'. The nature of accident should be described accurately. He must attribute his report to some authority. The source should be identified at the very start. The context in which the announcement is made, for instance, 'press conference' or 'interview', as the case may be, should be mentioned.

In reporting court cases, care is to be exercised in not giving cause to libel or contempt. Anything that reflects directly or indirectly on the personal character or conduct of identifiable persons or institutions or criticizes or hinders the process of law should be scrupulously avoided. The report should be a fair summary of evidence tendered, statements made by the counsel, and ruling given by the court. If the charges made by the prosecution are reported, the reply of the opposite party must also be incorporated in the story. The onus of proving that the report was in public interest is on the agency or the newspaper.

In reporting crime, murder, suicide, fire, sabotage, etc. the statement regarding the name of the person involved, motive, cause, etc. should be attributed to police or an appropriate source. 'Arrest' is different from 'taken into custody' or 'detained' for interrogation and as such correct nomenclature should be used. A person is presumed to be innocent until he is found guilty by a court. It is advisable to use 'alleged assailant', 'allegedly stabbed'. All information provided by the police should be attributed to them. A reporter should refrain from making comments or speculating the way the crime was committed nor should he draw any conclusion or support or discount a particular theory.

The communities are generally not identified as 'Hindus' or 'Muslims' while reporting communal clashes. Generalized allegation and accusation of being anti-national should not be made against a whole community. Fullest verification is necessary before giving facts and figures. Nothing should be included in the report which whips up communal passions. The source from which casualty figures, etc. are taken should be indicated. If the figures are not confirmed, the report must indicate that the figures are 'unconfirmed'. News of efforts aiming at restoring peace and harmony should be highlighted.

The death story includes the cause of death, its time, and place. The age, by whom survived, the name of the disease are to be mentioned. If it is not intelligible to the readers, it should be explained in the layman's language.

In reporting demonstrations and meetings, avoid adjectives and superlatives. Give as far as possible the factual account. In covering the presentation of budgets in Parliament and Assemblies, the new tax proposals, deficit, surplus, comparison between the previous and the new budget tax proposals, new schemes, reactions, etc., are to be reported. In reporting the debates, the names of speakers are followed by their party affiliations. In reporting the question hour, identification is not necessary. The report of the proceedings should be fair and objective and remarks if any made should be in public interest. The expunged portions should not be included in the report.

The reporter has to interview people for news. He should study the subject and should have at least a broad background of it before conducting the interview particularly on specialized subjects. The knowledge of shorthand and typing can help him a great deal. While interviewing people, he should be a good listener and should keep a pleasant and cheerful disposition. The reporter should have mastery over the techniques of interviewing people.

The reporter should also clearly understand the difference between different classification of news. Flash is a one-line news item about an event of major significance. It has an element of suddenness and tells about something unexpected. 'Snap' is used for important sports or commercial news. 'Top Priority' story is of one or two paragraphs while 'priority' story can be three or more paragraphs.

The press-reporters possessing press authority from newspapers or news agencies can send press telegrams including the 'Flash' press telegrams to their paper or agency. The rates charged for inland telegrams for minimum first 50 words are: ordinary Re.1 and express Rs.2. For every 5 additional words Re.0.10 and Re.0.20 are charged. The flash telegrams are limited to a maximum of 100 words and are charged at the same rate as for inland express private telegrams. The press telegrams may be accepted without payment, if the newspaper or the news agency had obtained previous sanction from the postal authorities.

Style

A news story must be written effectively. The introductory sentence or paragraph, the lead or the beginning, is crucial to the story. The function of the lead is not only to summarize the story but also to attract readers to the story. It sets the tone and the temper of the story. The news story should have the most important points in the first paragraph but the temptation to 'tell' too many things in introduction should be avoided.

Brevity is the quality in the presentation of news. In the news story there is not much place for subsidiary and background material. The news is written in terse, concise, and matter-of-fact style. There is not much room for colour, ornamentation, or dramatization. It is a hurriedly written piece to meet a deadline. Since it is limited to time and place, no attempt should be made to make it a self-contained story.

CHAPTER XXVI

Opinion Pieces

The opinion pieces include editorials, articles, reviews, columns, letters to the editor, etc. This type of writing has one common characteristic. It expresses opinions, passes judgement, or offers suggestions.

Editorial

Editorial is the mirror of the newspaper's opinion. It is the conscience of the paper. It projects the viewpoint of the paper on a given policy, programme, or event. It can inspire, motivate, excite, appeal, criticize, or reject an idea or a policy. The expression of opinion is intended to lead the public opinion and convert the readers to its point of view.

Editorials are written with reason and conviction. The writer should have heart in the subject on which he is writing. The editorial should not be repetitive of facts stated in the news story. It should give a digest of the facts, evaluate them, and arrive at a logical conclusion step by step.

The editorial writer can write straight off if he has a background on the subject. Prior to writing, it is necessary for him to find out his paper's past policy on the subject so as to ensure that the line he is taking is not contradictory.

The argument to be developed in the editorial should be seen in the context of the opposite viewpoint. Spontaneity and cool, logical approach is necessary to demolish the arguments of the other side. Abusive language or rhetoric will not help.

The style of writing of editorials differs from newspaper to newspaper. Though the writer has greater freedom in regard to the length, brief editorials, properly written, make greater impact. Lengthy editorials are generally not read. It is good strategy not to argue too much after developing a point or to include background or other material just for the sake of filling space. The structure of the editorial should be simple so that the readers can easily follow it.

The writer can have different moods in writing the editorial. Brian Nicholas in *Features with Flair* has indicated several moods in which a writer can begin his editorial – incredulous, questioning, counselling, constructively critical, differing, scornful, prophetic, appealing, understanding, and praising.

Reviews

The critics write reviews on a variety of subjects – books, plays, films, TV and radio programmes, etc. While writing reviews, the critics should keep in mind that they are not writing for themselves but are addressing the readers. Any attempt, therefore, to project too much of the critic's own viewpoint or to criticize the work for the sake of criticism or for the sake of controversy would not enhance the value of the writing. The efforts should be to find out something 'good' in everything.

The work to be reviewed should be adjudged in the proper context, i.e. the level of readers or audience for whom it is meant. The review should have two major elements – explain or describe and assess or evaluate the work. One salutary principle is that one should not write about a person anything which one is ashamed to tell him on the face. The pen should be used with great care.

The critic need not be a practising expert in a particular field but he should have sufficient background knowledge of the subject. The reviewer is free to give his own assessment, opinion, and judgement about the work provided it is not based on untruth or malice, but he need not be annoyed if the people do not agree or accept his viewpoint.

Article and 'Middle'

An article is an elaborate piece of composition written on some broad subject, well documented, and expresses the opinion of the writer who has studied the subject in all its aspects. Unlike features, the subject of the article is not very narrow, specific, or minute. The article is generally written in a sober style and the subject-matter is treated in a scholarly manner.

A write-up that generally appears at the centre on the editorial page – below the 'article' and above the 'letters to the editor' in a newspaper – is known as 'middle'. It is so called in journalistic parlance because of its middle position between two different types of opinion pieces on the same page.

The 'middle' is usually a humorous, entertaining, and crisply written piece; a satire; an unusual experience or a personality sketch. It may either deal with an off-beat subject or a topical matter or attempt to expose or ridicule a policy, programme, activity, or bring to public gaze some grievance or inconvenience. In all these cases, the 'middle' is written in a lighter vein so as to make it an interesting reading and providing entertainment to the readers.

The selection of the topic, general approach, treatment, style, etc. followed in the middle are akin to feature writing. Such compositions as a rule do not have much of statistics or documentation or scholarly or sober treatment of the subject as is generally found in an article. It is also shorter in length compared to an article. The language is simple but gripping and effective with small sentences. The focus or the thrust is always on a specific aspect or on a single point.

The success of the 'middle' lies in its holding the interest of the readers from the beginning to the end. The 'middle' is generally written by experienced people who have imagination and observation and have developed necessary expertise by constant practice in this type of writing.

The characteristics of an article and in what way it is different from features, etc. are dealt with in the chapter on 'Projection through Features'.

Letters to the Editor and Column

The letter to the editor is a sort of a feedback for the paper. In a letter to the editor, the individual expresses his personal opinion or grievance on a specific subject of his interest or offers suggestions to overcome the difficulty. Letters to the editor may also pertain to petty complaints. Such letters can be effective if they deal with a specific point and advance logical arguments. They should not indulge in abuse or deal the subject-matter in a round-about way. They are generally brief in length and intended to make a point or a counterpoint. In some cases, the letters are written in a very forceful style and they make a great impact on the readers.

The personal opinion of a column writer is expressed on a subject in a column. The writer has a fixed style of writing and he generally writes on fixed subjects. He has more or less a fixed point of view particularly on political and economic subjects. However, there are columns in a newspaper where other persons also contribute. There are also columns where the columnist writes on a variety of subjects. The subjects of column writers can be political, economic, cultural, or sports, film, radio, books, 'in town', etc. Generally columnists write once a week but there is no fixed rule.

PR and Opinion Pieces

Publicity through the medium of the press is most popular and effective. The PR man should make every effort not only to get into news columns but also to take advantage of other columns of the newspaper.

Apart from projecting the image of his organization through news stories, features, and articles, a clever publicist can also influence opinion pieces on the editorial page of the newspaper which comprises of opinion pieces such as editorial, comment, article, column; 'middle', letter to the editor, etc. in favour of the organization or to the point of view held by it. To achieve success, the publicist has to act in a persuasive and subtle manner.

The publicist can occasionally suggest subjects for editorials. He can also indicate the line of approach to a particular problem. This can be done through writing a letter to the editor and giving him relevant material for his consideration and possible use. Such communications should be signed by the highest authority of the organization. They should be written in a very persuasive, congenial, and convincing style.

Another method is to make a personal call on the editor and discuss the subject with him in depth. The editor or the leader writer can also be invited for lunch or dinner and the problem can be posed before him. If he is receptive, the matter may be further pursued and necessary material sent to him. In case the publicist feels that the editor has his own considered views on the subject, it is advisable not to pursue the matter further. However, if the paper's policy is not firmly committed to a particular line, it is worth while for the publicist to make all efforts to 'sell' his point of view.

The publicist can make clever use of letters to the editor column. He himself can officially write a letter to the editor contradicting a news item or the stand taken by the paper which adversely affects his organization or the point of view of the organization. A more effective way, however, is to get the letters written by individuals expressing the point of view which the publicist would like to project. Care has to be taken, however, that it is not overdone. Letters from the readers have not only more chance of publication but also have a greater impact on the public mind. As such, a very effective use can be made of this column.

The publicist can attempt to influence the column writer by sending relevant material which can be fitted into the subject of the column. Since every columnist has his own field and individual style, the publicist should provide him only appropriate material and also make it exclusive for his use. The publicist can also develop cordial relations with the column writer and in this way can influence him to his point of view to some extent.

To be successful in his work, the publicist must know that in newspapers there are different people to do different work. Every newspaper has a number of 'beats' - police, political, economic, social, cultural, sports, university, transport, etc. He must contact the right man to sell his stuff. If there is any doubt in the matter, the news editor or the chief reporter should be consulted.

It should be clear that the special representatives of newspapers deal with news of all-India importance in their respective subject fields while the reporters cover local functions and news of local interest. As such it does not serve any useful purpose to contact a special correspondent dealing with a particular subject field for local coverage. Similarly, for an event of all-India importance, the publicist should approach the concerned representative of the newspaper and not the local reporter.

If the publicist wishes to get some feature/article in the Sunday edition of the paper, he should first study the kind of material included in that edition. His material must fit in the broad framework of the paper. Also, such material has to be supplied to the magazine editor well in advance and on exclusive basis with good quality live photographs directly related to the subject. In this case, it is a good strategy if the publicist puts across the idea of the subject of the feature before the editor. Only if he agrees in principle about the subject, the matter should be pursued further. He should make it clear in the forwarding letter that the editor is free to cut the length of the feature or make appropriate changes and that no payment is claimed for the publication of the feature.

Though it is difficult to influence the cartoons in the newspapers, there is no harm in suggesting appropriate themes to the cartoonist of a newspaper once a while. Here also, success depends on the relations and the rapport which the publicist has established with the cartoonist.

CHAPTER XXVII

Getting into Newspaper Columns

Familiarity with Organizational Set-up

The PR man can get success in public relations work only if he has some idea about the newspaper organization. This is necessary to enable him to contact the right department and the right person for a particular work. For instance, the publicist should know that for the coverage of local functions, he has to request the chief reporter. But where the news about the organization and its activities is to be disseminated on the national scale, he has to contact the special correspondent dealing with his subject field. The local reporter or the chief reporter will not be of much help.

The organizational set-up varies from newspaper to newspaper depending on the size of the newspaper and the different services it offers for the readers. Therefore, the PR man should get himself acquainted with the organizational set-up of a newspaper before he approaches the concerned department and person.

Editorial Wing

The editorial or news department is the heart of a newspaper. It deals with news, features, columns, editorials, etc. It is headed by an editor or an editor-in-chief. The editor is assisted by assistant editors, correspondents, reporters, critics, etc.

Big newspapers also have special correspondents covering different subjects. They generally cover news of all-India importance. There can be separate feature, sports, finance, society, science, agriculture departments manned by assistant editors. For the Sunday or Magazine edition, there is generally a separate magazine editor. The photo editor provides photo coverage with the help of staff photographers. The editor is also assisted by leader writers, columnists, cartoonists, sub-editors, reference librarian, etc.

One important desk, namely, the copy desk and the functionary heading it, i.e. the copy editor or the copy writer whose name never appears in print, is the backbone of the newspaper. He edits the copy, writes headlines, and, in the final analysis, ensures the newspaper's reputation for accuracy and for attractiveness. He is virtually the last man between the newspaper and the public. It is his job to see that news, feature, or article, or editorial is free from mistakes of words, usage, spellings, punctuation, grammar, etc.

The editor of a small paper combines in himself almost all the functions, i.e. gathering, editing, and printing of news. He is not only the managing editor but his own reporter – collecting and writing local news. He is the copy editor and headline and editorial writer.

Business and Mechanical Departments

The second important department is the business department, which earns revenue for the newspaper. It is divided into two main divisions – advertising and circulation. The advertisement department may have further sub-divisions such as advertisements for local display, for national display, classified advertisements, etc. It may also have a research bureau and an art section to help the preparation of advertisements.

The circulation department deals with despatch of copies in the city and outside the city through road, rail, and air. It may also have a promotional wing to boost up the circulation of the paper.

The mechanical department is generally divided into four parts – composing, engraving, stereo-typing, and press. In the first, the copy is set into type. The engraving wing is concerned with photos and drawings and makes 'cuts' for printing. In the stereo-typing room, the plates for the press are cast in molten metal from the page form. The papers are printed, folded, trimmed, counted, and delivered to the mailing section by the press room.

The bigger newspapers have also separate administrative or coordinating as well as promotional departments. The administrative department looks after the administration of different departments while the promotional department deals with all promotional work in respect of advertisements and circulation. Also, it helps to build up the image of the newspaper and tries to earn goodwill and understanding of the clientele.

Competition for Space

In a democracy, with free press, the publication of information is not an easy task in newspaper columns except through paid advertisements. Newspapers have limited space. Nearly half or 40 per cent of this space is taken up by paid advertisements. There are also fixed items such as editorials, comments, letters to the editor, sports, cinema, and book review columns.

Newspapers also give coverage to international news and other important national events. Such news coming through national and foreign news agencies, radio broadcasts, and the newspaper's own correspondents occupy a great deal of space. As such, very limited space is available for information and public relations personnel for the coverage of activities of their organizations. There is a good deal of competition for this space among the government departments, the public and the private sectors, foreign embassies, and other organizations.

Whether it is a news story or a feature or an article, the successful placement or marketing of the finished product is absolutely essential to achieve the desired results.

If the publicity man is called upon to give information to the newspapers on a subject of great public interest in which a large number of readers are interested, it is not difficult for him to get into the newspaper columns. But the bulk of the information which the publicity personnel normally like to get into the newspaper columns does not fall in this category. The information may be important for the organization and also for a section of the community, but it may not be of that much interest to the general readers. The real question, therefore, before the publicist is how to get into newspaper columns in such a situation.

Exclusive Placement and Involvement of Reporters

If the news is not of that much importance, it can be placed exclusively with a particular paper or papers of a particular region or language. In such cases, instead of a prepared release, it is better to brief the correspondent of the paper on the subject and give him all relevant material. The correspondent may be asked to prepare his own story. The same story after a lapse of time can be placed with other papers with a different angle. As for papers other than daily newspapers, it is necessary to select the relevant periodicals that deal with the subject covered in the news item.

The placement of features and articles, on exclusive basis, is even more important than the news of secondary importance. In the case of features, it is very necessary and also desirable to involve the reporters. They can be approached and persuaded to do a feature on the subject. A request has to be made for this to the news editor or the chief reporter.

In such cases, it is absolutely necessary for the publicist to do all spade work. The reporter is a busy person. He has no background of the subject. He should therefore be given all the background material and other information. Interviews with persons concerned should also be fixed for him. The reporter may also be advised to bring his cameraman. The date and time convenient to the paper should be fixed. Transport, entertainment, and other courtesies should be extended.

The features and articles done through the newspaper reporters have a distinct advantage as their publication is more or less guaranteed. The projection of the subject is also more effective. There is of course an element of risk. Since the organization is exposed to a newspaper man, he may come to know the weaknesses or shortcomings of a particular scheme or a project, which is the subject-matter of the feature. This difficulty can be overcome if the publicist is able to explain things in their proper context and to the satisfaction of the reporter. The publicist's proper rapport with the reporter can help. However, it should not worry the organization too much if there is criticism here and there in the feature prepared by the reporter so long as the total impact of the feature is good.

For placement of publicity material, particularly features

and articles with newspapers and journals, one has to know the publications in the subject field, their readership (localized or wide, specialized or general), style, frequency, language, standard, etc. All this information is necessary to decide the placement of the publicity material.

Selection Guides

There are a number of standard guides that give details about the newspapers and periodicals – national and international. These guides are extremely useful for placement purposes.

The *Press in India* (2 volumes) is brought out annually by the Registrar of Newspapers for India. Part I deals with the various aspects of press in India, while Part II gives State-wise list of Indian newspapers. In each case, information about the place of publication, names of the publisher, printer, editor, printing press, name of the owner, circulation (paid and free), and subject classification is given. There is also a name index of the newspapers at the end of the publication.

The publication is extremely useful for freelancers, publicity personnel and other organizations for the selection of the papers for the placement of their publicity material. The only lacuna in the publication is that it has no subject index which makes it rather difficult for the subject specialists to find out at a glance the list of all papers in a given subject field. Despite this limitation, the publication is extremely important for marketing publicity material, particularly features and articles.

Syndicates/Agencies

Feature syndicates/agencies also supply articles, features, photographs, comic strips, cartoons, etc., on payment to newspapers and periodicals. The publicist can make available features to these agencies for placement in newspapers.

The following news-cum-feature agencies are accredited to the Government of India :

(a) Indian News and Feature Alliance; (b) Indian Press Agency; (c) National News Services; (d) News Bureau of India; (e) Press Asia International; (f) Foreign News and Features; (g) P O T Analysis and News Service.

Other feature agencies are : (a) Indian Press Service, Bombay; (b) National Press Syndicate, Bombay; (c) Asian Press Service, Bombay, (d) Press News Features, Delhi.

PR and Ceremonial Functions

On a number of occasions, the publicist is faced with the problem of disseminating news material when he has no hard or hot or spot news to 'sell'. He can succeed if he uses skill to turn his soft news into human interest features. How best this can be done and what techniques are required to be deployed are matters of vital interest to all publicists. The conversion of such news into features not only enables the publicist to get into newspaper columns, and in a much prominent way, but also in this manner he makes much greater impact on the readers.

One general difficulty for the PR man is to publicise ornamental or routine or ceremonial functions – award of prizes, valedictory functions, distribution of certificates on completion of training, inauguration of certain institutions, observance of some anniversary, etc. Usually a VIP is called on such occasions. The VIP's speech or inaugural address generally contains very little news value material. The result is that the press either does not take note of the function or dismisses it in a few lines. The organizers of the function who have spent a good deal of labour, money and time feel sore when they see the poor coverage in the newspapers the next day. They curse the publicist for his 'inefficiency' or his 'lack of rapport' with the press. Such occasions are both a challenge and an opportunity to the publicist. He is required to take a number of steps, rather advance steps, if he wishes to come out successful of such tricky situations.

In the first place, the publicist should make it clear to the organization that the holding of such ornamental functions is not of much help to him from publicity point of view. Newspapers are interested in news and such functions do not usually generate news of any significance. As such, the time, money and labour spent by the organization would not make much difference in securing publicity. The point is that the organization should not expect publicity commensurate with the effort it has put in to make a 'success' of the function. Such functions may be important for the organization for its own reasons, i.e. for building up contacts with the VIPs, etc. But from publicity point of view, these functions are not of much consequence.

The publicist should also advise the organization in regard to the venue and timing of the function. The venue should be at a place which is centrally located and easily accessible. The timing should preferably be forenoon or early afternoon so as to avoid evening news rush and also to reach the 'dak' editions of the newspapers.

The publicist himself can take care of other details such as press enclosure, i.e. reserving some vantage place for press representatives, etc. The publicist should also extend invitations well in advance to the press representatives and cameramen along with a brief backgrounder on the subject. If the speech of the VIP is available in advance, he can distribute its copies to the press representatives at the time of the function. If the press reporters do not come to the function, a handout can be issued by the publicist incorporating the main points of the speech of the VIP and other details of the function.

All these efforts on the part of the publicist may or may not result in the coverage of the function to the extent he or his organization desires or expects. What is the remedy?

Human Interest Angle

The best solution is to extract the human angle out of the function. This has to be done well in advance and if possible by involving the reporters, or the reporter if it is to be done on exclusive basis, depending on the nature and importance of the occasion.

For instance, if the valedictory function is for giving certificates to the trainees who have completed a course, the trainees can be interviewed either by the publicist or preferably by the newspaper reporters so as to find out from them about the nature of the training – its good points, drawbacks, suggestions, etc. – and also to elicit information as to how the training is going to be useful for their future career towards employment or self-employment.

A feature based on such interviews is definitely more 'saleable' than the ornamental coverage of the function. This technique can be utilized profitably whether the training pertains to the unemployed educated or the ex-servicemen getting ready for a 'second career' in civil life or the widows of service personnel or the disabled and the handicapped. A feature identifying the person or the persons with their family background, etc. and relating it to training and career opportunity can have a far-reaching impact on the public mind. The press reporters who are generally allergic to the VIP speeches would welcome an opportunity to talk to the beneficiaries and do a human interest story. Incidentally, the publicist can always request the reporter that he may also mention about the VIP's speech and other details. Such requests are generally accommodated by the reporters. The feature treatment of soft news in such cases highlights the effort of the organization in a much bigger way than is otherwise possible.

Photographers should also be encouraged to take action-oriented photographs rather than concentrate on ceremonial or ornamental pictures which are usually not used by newspapers. Photographs with human angle can be taken and each newspaper can be given pictures on exclusive basis. All this requires proper and advance planning and a good deal of effort but there is no other way to effectively publicise such ornamental functions.

Socio-economic and Welfare Programmes

Many of our socio-economic and welfare measures can be highlighted by the PR man through a series of human features, clearly identifying the persons and places.

Take the question of the price rise of essential commodities. One way to project the success of the government on the price front is to give statistics about the wholesale price index or consumer price index. Very few people understand the significance of rise and fall in the price index. The more effective way is to find out the reactions of persons directly involved – housewives, shopkeepers, and consumer cooperatives. A feature based on interviews with these people can indirectly bring out the steps the government has taken, such as price tags, better distribution machinery, and speedier movement of goods, to halt the price rise. Even if the intention is to project the failure of the government and to highlight the sufferings of the people, the same technique can be adopted. The feature need not take extreme positions. It can be balanced, and in that case the difficulties of the situation and specific suggestions to solve the problem can also be incorporated.

It will not convince the general public if the publicist gives detailed statistics about the availability of essential commodities, text-books, stationery, etc. for students in colleges and hostels at reasonable prices. The question is what the beneficiaries have to say in the matter. The favourable reaction of the teachers and others on the subject, if projected through a feature, can result in a more meaningful publicity.

Under the National Permit Scheme, the permit holder can transport goods in several States. How has this scheme removed the bottlenecks such as detention of vehicles at check-posts resulting in harassment and delay? The reaction of transporters, traders, and consumers testifying that the scheme has resulted in speedier movement of goods is the best way of publicising the success of the programme.

Welfare schemes pertaining to rural areas – land to the landless, abolition of bonded labour, allotment of house sites, and the gains of 'Antodaya' scheme (upliftment of poorest of the poor) can best be projected through human interest features rather than statistics of acreages or sites or the number of persons benefited or amount of money spent on projects. The story based on the experience of persons who have received land or house sites or who are liberated from bondage or who received assistance for upliftment will be of great human interest. The feature writer can successfully project the beneficiaries' happiness, change in their life style, and the way in which they are taking advantage of the situation for the betterment of their families. Such features project through beneficiaries themselves, the good work being done by the various agencies – social and extension workers, banks, etc. Also, through the same technique, the weaknesses of the programme can be exposed, difficulties pointed out, and solutions suggested.

Provision of more drinking water, better medical, schooling, and communication facilities, particularly in rural areas need not be talked of only in statistical terms. More purposeful publicity is to find out from the beneficiaries themselves as to what extent they have benefited and how the provision of facilities meant a difference in their day-to-day life. The flash-back technique of the situation as it existed in the past and as it exists now can be highlighted in a feature by interviewing some old people in the village who can give good material to contrast the two situations. This can be projected through a feature. It would make a significant impact on the public mind.

The new deal given to lakhs of handloom workers in the country by making necessary inputs available to them at reasonable prices, reserving certain areas of production for handloom, and setting up of export-oriented pilot production centres can best be brought out through a feature based on interviews with the handloom workers themselves. Their specific gains leading to a better life can be brought out through a feature.

Cataloguing of the functions of the new rural banks opened for the benefit of the people to enable them to take advantage of modern farm technology by giving them investment support through credit from the banks at concessional lending rate of interest and easy instalments can be brought out more powerfully through a feature rather than through a news item. The real point to be projected is in what way these banks have made a difference to the people of the area in getting seeds, fertilizers, pesticides, etc., and to what extent they are now free from the clutches of age-old blood-sucking money-lenders. Another point to be brought out is how these banks are different from the commercial banks and other cooperative credit institutions operating in rural areas for a long time. A similar approach is necessary to bring out the specific gains to the people of new industrial centres in the districts which provide package assistance at one point to potential entrepreneurs, in the field of small-scale sector and rural industries.

An announcement is made about simplification of procedure in regard to export, such as setting up of export production and export planning cells to help exporters, incentives to exporters, removal of certain constraints, etc. A feature based on the exporters' reactions to these measures and linking it with increase in exports is a better way of projecting the beneficial effects of these measures.

The extension of the Apprenticeship scheme to more industries and trades so as to extend the benefit of the programme to more apprentices in the country can be publicised by giving statistics through a news item. However, better publicity would be to project the reactions of the beneficiaries, their difficulties and suggestions, through a feature.

Information is disseminated in regard to the facilities available to eligible couples in respect of family welfare programme and other related matters. The feature writer can interview the hospital authorities, family welfare centres, eligible couples, etc., to find out whether the facilities actually exist on the ground and to what extent they are being availed of by the persons concerned. A probe into the matter through a feature can test the claims of the authorities. It can also bring out the weakness and the lacuna in the programme.

At the time of famine or floods, a good deal of information is given out about relief measures by the governmental agencies and voluntary organizations. Aid in cash and kind, medical assistance, etc., are given due publicity. This effort can be supplemented through feature stories giving the favourable reactions of the people. The feature writer can interview old people who can narrate the present happy experience and contrast it with the past when such relief measures were not available to them.

The effects of social evils such as dowry, alcoholic drink, untouchability, etc., can also be projected by relating them to specific cases and identifying the persons and the places. A feature can vividly portray the human sufferings. Such publicity can make a direct appeal to the people's conscience and help mitigate these evils.

Private Sector Projection

The private sector enterprises in India, even with their elaborate public relations set-up and enormous financial resources, rarely employ feature techniques to boost up their publicity. Their effort is generally confined to conventional publicity, i.e. issue of advertisements and supplements, bringing out publicity folders, brochures, house journals, and conducting publicity through cinema slides, films, etc. All this is too direct a publicity. There is no coordinated effort to exploit the favourable consumer reaction to their product in an intelligent manner. It is true that direct mentioning of the name of the firm may not be possible in the news columns of newspapers. But favourable reactions can be cleverly projected in an indirect manner.

Take, for instance, a firm dealing in pesticides and interested in popularizing its product. A series of interviews can be conducted with farmers in regard to pest problems faced by them and the way in which they have tackled the same. In the course of interviews, along with many other things, the farmers can mention that a specific product has helped them in killing a particular pest. This information can be utilized by the publicist in a variety of ways

Similarly, reports on trials on pesticides conducted at the agricultural university experimental farms can be used for preparing features. The same technique can be adopted in popularizing some medicines. Interviews can be conducted with patients and doctors for this purpose.

Surveys conducted by private concerns about the use of their products in particular areas can be used for preparing features and articles. Even if daily newspapers do not take such stuff in their news columns, the publicist can make use of this type of material in preparing advertisements and in writing articles in specialized magazines and house journals. This material can also help in influencing the leader (editorial) and column writers of newspapers.

CHAPTER XXVIII

Interview Technique

For preparing news stories and features, it is necessary for the PR man to interview people. Interviewing people has developed into a fine art. As such, the interviewers should know the different types of interview and also the techniques for a successful interview.

Types – News/Symposium/Personality

Though interview stories are of many kinds, they can be broadly classified in three categories:

1. News interview.
2. Symposium or group interview.
3. Personality interview.

In some stories, different types of interview are combined.

The 'News interview' is intended to give the readers expert comments and illumination on a subject current in the news from persons directly or indirectly connected with the news item. In the case of an accident, the news reporter tries to meet as many eye witnesses as possible to prepare his story. The news item about the announcement of a new car factory gives the details as to who will put up the factory, how much it will cost, where exactly the new plant will be set up, how many persons will be employed, when the factory will go into production, etc. All these are 'simple' facts.

A feature writer who would like to probe the subject deeper to find out many other aspects, not covered in the news item, would try to find out the likely housing problem to come up, the rationale for the selection of the site, the prospect of reduction in consumption of petrol in the new model, the likely cost structure of the new car, etc. In all these cases, it is necessary to interview several persons connected with the subject such as the mayor of the city, the manager of the company, the bankers, the builders, and the contractors to find answers to the questions. Also, the effect on the local economy, the availability of water and power, transportation, and marketing problems can be possible subjects of features.

In the above example, the feature based on interviews of different people adds significantly to public knowledge and understanding of the subject. The interviews not only illuminate and explain several points but also provide better understanding of the subject by clearing many clouded and puzzled facts.

In the 'Symposium or group interview', the reporter gets his information not only from a few persons who are connected with the event as in the case of an accident, but from several other persons who may not be connected with the event. In symposium interviews, the interviewees are selected not for their authority on the subject or topic but as ordinary citizens whose views are worth reporting. There is no fixed rule as to how many persons are to be interviewed. The story must indicate how extensively the survey was conducted. Also, the same questions, in substantially the same words and in the same manner, should be asked from the different respondents. For instance, the desirability or otherwise of dissolution of the State assemblies consequent on the defeat of the Janta in the Lok Sabha in 1980 or the constitution of special courts to deal with particular offences can be referred to a number of persons and their views obtained. A feature can be built on that basis. This can yield the opinion of a cross-section of the people who are not necessarily experts on the subject.

The 'Personality interview' is done to reveal the personality of a person who is being interviewed. It is different from a biographical sketch. The biography gives all details as to when the person was born, the number of children he has, when he became the ambassador, etc. The biography is helpful in writing obituaries but it rarely brings out the qualities of the person and also lacks the warmth and intimacy.

In personality interviews, the interviewer selects a man/woman who either is a newsworthy personality or has become newsworthy because of certain traits in personality – eccentricity, oddity of habit, or because of certain circumstances. For instance, a beggar becoming a millionaire is certainly a newsworthy personality.

Art of Interview

Before any interview is conducted for either a news story or a feature, the interviewer should fully prepare himself. He should thoroughly know his subject. If necessary, he can dig up material from a library or a newspaper office and acquire a thorough understanding of the topic. For instance, a person interviewing a musician should know something about music.

The interviewer should not only know his subject but also have some idea about the person whom he has to interview. Since interview is a face-to-face situation, a sharply personal affair, a rapport with the interviewee is absolutely necessary. The interviewer, therefore, should know something about the person, his age, his habits, and his interests. Some of this information can be obtained from his host, relations, or friends, or from other sources.

The interviewer should go on his task in a straightforward manner. First of all he should get an appointment with the interviewee either on telephone or by meeting him personally. In all cases, clear indication of the time should be given. Appointment should be on a date and time convenient to the interviewee. The same is also true about the venue of the interview. It is better if the interview is conducted at a place where there is not too much disturbance.

The interviewer should also decide whether he is going to meet the person concerned alone or he would like to meet him in the presence of some other person. Generally speaking, people are not frank in the presence of others. As such, it is better to meet the person alone unless is it necessary to have other's presence, so that the other person acts as a witness in case the interviewee later denies his statement.

The interviewer should prepare in advance meaningful and intelligent questions which have direct relevance to the news story, feature, or article so that no time is wasted.

The interviewer should take care not to impose his personality on the interviewee. He should not talk too much. He should be a good listener. His job is to lead the conversation by putting specific and relevant questions.

The interviewer has also to guard against intentional falsehood, faulty memory, lack of information, etc. on the part of the interviewee.

In personality interviews, the verbal and physical mannerism of the interviewee is also worth reporting. In the news interview, the emphasis is on what the man says. In the personality stories, the manner in which the man speaks is also relevant.

Since it is not possible to have a photographic memory so as to retain the information obtained through interview, it is necessary to have some accurate record. The knowledge of shorthand is an asset for an interviewer. Otherwise, he has to devise his own shorthand symbols, key phrases, etc. and to take notes, particularly of those aspects which are more pertinent to his story. Experienced reporters who have a thorough knowledge of the subject can interview without taking any notes. But this stage is reached after considerable experience. Generally, the interviewer should take notes as the interview progresses.

The purpose of the interview is to reveal the personality or the achievements of the interviewee. It is therefore necessary not to cause any personal annoyance or injury to him. The interviewer should always keep the confidence of the interviewee. Those aspects which are revealed for the interviewer's background information only and requested to be kept off the record should not be used in the story. Once the interviewer betrays the confidence, he dries up not only that source of information but also other sources. However, the interviewee should be told that the purpose of the interview is to do a story and therefore it would not be fair on his part if the bulk of the interview is intended to be kept off the record.

A tape-recorder can be used to eliminate taking of notes. However, it should be used with the full consent and knowledge of the interviewee. There are advantages and disadvantages in using a tape-recorder. The disadvantage is that the reporter has to play the lengthy tape to find out the important segments of the talks. It is advantageous if the text of the interview is to be reproduced in the story as in the case of an interview with Prime Minister/VIP where the story is to be based largely on questions and answers. The via media is to take notes and listen to the tape only to check accuracy. In a routine interview, the use of a tape-recorder is an unnecessary luxury.

In certain circumstances the interviewer can show the draft of the story based on the interview to the interviewee. The promise to clear the story makes it easier for the interviewer to get free and frank answers. It also enables him to check errors and to avoid mis-reporting. This is more important for the beginners and also when the interview is on technical or legal subjects. In all other types of routine interviews this formality is not necessary as it means unnecessary delay and may create other complications and difficulties.

For a successful interview, it is necessary to create at the outset a relaxed and informal atmosphere. At the same time, time-consuming preliminaries are to be avoided. The interviewer should not enter into conversation or discussion if the interviewee is in a tense mood.

The interviewer should always keep to his appointment. Even if the interviewee delays the interview, the interviewer should not give agitated look or grumble. It does not help.

While it is necessary to be polite and courteous, the interviewer should be firm to direct the interviewee into the area to be covered. The interviewer should hold him gently on the track and should not allow him to wander or talk too long on unrelated matters, as that would mean waste of time for both.

CHAPTER XXIX

Development Journalism

A relatively new subject – Development Journalism – included in the syllabus of the Post-Graduate Diploma Course in Journalism at the Indian Institute of Mass Communication, New Delhi – deals with the role of mass communication agencies for developmental purposes. In other words, the subject spells out the techniques to be employed to support developmental effort through mass media.

The Concept

The concept of development journalism is undergoing a much wider meaning in developing countries, particularly in India. It is something more than mere dissemination of scientific and technological information relevant to development in a particular area or a community to the potential beneficiaries. Nor is it confined to the presentation of impressive statistics in terms of dams, megawatts, miles of railway track or roadways, tonnage of steel and aluminium, number of housing units, or increase in per capita income. It is also not simple feedback of information from developing areas to the planners and administrators.

Development journalism concerns itself with spelling out the gains and the losses in concrete terms rather than mere cataloguing of achievements and failures. It means identification of developmental gains in terms of beneficiaries, places, degree of progress, etc. so as to make the projection more effective and purposeful. Again, the scientific knowledge to be disseminated by the mass communicator to the rural community or to specific areas has not only to be in an acceptable form but also to be related to specific fields such as agriculture, education, health and hygiene, rural water supply, family welfare, etc. The message should not be in general terms.

The mass communicator engaged in collecting feedback information in a developing area or community would be successful in his task only if he makes a searching probe into the interaction between a new material achievement of the state or of a region or of a community and its effects upon the various sections of the people. For a real feedback, the communicator has to study the effects of the material development on the people, that is in what way the people are to profit or to suffer from the development process.

Development journalism is thus an all-comprehensive concept. It can serve as a catalytic agent to socio-economic progress in developing countries and in bringing the benefits of scientific and technological advances to the people in undeveloped areas.

Responsibilities and Obligations

The concept of 'development' is different from that of economic growth. Development necessarily has a mass dimension, which economic growth, as such, may or may not have. In the same way, development journalism is newer and wider in its embrace than financial, commercial, or agricultural journalism. It is closely related to the mass functioning of the mass media.

Development journalism is not 'propaganda' and certainly not 'government propaganda' as it is commonly understood. Development journalism propagates ideas which motivate people and governments. It is only in that sense that development journalism can be considered to be propaganda but it is propaganda about the needs, problems and demands of the people.

The most important reason why development journalism is suspected to be 'government propaganda' is that many short-sighted restrictions are placed upon the media in the name of development by some governments. Sometimes journalists also do not show the enterprise, self-confidence, and professional skills required for independent and vigorous practice of development journalism. This results in a bad name to the very concept of development journalism, its credibility and effectiveness.

What should be the correct relationship between the government and this special brand of journalism? Development journalism is a partner of the government in discovering what kind of development the people want and need, and what sort of policies the government might pursue. But beyond this relationship, development journalism is equally an independent investigator. It is an honest and free critic in pointing out what may be going wrong and what dangers may be building up as a result.

The mass media should not only help in the fulfilment of the national objectives but also help in deciding what the objectives should be. The mass media should work for the attainment of national objectives by spreading awareness about the objectives among the people and by securing their participation in national tasks. The mass media should also take part in identifying true national interests and aspirations, otherwise temporary expediency may be mistaken for national interest. They should also scrutinize and monitor the implementation of national programme so that public policies may be altered whenever they go wrong or threaten to produce unforeseen and undesirable consequences. Many of the adverse social and economic distortions resulting from the 'green revolution' could have been avoided if the authorities had been alerted about them in time by the mass media, which are professional observers and reporters of the social and economic scene. It is, therefore, necessary that training in development journalism should be improved and expanded further.

'Entertainment journalism' is always more entertaining than serious journalism, Similarly an 'event' is more interesting than the 'process' which produces it. Development journalism deals more with the process than the event. But development journalism can also be 'popular' in the best sense of the word. Development affects the lives and problems of the mass of the people, their wages, the price they get of what they produce or manufacture, the price of what they buy, the value of the money in their pockets, their rights to education and social equality, etc. This is also the stuff of development journalism and if these themes are discussed and reported with skill, they can make development journalism as popular as any other branch of journalism. To some degree, development journalism has made itself dull because of the way in which it has been practised. But that is less the fault of the concept of development journalism than that of some of its practitioners.

Development effects fundamental, social, and economic changes. It brings large majorities of people into the full stream of social and political processes, from which they have been excluded by history in many developing countries. Development journalism is an ally of these revolutionary changes.

The successful practice of frank and honest development journalism in any country depends upon the state of public awareness of the value of the freedom of the media, because journalists alone cannot practise it in isolation. But there cannot be much public appreciation of the value of the freedom of the media if journalists do not exercise, with responsibility as well as courage, such freedom as they may have in any given situation.

The role of development journalism in arousing and motivating people can be practised effectively by the media only to the extent that they perform it with a spirit of independence and are seen by the people to be doing so. The media, particularly the independent segments, should not allow their independence to be eroded by their relationship with the authorities in power.

A frequent dialogue between the government and the media can help both towards a better understanding of the need for free and responsible development journalism. The lack of such understanding creates avoidable conflicts and results in unnecessary and harmful restrictions on the freedom of the media.

CHAPTER XXX

Freedom of the Press

Article 19(1)(a)

The expression 'freedom of the press' as such has not been defined or referred to in the Indian Constitution. However, Article 19(1)(a) of the Constitution dealing with one of the fundamental rights says: 'All citizens shall have the right to freedom of speech and expression.'

This freedom is referred to in general terms, and includes not only freedom of speech which manifests itself through oral utterance, but also freedom of expression, whether such expression is by written or printed matter.

The original Article 19(1) and (2) of the Constitution (before amendment of the latter in June 1951) read as follows:

19(1) All citizens shall have the right

(a) to freedom of speech and expression;
(b) to assemble peaceably and without arms;
(c) to form associations or unions;
(d) to move freely throughout the territory of India;
(e) to reside and settle in any part of the territory of India;
(f) to acquire, hold and dispose of property;
(g) to practise any profession, or to carry on any occupation, trade or business.

(2) Nothing in sub-clause (a) of clause (1) shall affect the operation of any existing law insofar as it relates to, or prevent the State from making any law relating to, libel, slander, defamation, contempt of court or any matter which offends against decency or morality or which undermines the security of, or tends to overthrow, the State.

By the Constitution (First Amendment) Act of 1951, sub-section 3 of Article 19(2) of the Constitution was replaced in the form in which it exists at present. Clause (2) of Article 19, as it stands now, reads as follows:

> Nothing in sub-clause (a) of clause (1) shall affect the operation of any existing law, or prevent the State from making any law, insofar as such law imposes reasonable restrictions on the exercise of the right conferred by the said sub-clause in the interests of the security of the State, friendly relations with foreign states, public order, decency or morality or in relation to contempt of court, defamation or incitement to an offence.

Compared with Article 19(2) as it originally stood, the additional subjects with respect to which legislative restrictions could be imposed on the right of the freedom of speech and expression were (1) friendly relations with foreign states, (2) public order, and (3) incitement to an offence. The amended Article 19(2), however, stated that the restrictions were to be 'reasonable'. The courts were given power to decide in a given case whether or not the restrictions in respect of the various subjects were 'reasonable'. The restrictions under Article 19(2) thus became a justiciable matter, just as other restrictions enumerated in clauses (3), (4), (5), and (6) of Article 19 were justiciable issues from the very beginning.

Press Laws Enquiry Committee

Long before the Constitution (First Amendment) Act was placed on the statute book (on 18 June 1951), the Government of India had set up the Press Laws Enquiry Committee to

(a) examine and report to the government on laws regulating the press in the principal countries of the world including India;
(b) review the press laws of India with a view to examining if they were in accordance with fundamental rights formulated by the Constituent Assembly; and

(c) recommend to the government any measures of reforms in the press laws considered expedient upon such review.

The Committee, which submitted its report on 21 March, 1948, considered comprehensively the Indian Penal Code, the Criminal Procedure Code, the Sea Customs Act, the Indian Telegraph Act, and the Indian Post Offices Act. It discussed the Press and Registration of Books Act, the Indian States (Protection against Disaffection) Act, the Indian Press (Emergency Powers) Act, the Foreign Relations Act, and the Indian States (Protection) Act. It reviewed the working of ten State Acts adopted between 1947 and 1948 in the interests of public security.

The recommendations of the Committee generally favoured the abolition of laws specially concerning the press and the incorporation of their major provisions in the ordinary laws of the land.

The Committee, however, supported the provisions of the Indian Telegraph Act, the Post Offices Act, and the Sea Customs Act which provided the right of interception of messages and literature. It recommended the retention of the Official Secrets Act and the three sections of the Indian Penal Code dealing with disaffection, communal hatred, and tampering with the loyalty of the armed forces. It suggested that suitable alterations should be made to exclude peaceful agitation for social and economic change.

The Press (Objectionable Matters) Act

Introduced in Parliament on 31 August, 1951, the Bill attempted to give effect to some of the recommendations of the Committee. It was directed against encouragement of violence or sabotage and certain other grave offences and against the publication of scurrilous matter. Under the Act, the following laws were repealed:

1. The Indian States (Protection against Disaffection) Act, 1922.
2. The Press (Emergency Powers) Act, 1931.
3. The Foreign Relations Act, 1932.

4. The Indian States (Protection) Act, 1934.
5. Five Press Acts in force in the acceding States of Hyderabad, Madhya Bharat, Mysore, PEPSU, and Rajasthan.

The government had the power, under the Act, of demanding and forfeiting security on a judicial decision, of declaring certain publications confiscated, of seizing and forfeiting undeclared printing presses producing unauthorized news-sheets, of detaining imported packages containing certain documents, of prohibiting postal transmission of certain publications and messages, and of seizing and destroying unauthorized news-sheets and newspapers.

The Press (Objectionable Matters) Act was severely criticised. It came to be known as the 'Black Act'. Eventually, in 1957, the Act was repealed.

Parliamentary Proceedings (Protection of Publication) Act

In 1956, the Parliamentary Proceedings (Protection of Publication) Act was passed, at the initiative of Feroze Gandhi. It gave immunity to the press in regard to faithful reporting of parliamentary proceedings. The Act conferred immunity from any liability in respect of the publication in a newspaper of a substantially correct report of any proceedings of either house of Parliament unless the publication is proved to have been made with malice. The Act permits the press to report defamatory statements in Parliament without committing a breach of privilege of the Parliament and by implication no libel action for the publication of any such statement referring to any outsider would lie. This Act applied only to the Proceedings of Parliament and not of State Legislatures which were left free to enact their own legislation in that respect. The Constitution (Forty-fourth Amendment) Act, 1978, however, now provides immunity to the press in respect of proceedings of State legislatures.

Three Ordinances

Three Ordinances were proclaimed after the promulgation of Emergency on 25 June, 1975, to effect changes in certain press laws. The government armed itself with special powers to restrain the individual's freedom of expression. One of the Ordinances provided for the repeal of the Press Council Act, 1965. The second was the Prevention of Publication of Objectionable Matter Ordinance. The third Ordinance repealed the Parliamentary Proceedings (Protection of Publication) Act, 1956.

The Press Council was established in 1966 with the aim of evolving a code of conduct for the press and bringing about a fusion of rights and responsibilities on the part of the press. Since these objectives had not been served in government's view, it repealed the Press Council Act of 1965 and abolished the institution with effect from 1 January, 1976. The Council was revived with some changes in September, 1978.

The repeal of the Parliamentary Proceedings (Protection of Publication) Act of 1956 was officially held to be a natural consequence of the decision to promulgate the ordinance to prevent publication of objectionable matter. According to the government, the immunity conferred on the press by this legislation was 'largely misused', bringing about a lowering of the standards of journalism.

The Prevention of Publication of Objectionable Matter Ordinance, 1975, provided 'for action mainly against publications which are likely to excite disaffection against the constitutionally established government, incite interference with production, supply or distribution of essential commodities or services, create disharmony amongst different sections of the society and indecent or scurrilous or obscene writings.'

The Ordinance provided for security to be demanded from the printer, the publisher, or the editor responsible for the publication of objectionable matter as defined. Any words, signs, or visible representations, which were defamatory of the President, Vice-President, Prime Minister, or any other member of the Council of Ministers, the Speaker of the Lok Sabha, or the Governor of a State, became an offence, punishable under the Ordinance.

Constitution (Forty-fourth Amendment) Act

In March, 1977, the censorship of newspapers was abolished and the Prevention of Publication of Objectionable Matter Act was repealed and the Parliamentary Proceedings (Protection of Publication) Act was re-enacted. The Constitution (Forty-fourth Amendment) Act, 1978, passed by Parliament, provides constitutional authority to the Feroze Gandhi Act. It also extends the protection to journalists in respect of publication in newspapers of proceedings of State Legislatures as well. The new article 361-A inserted in the Constitution provides that no person shall be liable to any proceedings, civil or criminal, in any court in respect of publication in newspapers of a substantially true report of any proceedings of either House of Parliament or either House of the State Legislature unless the publication is proved to have been made with malice. This provision cannot be suspended even during an emergency.

The government dismantled the Samachar and restored the status quo ante in respect of the four news agencies. The Press Council was revived. It also set up a new Press Commission. In June, 1980, the Press Commission was reconstituted with wider terms of reference.

Self Regulation

The advocates of press freedom in India are of the view that all subtle forms of influence over the press should come to an end. They feel that subsidized housing and other perquisites to correspondents including sponsored tours, reprehensible practice of fixing advertisement rates for newspapers, and not allowing newspapers to directly import the newsprint they require should come to an end.

They would like the government to make a constitutional provision to ensure that the press freedom was not interfered with in the future. They concede that the Press Council is necessary, but are of the view that the government should have nothing to do with it. They suggest that cess should be collected on newsprint and be distributed to the press to finance the Press Council and the news agencies. The press, they argue, is one of the four pillars on which the mansion of democracy stands. If one pillar collapses, the whole structure would crumble.

The press should, therefore, evolve a code of conduct to regulate itself. Outside regulation or interference is neither desirable nor called for.

Criticism and dissent are essential in a democracy. The press, however, has to ensure that it is objective and unbiased and not influenced by 'favours, money, or the bottle'. Only then the press can play the vital role of mobilizing public opinion and also act as 'watch-dog' in safeguarding people's liberties.

No freedom, however sacred it may be, can be absolute. All freedoms are relative and subordinate to freedom of society. This is also true of press freedom. Not only the freedom of the press is subject to the laws of the land, such as law of contempt and libel, but also to the privileges of the Parliament and State Legislatures.

The stress should be not so much on the freedom of the press, but on 'free and responsible press'. The press should no doubt be free of outside regulation or interference, but at the same time it should also be responsible to the society it serves. It should accept certain responsibilities or code of conduct to regulate itself to discharge its functions.

The press has an obligation – voluntary and self-imposed – that in the presentation of truthful news and fair comment, it adheres to certain norms of decency and decorum and that it does not indulge in vulgarity, obscenity, character assassination, violation of citizens' privacy, and incitement to violence, disorder, and disintegration of the country.

The role of the press in India should be neither that of an 'adversary' as in the West nor that of an 'unquestioning ally' as in the Socialist countries. It has to play a middle role to help in the development process.

Guidelines for the Press

In 1966, the Press Council evolved certain guidelines for the conduct of newspapers. Explaining the rationale behind these guidelines, the Council stated that 'While it is the legitimate function of the press to draw attention to the genuine and legitimate grievances of any community with a view to having the same redressed by peaceful, legal and legitimate means, it is improper and a breach of journalistic ethics to invent grievances or to exaggerate real grievances, as these tend to promote communal ill-feeling and accentuate the discord.'

According to these guidelines, the Press should avoid:

- distortion or exaggeration of facts or incidents in relation to communal matters or giving currency to unverified rumours, suspicions or inferences, as if they were facts and base their comments on them;
- employment of intemperate and unrestrained language in the presentation of news or views even as a piece of literary flourish or for the purposes of rhetoric or emphasis;
- encouraging or condoning violence even in the face of provocation as a means of obtaining redress of grievances whether the same be genuine or not;
- scurrilous and untrue attacks on communities or individuals, particularly when they are accompanied by charges attributing misconduct to them due to their being members of a particular community or caste;
- falsely giving a communal colour to incidents in which members of different communities happen to be involved;
- emphasizing matters that are apt to produce communal hatred or ill-will or fostering feelings of distrust between communities;
- publishing alarming news which are in substance untrue or making provocative comments on such news or views which are otherwise calculated to embitter relations between different communities or regional or linguistic groups;
- exaggerating actual happenings to achieve sensationalism and publication of news which adversely affects communal harmony with banner headlines or in distinctive types; and
- making disrespectful, derogatory or insulting remark on or reference to the different religious faiths or their founders.

While the press in a democratic country like India has a primary duty to report events objectively and faithfully, it has also a larger obligation to the nation to defend and to preserve the democratic way of life. It is, therefore, necessary for the press to voluntarily adopt a policy not to play up or give undue publicity or to give 'celebrity' treatment to news which tends to promote authoritarianism and dictatorial trends or to aggravate communal or regional tensions. In defending democracy and the rule of law, the press, in fact, is defending its very existence, as freedom of the press can survive only in a democratic set-up.

CHAPTER XXXI

The Press and the Law

Those engaged in PR work should be familiar with the laws which affect them in their professional work. The most important among them are law of libel and defamation, contempt of court and legislatures, copyright, etc.

Libel

It is a writing tending to injure and degrade the character of a person who is the object of it. It is a defamatory statement published in the press or otherwise, while slander is oral defamation. Libel is the publication of a false and defamatory statement expressed in writing, printing, or by signs, pictures or in some form which is permanent, published without lawful justification or excuse concerning a person and which injures his reputation. Libellous statements are divided into the following categories:

1. Exciting hatred, contempt, scorn or ridicule.
2. To be shunned or avoided by society.
3. Affecting profession, calling or office.
4. Affecting trade or business.

For instance, calling a person a liar, a villain, a jackal, or a swine, or making a dishonourable comparison of the persons to characters in history, fiction, or mythology or making erroneous announcements are libellous statements.

The defence usually put up are justification, privilege, fair comment, and innocent dissemination. To impute the truth about a person for public good or to express in good faith any opinion about the conduct of a public servant in discharge of his public function or of any person touching any public question is not libel. Similarly, to publish a substantially true report of the proceedings of a court of law or to comment in good faith on merits of civil and criminal cases is not considered defamatory.

A reporter can express in good faith an opinion on the merits of the case, which has been decided or the merits of any performance which its author has submitted to the judgement of the public. He can also make an imputation on the character of another person in good faith if it is for the protection of the person making it or of any other or for the public good. Similarly, he can convey a caution to one person against another or prefer an accusation or censor the conduct in good faith of a person over whom he has authority.

The acceptance of defence as indicated above depends upon the interpretation of the statement made and the appreciation of evidence by the court.

The remedies available to the aggrieved person in India are of two kinds – civil action under the common law, or criminal proceedings for defamation. In the first, the claim is essentially for damages by monetary compensation. In criminal proceedings, it is punishment with fine and/or imprisonment.

Parliamentary Privilege

Journalists have to take care while reporting the proceedings of the Parliament or the State Legislatures. The Parliamentary Proceedings (Protection of Publication) Act, 1956, provides that no person should be liable to any proceedings – civil or criminal – in respect of publication in a newspaper of a substantially true report of any proceedings of either House of Parliament. This Act was repealed during the Emergency but has now been again re-enacted. The provisions of the Act have been discussed in the chapter on 'Freedom of the Press'. The State Legislatures, however, do not have such Acts at present.

While reporting the proceedings of Parliament or State Assemblies, care should be taken that the writings do not constitute a breach of privilege or contempt of the House. The general principle is that the writings which tend to destroy the image of the House and its members in the performance of their functions and duties by diminishing the respect due to them and by bringing them into odium, contempt, and ridicule would constitute a breach of privilege and contempt of the House.

There is no legislation enacted so far defining precisely the circumstances in which the publication may constitute a breach of privilege. However, action has been taken in the following types of cases:

(a) Inaccurate reporting;
(b) Distorted, unfair, wilful, mendacious rendering of proceedings, or a wilful suppression of an account;
(c) Publicising the expunged proceedings and publication of reports or proceedings of sub-committees of the House or resolutions or questions or motions, etc. before they are brought before the House.

Contempt of Court

Any act done or writing published calculated to bring a court of law into contempt or lower its authority or to obstruct or interfere with due course of justice or lawful process of the court is contempt of the court. For instance, publication of proceedings of a case being heard in camera, false and grossly inaccurate reporting of court proceedings, publication that may tend to interfere with orderly administration of justice, or publication that scandalizes the court, the judges, the counsels, the parties, or the witnesses are contempt of court. Also no comment should be made and proper care should be taken in reporting when the case is sub judice.

The press does enjoy the privilege of fair comment but personal attacks on judges attributing incompetency, corruption, partiality, judicial dishonesty, political bias, improper motives, or 'other considerations' in the court are contempt of court.

The Contempt of Court Act XXXII of 1952 says: 'Save as otherwise expressly provided by any law for the time being in force, the contempt of court may be punished with simple imprisonment for a term which may extend to six months or with fine which may extend to Rs.2,000 or both.' It is provided that the accused may be discharged or the punishment awarded may be remitted on an apology being made to the satisfaction of the court.

Copyright

Copyright is a right accruing to a person in respect of a work produced by him as a result of exercise of skill, judgement, and labour. Under the Copyright Act, protection is afforded to literary, dramatic, musical, artistic, archaeological, or any work relating to craftsmanship, engraving, and also to films, television, broadcasting diffusion. In such cases, the author has the exclusive right for publication, production, reproduction, performance in public, translation, etc. However, a fair dealing with literary, musical, artistic work for the purpose of research, criticism, review, reporting current events in a newspaper or magazine or for judicial proceedings, etc. do not constitute an infringement of copyright.

Under the Copyright Act, 1957, registration of any work in which copyright exists is entirely voluntary. In the absence of registration, redress for infringement would be under common law.

Press and Registration of Books Act, 1867

The Press and Registration of Books Act regulates printing presses, newspapers, registration of books and newspapers printed in India. It places a duty on the publishers of any newspaper to furnish annual statement, etc. to the Registrar of Newspapers along with returns and reports. (Also discussed in chapter on 'PR through Publications and Journals'.)

Under the Act, one copy of newspaper published in English, Hindi, and Urdu is required to be sent to the Press Registrar, New Delhi. The following offices of the PIB receive the copies on bebalf of the Press Registrar of India in other languages as under:

Calcutta	Bengali, Oriya and Assamese.
Madras	Tamil and Telugu.
Ernakulam	Malayalam.
Bombay	Marathi and Gujarati.
Bangalore.	Kannada.
Delhi	Any other language.

Delivery of Books and Newspapers (Public Library) Act, 1954

Under the Delivery of Books and Newspapers (Public Library) Act, 1954, books and copies of newspapers are to be delivered free to the four national libraries : (i) National Library, Calcutta; (ii) Connemera Public Library, Madras; (iii) National Central Library, Delhi; and (iv) Central Library, Bombay.

The Official Secrets Act, 1923

This Act consolidates the law relating to official secrets and deals with two kinds of offences: (1) spying, and (2) wrongful communication, etc. of secret information.

Under Section 3 of the Act, it is an offence if any person for any purpose prejudicial to the safety or interests of the State (a) approaches, inspects, passes over, or is in the vicinity of, or enters any prohibited place; or (b) makes any sketch, plan, model, or note which is calculated to be or might be or is intended to be directly or indirectly useful to an enemy; or (c) obtains, collects, records, or publishes, or communicates to any other person any sketch, plan, model, article, or note or other document or information which is calculated to be or might be or is intended to be directly or indirectly useful to an enemy.

Miscellaneous Acts

The Working Journalists Act, 1955, aims to settle the service conditions of the working journalists pertaining to their salaries, provident fund, gratuity, and to regulate hours of work, holidays with pay, notice period of termination of service. It aslo deals with constitution of wage boards.

The Prize Competition Act, 1955, aims to prohibit advertisements of prize competitions except as provided in the Act. The Act prohibits promoting or conducting any prize competition in which the total value of the prize or prizes whether in cash or otherwise to be offered in any month exceeds one thousand rupees and in every such competition the number of entries must not exceed two thousand. Licence is also needed under the Act.

The object of *The Drugs and Magic Remedies (Objectionable*

Advertisement) *Act*, *1954*, is to prevent self-medication and self-treatment, and to prohibit advertisements commending certain drugs and medicines.

The Indian Telegraph Act empowers the government to take possession of telegrams and to order interception of messages, while *The Indian Post Office Act* gives power to intercept postal articles under certain conditions. *The Sea Customs Act* authorizes the government to prohibit and restrict importation or exportation of goods including packages containing certain publications imported into India.

CHAPTER XXXII

Press Council

Set-up prior to Emergency

The Press Commission (1954) in its report recommended the setting up of a statutory all-India Press Council to look after the editorial independence, objectivity of news presentation, and fairness of comments, etc. on the part of newspapers. The Council, according to the Commission, was also to foster the development of the press, protecting it from external pressure and regulate its conduct in matters of such objectionable writing as was not legally punishable. In pursuance of this recommendation, the Press Council of India was constituted by the Government of India in 1966 under the Press Council Act, 1965, which was later amended on 31 March, 1970. The Council's term which expired in December, 1975, was not extended during the Emergency.

The Council, prior to its termination, consisted of a Chairman and 26 members. A committee consisting of the Chairman of the Rajya Sabha, the Chief Justice of India, and the Speaker of the Lok Sabha nominated six editors, seven journalists other than editors, six persons either owning or in the management of newspapers, and one person representing the management of news agencies. A member each was nominated by the University Grants Commission, the Sahitya Akademi, and the Bar Council of India. Two members were nominated by the Speaker of the Lok Sabha and one by the Chairman of the Rajya Sabha.

The Press Council was an autonomous body. Its object broadly was to preserve the freedom of the press and to improve the standards of newspapers and news agencies in India. The Council could censure, warn, or admonish a newspaper or a news agency for any professional misconduct or breach of the code of journalistic ethics or an offence against public taste. It could also ask the newspaper to publish the Council's findings or observations against a defaulting paper. It could also condemn the government or other organizations for interfering with the freedom of the press. It enjoyed the same powers while holding an enquiry under the Press Council Act as is vested in a civil court while trying a suit under the Code of Civil Procedure. These provisions remained more or less unchanged in the revived Press Council (31 August, 1978).

Revived Press Council

The functions of the Press Council of India, according to the Press Council Act, 1978, are 'to preserve the freedom of the press and to improve standards of newspapers and news agencies in the country'. The Council is also to build up (not formulate) a code of conduct for newspapers, news agencies, and journalists in accordance with high professional standards and to encourage the growth of a sense of responsibility and public service among all those who are engaged in the profession of journalism. The code is to be evolved through case law and conventions over a period of time.

The Council is empowered to hold enquiries on complaints made to it or otherwise against the offending newspapers and news agencies. For the purpose of performing its functions or holding any enquiry, the Council shall have the same powers throughout India as are vested in a civil court while trying a suit under the Code of Civil Procedure in certain respects. These powers include summoning and enforcing the attendance of persons and examining them on oath, requiring discovery and inspection of documents, receiving evidence on affidavits, requisitioning any public record and issuing commissions for the examination of witnesses or documents.

The Council is to be a body corporate having perpetual succession and consisting of a Chairman and 28 members. The Chairman of the Council is to be nominated by a three-man panel comprising the Chairman of the Rajya Sabha, the Speaker of the Lok Sabha, and a person elected by the members of the Council. Thirteen of the members are to be nominated in accordance with such procedures as may be prescribed from among the working journalists including six editors. The number of working journalists representing newspapers published in Indian languages has been raised from three to four.

Six of the 28 members are to be nominated from among those persons who own or carry on the business or management of newspapers. Three members are to be nominated on the Council from the Lok Sabha and two from the Rajya Sabha. There is no distinction between languages in so far as the representation of owners or managers on the Council is concerned.

Besides, one representative from among persons who manage news agencies and one member each from the field of education and science, law, and literature and culture are to be nominated by the University Grants Commission, the Bar Council of India, and the Sahitya Akademi respectively. No member on the Council is to be nominated by the government.

The power to apppiont the Chairman and a member of the Press and Registration Appellate Board under the Press and Registration of Books Act, 1867, has been given to the Council. The Board deals with appeals by newspapers concerning their declaration before district magistrates.

The Act also contains an enabling provision empowering the Council to levy graded fees on newspapers with over 5,000 circulation and on news agencies for the services it proposes to render. This reduces its dependence on the government's financial support and provides scope for the development of a sense of participation of the newspapers in the affairs of the Council.

Like the former Press Council, the revived Council is also a statutory quasi-judicial and self-regulating body without 'teeth' (power to impose legal penalties). However, it differs from the earlier body in three important respects, namely, in regard to the procedure of appointment of its Chairman and composition (English papers would not dominate as also the newspapers chains); the power to consider complaints against the government and criticize the governmental actions; and to levy fees on the newspapers and others for its work.

Press Council and Freedom of Press

Also, the Press Council has residual powers to undertake any studies suo moto relevant to the discharge of its functions. The

Press Council's reports are to be placed before Parliament and as such the members of Parliament are in a position to criticize the government on the basis of the Council's observations.

It is expected that the Council in course of time would be not only a mechanism for self-regulation for the press but also a 'bulwark' against any attack, pressure or encroachment on the freedom of the press from any source – government, proprietors, advertisers, political parties, trade unions, and other interested groups. It has also been empowered to look into the ownership pattern of newspapers or news agencies which may impinge on the independence of the press and to help the press maintain its freedom.

The effectiveness of a self-regulatory body such as the Press Council has been recognized in several countries. In the UK, the Council came into existence in 1953. The Japanese body came into being as early as 1946. In West Germany and Israel, similar institutions were set up in 1956 and 1963 respectively.

CHAPTER XXXIII

News Agencies

Newspapers and other media depend to a large extent on news agencies for general news coverage. Even big papers do not have countrywide news network. They have their representatives at the State capitals and at some other important places. In some cases, newspaper representatives are also connected with their own teleprinter lines. Despite this, it is almost impossible to cover all news through their own sources. The media representatives as a rule concentrate on important happenings. For other news, they depend on news agency coverage. The medium and small newspapers cannot afford to have their own representatives. As such, they are more dependent on news agencies.

The basic function of a news agency is to purvey news and provide news reports of current events to the newspapers and others who subscribe to its service. The UNESCO definition of a news agency is 'an undertaking of which the principal objective, whatever its legal form, is to gather news and news material of which the sole purpose is to express or present facts and to distribute it to a group of news enterprises and in exceptional circumstances to private individuals with a view to providing them with as complete and impartial news service as possible against payment and under conditions compatible with business laws and usage'. No modern state can survive without an adequate set-up of information collection and its judicious dissemination.

PR and News Agencies

The publicist feeds the press with a variety of material – news, photographs, features, articles, advertisements, etc. either directly or through agencies. News stories or spot stories as they are called are handled by news agencies, photographs by photo agencies, features and articles by feature syndicates or feature agencies, and advertisements by advertising agencies.

The dissemination of information through a news agency by the publicist has certain advantages. The news agencies can transmit his message to local newspapers through the teleprinter network in the quickest possible time. As such, the publicist is saved from the botheration of sending his handout to local newspapers individually. Also, through news agencies the publicist reaches the outstation papers in no time which would be otherwise difficult. However, it is not a wise policy, except in the case of very important news items, to send the news material only to the agencies and not to the newspapers. News agencies may not use the publicist's copy or reduce it drastically before creeding it to the subscribers. In that case, newspapers are deprived of the full version and even if they wish to publish the story they are not in a position to do so.

While the news agency has the biggest merit of reaching the widest newspaper coverage in the quickest possible time, it also has the disadvantage of not being used by newspapers. By and large, a newspaper does publish a news item in full given by its own correspondent.

The general principle, therefore, is to send the item to both the agencies and the newspapers unless it is decided to 'sell' the story on 'exclusive' basis to a news agency or to a single newspaper or category of newspapers based on language, region, or frequency. Where news is given out on 'exclusive' basis to a news agency, the news agency correspondent should be clearly told about it so that he may do full justice to the material.

Role in a Democratic Set-up

The role of news agencies in a democracy with free press is of crucial importance. There are some basic principles which should govern the functioning of news agencies in a democratic set-up. Some of these are:

1. There should not be any monopoly of one news agency.

Competitive service freely available to all users is absolutely necessary.

2. The news agencies should not be state-owned or state-controlled. The government should not participate in ownership, nor have any voice in the control of the agency either editorially or administratively.
3. Financial assistance in the form of loans, etc. may be given by the government but without any strings. The payment made for services rendered comes altogether in a different category.
4. The set-up of news agencies should be a public corporation formed on the basis of cooperative efforts of newspapers and other users and interests.
5. In functioning, they should have the overall interests of state and of society. They should abide by the laws of the country as well as by the code of professional conduct.
6. They should develop coverage of foreign news by having their own correspondents at major foreign capitals and use their despatches to supplement and correct, where necessary, the services of foreign agencies which have the monopoly of world news. Also, they should provide the country's news to newspapers in foreign countries.
7. They should provide adequate coverage of regional news and meet the requirements of regional newspapers.
8. The agencies should provide different types of service – full or comprehensive, brief and summary (for district papers) for different categories of subscribers.
9. The tariff should be so devised that the subscribers should be charged in an equitable manner or according to the use made of the service. The subscription rate to be charged from newspapers should be in relation to number of pages, circulation, income, and other factors.
10. In addition to the services provided to newspapers, the news agencies also provide news service including commercial and special services to individual subscribers – Central and State government departments, public sector undertakings, business houses, etc. In India, All India Radio, Doordarshan, External Affairs Ministry are important subscribers of the services of news agencies. The payment of subscription from official agencies should be

based on sound principles and not on ad hoc basis.

11. The news coverage should be fast, objective, comprehensive, and accurate.
12. Only those items which have a 'news value' should be selected. While determining the news value, the appeal to the readers and the significance of the event are to be taken into consideration. The criterion of 'news value' must undergo changes as social, political, and economic developments take place in the country.
13. In the selection of news, the agencies should have integrity and disinterestedness. Selection of news should be made on the basis of the importance and priority attached to individual facts. All relevant facts of significance should be reported.
14. The news agencies should not have any specific editorial policy. The agencies should avoid views or comments while reporting news. The privilege of comments should lie with the newspapers.
15. The agencies, in giving news, should be fair to different points of view. The views of opposition should be treated fairly and equitably in the matter of length and coverage. Since the agencies cater to subscribers of diverse and contradictory views, it is not proper for the agency to select news to suit the interests of any particular client. The interests or prejudices should not influence the agencies in the selection of news. In fact, the conflicting trends in the country and the society should be projected but in a balanced manner and in their proper perspective.
16. News agencies should be free from bias. It should also be immune from pressure from any quarter – governmental or big business, or proprietorial.
17. As far as possible, news agencies should be viable.

In brief, the news agencies in a democratic society should provide complete, impartial, objective, accurate, countrywide competitive news services free from slant, pressure, or interference from any source or quarter.

Four Agencies

Prior to Emergency, there were two English news agencies,

namely, Press Trust of India and United News of India. The two other agencies – Hindustan Samachar and Samachar Bharati – provided services in Hindi and regional languages respectively.

The history of news agencies in India dates back to just over 30 years. Before independence, Reuter owned and operated Associated Press of India. After independence API was transferred, in 1948, to Indian ownership and named the Press Trust of India. For years PTI remained virtually a monopoly. It faced no worthwhile competition from the United Press of India which merely provided an outlet for nationalistic activities. UPI was financially weak and was wound up in 1958. For three years thereafter PTI was alone in the field. The United News of India was born in 1961 largely as a result of newspapers' dissatisfaction with the performance of the monopolistic PTI. Both PTI and UNI were owned by newspapers as cooperatives.

The PTI, has 400 subscribers, 45,000 km of teleprinter lines commanding 87 bureaux all over India and has about a dozen correspondents stationed in different parts of the world. The UNI has 50 branch offices and a network of 40,000 km of leased teleprinter lines and has about 400 subscribers. The wordage of PTI and UNI was about 1,00,000 and 50,000 a day respectively.

India's first multilingual news agency, Hindustan Samachar, was set up in 1948. In 1957, it became a society called the Hindustan Samachar Cooperative Society. It has 51 teleprinter centres and a network of 35 bureaux. The agency feeds news to more than 135 subscribers in 11 Indian languages.

Samachar Bharati, the second language agency, came into being on 2 October, 1966, but became operational only in 1967. It has 200 teleprinters connecting a network of 30 bureaux. The agency supplies news to 160 language papers, particularly the small and medium newspapers, All India Radio, and State information agencies.

Samachar and Kuldip Nayar Committee's Report

The four agencies merged on 1 February, 1976, and a news agency, 'Samachar', was formed. Samachar was expected to collect and disseminate news within the country and abroad and to provide complete, impartial, objective, accurate, and countrywide news service.

The government in March, 1977, appointed an expert committee under the chairmanship of Kuldip Nayar to examine the functioning of Samachar taking into consideration the freedom of the press, independence of news agencies, and possibilities of competitive service freely available to all users.

The committee recommended that Samachar should be dissolved and re-structured by the creation of two news agencies – 'Varta' and 'Sandesh'. These in their turn should jointly set up an organization for international news services which may be called 'News India'. News India would buy foreign agency services and make them available to subscribers of Varta and Sandesh.

While Varta was suggested as a news agency to organize and develop news services in Indian languages, along with an English service, Sandesh was visualized as an exclusively English news agency. News India was not to be a separate news agency as such but would be financed and managed in partnership by the two agencies jointly. News India was to be a monopoly in foreign news. The committee also recommended that an interim body be set up by the government to bring about the reorganization within a period of three months.

Two of the members, C.R. Irani and A.K. Sarkar, differed from the recommendations regarding the basic structure. They suggested that the Samachar should be split into two news agencies primarily in the English language, since, in their view, the service was demanded in this language. These agencies should also be 'given back' their previous names. As regards news services in Hindi and other Indian languages, these two agencies should be left free to develop them as they might consider best. They should also be free to organize international services of their own separately. They were opposed to granting monopoly to News India in international news coverage.

For the services given by news agencies to All India Radio and Doordarshan, the Kuldip Nayar committee recommended a formula of payment based on the number of radio and TV licences (Re.1 per radio licence and Rs.5 per TV licence).

The acceptance of the Kuldip Nayar committee report, it was argued by the critics, would have created three monopoly news agencies – one each in the field of English language, Indian languages, and international news service. In fact, the critics argued that each would be a monopoly in its field – News India in foreign news, Sandesh in English news at home, and Varta in languages. There could hardly be any competition between Sandesh and Varta, because Sandesh would be only in English and therefore faster, and Varta in a number of languages and therefore would have to take to time-consuming translation at each major centre. The set-up would not have the merit of competition. Also, if the government had to make up the budget deficit of Rs.1.7 crores every year in respect of the proposed three agencies, the agencies would hardly enjoy any independence. As such they would also not have the advantages of self-supporting agencies. Thus the objective of having news agencies 'completely independent of the government and not given the right to monopoly' would not be fulfilled.

News Agency or Agencies

The Government of India decided on 14 November, 1977, to reject the Kuldip Nayar committee report. It was decided to split Samachar and to restore the status quo prior to the merger of the four news agencies. The agencies started functioning separately from 15 August, 1978. The Government of India's decision has been criticized on the following grounds:

1. The decision indicates that the government has no responsibility, whatsoever, in the matter. It is argued that the media should be treated as public utility and the government must frame its policy towards the media as it has done in the case of science, technology, and other subjects. In the name of freedom of the press, the government should not abdicate its responsibility in such an important matter.

2. In the name of competitive news agencies, there will be a lot of duplication in respect of dissemination of news which the country at this stage of development with meagre financial resources can hardly afford.

3. For foreign news coverage, the country will have to depend on foreign international news agencies with all its drawbacks such as poor coverage of Indian news, slanting, etc. At present, Samachar has only five correspondents located in London, New York, Moscow, Kathmandu, and Colombo. It

was proposed to appoint 25 more correspondents for a period of two years particularly in South East Asia, Latin America, and other countries. This scheme will now become a non-starter. The decision will also create difficulties in the functioning of the non-aligned news agency pool.

4. The government decision is contrary to the Press Commission's recommendations that the news agencies should be converted into a public corporation under parliamentary enactment.

5. Different news agencies will be more subject to the pressure of big newspapers and other vested interests. This will not be conducive to their proper functioning.

6. None of the news agencies will be viable as they will depend on subsidy and/or support from the government or big business.

7. It will retard expansion of news agencies' network both within the country and abroad which is badly needed in the present stage of the country's economic development.

8. The split will badly affect development of Hindi and other Indian language news services.

9. The employees of Samachar will be adversely affected in regard to their emoluments and other service conditions.

10. The country needs a national viable news agency and Samachar could have been restructured so as to make it independent of the government or other control. The leading newspapers could have set up their own competitive news agencies, if they so desired.

11. Competition is a misnomer as newspapers are free to publish or not to publish news items and reports from news agencies. Also, many newspapers have their own correspondents who can act as a check on one-sided news stories emanating from a single news agency.

A contrary view on the subject is held by equally eminent leaders in the newspaper profession. Their reasonings are as under:

1. The government's decision to split up Samachar is intended only to undo the 'merger' of the erstwhile news agencies. The decision is a part of a larger commitment of the government to allow free and unfettered atmosphere for the functioning of all democratic institutions including the news agencies.

The decision, however, does not rule out voluntary cooperation or coming together or merger of news agencies, if they so desire.

2. The question of resources is not a valid argument as Samachar during its one year of existence was given about Rs.75 lakhs by the government. The merger of news agencies therefore did not result in viability.

3. The argument that Hindi and Indian language services would suffer with the revival of a number of news agencies is also not correct. They can certainly develop as a part of the main news agencies in the country. For instance, PTI and UNI can have effective Hindi and language wings. In any case, news agencies have to be based on actual demand of news from news enterprises and not on any other considerations. The government has, however, announced that it would extend financial help for the development of news services in Indian languages.

4. It is true that wherever there is more than one news agency, it does result in a certain amount of duplication in the dissemination of news. This is avoided in dictatorial and totalitarian countries where there is only one official news agency. Ours is a democratic society and we have to pay this price.

5. In 1954 the Press Commission recommended: 'However objective a news agency strives to be, there are certain drawbacks which arise from monopoly and which could be obviated only by competitive service available freely to all users.' The Government of India on 22 July, 1971, accepted this recommendation as was evident from the reply to a question in the Rajya Sabha by the Minister of Information and Broadcasting.

6. India is in the process of rapid economic development and there is considerable scope for more than one news agency to develop. It is true that democratic countries such as the UK and France have only one news agency. Considering the area, population, geography, language, and other factors there is ample scope and future for more than one news agency in India.

7. The basic criteria of news agency services in a democratic set-up are competition and independence. Effective competition is possible only if there is more than one agency. The agency cannot be independent if it is controlled financially or otherwise by the government or other vested interests. The payment for services rendered by the news agencies to TV and AIR is,

however, a different matter. This is purely a commercial transaction and not a financial subsidy.

8. The decision to split Samachar is not going to affect India's participation in the news agencies pool of non-aligned countries. The agencies can participate individually or jointly through some cooperative arrangement in the pool and the government has announced its willingness to consider giving financial help for this purpose. The projection of the Indian picture abroad can perhaps be better done by independent news agencies rather than by a single officially-sponsored news agency.

9. The Kuldip Nayar committee had suggested that the government should pay its subscription under an automatic formula at Re.1 per radio licence and Rs.5 per TV licence. The collection should be shared between Varta and Sandesh. Since the government is committed to give AIR and Doordarshan autonomous status, it is extremely doubtful if this formula finds acceptance with the new corporation. The corporation may like to develop its own news gathering sources.

10. The emoluments of Samachar employees are to be protected by the government through grant-in-aid on a tapering basis for a period of six years. In any case, this cannot be a justifiable argument for retaining one agency.

11. The via media can be on the lines of the French news agency. For the news supplied by the news agencies to official organs such as AIR, TV, government departments, External Affairs Ministry, the government can give matching grants to the agencies equivalent to their income from the non-official sources.

Foreign News Agencies

According to the UNESCO Report on World Communications (1975), there are news agencies in 90 sovereign countries of the world. More than 40 countries including 25 countries with a population of more than one million have no news agencies. News agencies are directly controlled by the state in 50 of these 90 countries; in 40 others, the agencies are cooperatively owned and run by the newspapers and other media. In many of the countries, even where the agencies ostensibly are autonomous corporations, tied to the political set-up, the State casts a big shadow on the news agencies. By virtue of the size of their operations and their financial and technological strength, the five world agencies are breathing down the shoulders of the rest. These are the Associated Press of America, Reuters, Agence France Presse, TASS, and the United Press International.

A few other important foreign agencies are:

1. Kyodo (Japan)
2. Deutsche Presse-Agentur (Federal Republic of Germany)
3. Ansa (Italy)
4. Central News Agency of China
5. Tanjug Yugoslav Press Agency (Yugoslavia)
6. Polish Press Agency (Poland)
7. Iraqi News Agency (Baghdad)
8. Bangladesh Sangbad (Dacca)
9. Novosty Press Agency (USSR)
10. Depth News Asia Manila (Philippines)

Other Sources of News

News agencies – Indian and foreign – are no doubt major sources of news for newspapers and other news media. Other sources are: news media's own reporters, correspondents, and special representatives; monitored broadcasts of different radio stations; press notes, handouts and other publicity material from the government departments, embassies, business houses, political parties, and other organizations, reports of committees or commissions and other material emanating from educational, scientific, and learned institutions including research papers, evaluation studies, etc.

CHAPTER XXXIV

Non-aligned News Pool

While the Indian press is fed by a large volume of foreign news, India has not been able to sell any news service abroad even in the countries of Asia, Africa, West Indies, etc., where there is a great deal of interest in Indian affairs and events.

There is considerable potential for exporting Indian news but this perhaps could not be done in the past because the news agencies did not have the necessary facilities. The PTI had a few correspondents while the UNI had none. Samachar had five correspondents abroad. India, therefore, received world news through English, American, French, or Russian eyes. There was also no separate international news service which could draw foreign news for the country's press and disseminate Indian news to the world press.

The Pool

The non-aligned countries, numbering about 100 and comprising almost entirely the less developed regions of the world, felt concerned about the media situation. (Seventy per cent of the world population lives in Asia, Africa, and Latin America but only 26 per cent of world's daily newspapers are bought in these regions.) Also, 70 per cent of the news served by transnational agencies is about the industrialized West.

The conference of Foreign Ministers of non-aligned countries held in Lima in August, 1975, decided that a constitution for the news agency pool of non-aligned countries should be framed. A special conference for this purpose was held at New Delhi in July, 1976, in which the Information Ministers and news agency representatives from 62 countries participated. The decisions were ratified at the Summit Conference of the non-aligned countries in Colombo in August, 1976.

The New Delhi conference prepared a broad constitution for the Press Agencies Pool. The underlying principles were:

1. The aim is not to restrict but to supplement and expand the existing flow of news.
2. The pool is not to acquire hard contours and become a supra-national news agency; the pool would imply a set of arrangements.
3. Following from the above, there would be no need for the pool to have either a secretariat or a fixed headquarters.
4. The utilization of the wordage received by an agency would be fully within its discretion.

Before the initiation of the non-aligned pool idea, Samachar relied for the bulk of its international news on Reuter (UK), AP (USA) and AFP (France). In addition, it had bilateral agreements with 12 news agencies. Out of these, five were from non-aligned countries.

After the acceptance of the news agency pool scheme, Samachar finalized arrangements for exchange of news with 16 news agencies from the non-aligned world. As such, arrangements existed with a total of 28 news agencies including 21 from non-aligned countries, namely, Cuba, Indonesia, Vietnam, Yugoslavia, Bangladesh, Iraq, Sudan, Algeria, Qatar, Morocco, Kenya, Ethiopia, Zambia, and Malaysia. The other countries were USSR, Poland, Czechoslovakia, Japan, Romania, and Italy.

The arrangements visualized a two-way flow of news on a selective basis between Samachar and these agencies. The exchange of news between Samachar and a number of national news agencies in the non-aligned world began on 3 August, 1976. Samachar provided 300 to 400 words a day to each of its pool partners, comprising four or five news items drawn from its domestic files, as also despatches from its own staff overseas. To most of these agencies, Samachar provided news by international telex. Samachar and Bangladesh, however, exchanged news on their jointly leased teleprinter link between Calcutta and Dacca, while the Sri Lanka Broadcasting Corporation received news from Samachar's Madras-Colombo teleprinter link. Samachar exchanged news with the RSS of Nepal by telegram to and from Kathmandu. Consequent on the winding up of Samachar, PTI took over this work.

The non-aligned news pool is a self-paying project in the sense that the sender of the news pays the cost of the transmission. There is no special investment involved on staff or central headquarters. The recipient is also free not to use the news material received if it decides that it is unsuitable for circulation among its constituent newspapers.

Arguments Against the Pool

The non-aligned news pool has the potential to develop into a good instrument of inter-governmental cooperation particularly in the economic and social fields, but it is argued that it is no substitute for a foreign news agency. According to its critics: It is a pool of official publicity material or exchange of government handouts as most of the pool partners and the agencies disseminating the news are not free of official control. They suppress dissent as a matter of course. The non-aligned pool countries are mostly non-democracies (dictatorships, governments of monolithic parties, or bureaucratic oligarchies) and as such the agencies have no free hand in the selection of news items. The pool arrangement is at best an investment in international cooperation and not in any foreign news service. In fact, the critics say that the press attaches of the concerned embassies/high commissions can also undertake this type of work – exchange of official news. Other constraints on the rapid growth of the news pool are the non-existence of even a daily newspaper in some of the non-aligned countries and the lack of technological resources and skilled manpower to run the pool.

S.M. Mulgaokar, Editor-in-Chief, *Indian Express*, is of the view that in non-aligned news agency pool 'no thought has been given to ensuring objectivity and credibility. Indeed these are qualities which the non-aligned news agency pool has specifically rejected as irrelevant. Each country in the pool is responsible for gathering news within its borders and contributing to the pool what it considers fit for dissemination to the outside world. This amounts to acceptance of the totalitarian conception of information as an instrument of state policy since in most countries in the non-aligned bloc such national news agencies as do exist are controlled by the government.'*

Another veteran journalist, A.S. Abraham, is apprehensive of the utility of non-aligned news pool. According to him, the theoretical justification for the pool is sound. Western media, to a large extent, determine not only how non-western countries see the world but often even how they see themselves. Western media do monopolize the flow of information and that monopoly must end.

Abraham is of the view that this can and must be achieved only by the media in non-western states doing no less efficiently what the western media now do. In precise terms, they must aim to be as independent, as fearless, as investigative, and as committed to the truth as the western media, by and large, are. If this requires more and better equipment, greater professionalism, more effective training schemes, more liberal publishing laws, cheaper newsprint and transmission rates, then that is what the UNESCO should, by promoting worldwide cooperative endeavour in these areas, seek to make available.

Commenting on the role of media in a democratic set-up, Abraham says that there can be no compromise on, no dishonesty about, the basic assumption that the media in any truly open society cannot be an appendage of the state. No news pool, non-aligned or otherwise, will achieve parity with western media by propagating state-manipulated information. It is sometimes said that while for western media news means events, for those in the poor world, concerned with development, news is a process. Consequently, the argument runs, they cannot assume the adversary relationship with their governments that western media have with theirs. This position is not correct. As for news being an event or a process, reporting or commenting on it in any form can be truthful (and so possibly inconvenient to authority) or expedient (and so always acceptable to authority). It is not as if reporting a process, as against an event, automatically eliminates the choice between truth and the suppression of truth.**

*S.M. Mulgaokar, 'Editor's Note Book', *Indian Express*, 21 September, 1978.
**A.S. Abraham, 'Towards Freer Information – UNESCO Proposals Pose Grave Danger', *Times of India*, 25 September, 1978.

In Defence of the Pool

The supporters of the pool argue that in any case it is a good start towards the exchange of direct information among the non-aligned countries. The objective is to supplement and not to supplant the existing transnational news agencies. The idea is to create better direct awareness among the members. There is no intention to have any confrontation with multinational or global news agencies which have vast resources and superior technology enabling them to land their news in any part of the world at top speed and at throwaway costs. The pool is not an inward looking closed circuit system of information. It is only an attempt at greater flow of information among the non-aligned countries. The receiving countries are free to kill any item. The experience has been that while political items are not used much, economic and social news is disseminated more or less freely.

According to Mr. D.R. Mankekar* the four western news agencies, namely, Associated Press and United Press International of the USA, Reuter of Britain, and Agence France Presse of France, hold the monopoly of world news. The news sent out about the developing countries by these transnational agencies give a prejudicial image of the developing countries. The developing countries hardly get any regional news and the world news received by them is qualitatively as well as quantitatively western in content and angle. This is understandable as these agencies primarily gather, compose, and edit news for their home markets. The newspaper readers in developing countries often find such news out of tune and irrelevant or unsympathetic and woefully inadequate or prejudicial and destructive.

Mankekar is of the view that the non-aligned news pool is an attempt to remedy the vital gaps in the western agencies' services, by their own efforts, through a system of pooling their news resources and exchanging regional news of interest to non-aligned and developing countries. It is an important step to correct certain imbalances, deficiencies, or communication gaps in the field of information in the developing world. The

*D.R. Mankeker, 'Bridging the Information Gap', *Indian and Foreign Review*, 1978.

'imbalances' are of three kinds: (i) 'Inward file' that is in respect of content, quality and to some extent volume of news received by the developing countries from the outside world through western news agencies. The quality and content of news received at times is destructive and irrelevant, if not harmful. (ii) Lack of flow of news within a region, between neighbouring developing countries. Even when western news agencies cover regional news from developing countries, the story is western angle and out of tune with the requirements of the region. (iii) 'Outward file', that is news transmitted to the outside world from developing countries by the western news agencies. It is often distorted, prejudicial, or frivolous. News is seen through unsympathetic western eyes and written, edited, and selected to cater primarily for the needs of their home markets.

He is also of the view that while it is true that non-aligned nations distributed over four continents, in varying stages of development, all of them do not command competence and skill in equal degree, but collectively they certainly have the professional competence and organizational skill to operate the news pool. Also, the argument that several of the non-aligned countries have authoritarian rule and have no independent news agencies and therefore the news put out by the non-aligned news pool is packed with official propaganda should not stand in the way of the developing countries to set up national news agencies. The agencies can be converted in course of time into independent entities. In any case, some beginning has to be made and this is what the news pool seeks to achieve.

It is particularly in the sphere of regional exchange of news that the non-aligned news pool can play a vital part. The western agencies do not consider it worth while or viable to gather and distribute the regional type of news because their home markets are not interested in it. The pool can also deal effectively with developmental news, socio-economic reform, agricultural and industrial progress, cultural activities, and news of human interest. The content and angle of news received from western agencies by the non-aligned world can also be rectified if non-aligned news agencies can expand their corps of foreign correspondents.

Since the news pool service is of a supplementary character and is not intended to compete with transnational media in technical efficiency and speed of transmission, it has generally to step off spot news. It should, on the other hand, look for exclusive stories and concentrate on news on economic, commerce, developmental, cultural, and human interest relating to agriculture and land reforms, trade and commerce, industrial progress, etc. These should take the forms of news features, special articles, situationers, and backgrounders.

The news stories received from the pool disseminated by the national news agencies can be given credit line of the pool and the country from which it has originated so as to make it clear about the origin of the news story. Most of such material is bound to be somewhat lengthy in wordage and would not be affected by the time element and, therefore, could with advantage depend on air mail for their transmission, reserving the expensive electronic transmission channels for important spot political stories of special interest to the developing countries.

The actual experience of handling of the non-aligned news pool by India is that basically it is a news service of economic, developmental, cultural, and human interest. The high cost of transmission is a serious bottleneck. An effort is being made by the coordination committee of the non-aligned news pool to get appreciable concessions in cable transmission rates on the analogy of pre-Second World War 'penny a word' British Commonwealth cable rate. Also, the financial burden of an international effort of this kind, aimed at bringing closer the non-aligned nations, scattered over four continents, in goodwill and understanding, through exchange of news and information, cannot be borne by the news agencies themselves. As such, the participating governments have to foot the bill.

The non-aligned news pool has already become operational and the proposed Asian news exchange network backed and sponsored by the UNESCO and other similar ventures are expected to remove the imbalances and deficiencies now prevailing in the news system in the developing countries.

India's Image Abroad

While it is necessary to project the country's balanced picture across the world, it is extremely doubtful that this can be achieved by any official or officially-sponsored international news agency. It is well-known that responsible newspapers think several times before accepting any material emanating from the government-sponsored agencies. It is automatically considered propaganda stuff. In India also, no newspaper worth its name accepts material at its face value sent out by the USIS or the TASS agencies.

Newspapers everywhere give priority to national news and for the limited space left after national news has been accommodated, over 100 foreign countries compete. Each can at best hope to get attention only for news of the widest readers' interest. It is, therefore, clear that government-sponsored agencies by whatever name they are called are not at all suitable for giving out Indian news to foreign newspapers.

News material has a slightly better chance of acceptance if it is given out by independent news agencies such as PTI and UNI. It will be more effective if these agencies are encouraged and given facilities to expand their operations overseas. The setting up of an official international news agency will be of little help. Even for PTI and UNI, it will take quite some time before they are able to make any impact on foreign newspapers.

The best way, however, to get into foreign information media is through their representatives functioning in our country. Newspapers, radio, and television media all prefer to get their impressions of foreign countries through their own representatives and their own nationals. The foreign correspondents, therefore, constitute the best channel through which a balanced picture of India can be projected. It is they who write in depth about the country and not the news agencies which generally confine themselves to spot news. The evaluations of foreign correspondents are readily accepted by their principals. The foreign correspondents should, therefore, be provided all facilities to observe, understand, and write. India is a democracy and if some foreign observer at times takes a slanted view we need not get upset or lose our balance.

APPENDIX 1

Glossary

ABC – Abbreviation for Audit Bureau of Circulations, an organization compiling statistics on circulation.

Ad – Abbreviation for advertisement; generally display advertisements – persuasive material. It is paid for and therefore fully controlled in text, presentation, medium, and time by the sponsoring party.

Add – Additional news matter.

Agate – Type $5\frac{1}{2}$ or 6 point in depth; smallest type used by newspapers.

A.M. – A morning newspaper.

Angle – A slant or special aspect of a story.

A.P. – Associated Press.

Art – General term for all newspaper illustrations.

Assignment – Any news-gathering task allotted to a reporter. He may be assigned to obtain a news story, or one angle of such a story, or pictures, etc.

Audience – Group or groups to whom the public relations programme or any part thereof is directed.

Author's alterations – Changes made in subject-matter after proofs have been submitted, changes not due to errors by the type setter.

Backroom – The mechanical section of a small newspaper plant, as distinguished from the front office.

Banner – A headline stretching over the top of a page. Also called 'streamer', 'line', or 'ribbon'.

Bastard type – Type that does not conform to the standard point system.

Beat – Newspaper slang for a news item that is the exclusive property of one paper; a scoop; also applied to special territory assigned to reporters, as police beat.

Big newspaper – A paper which has a circulation of more than 50,000 copies per publishing day.

Black and white – Reproduction in one colour only, as distinguished from two or more colours.

Blanket head – A headline topping all the columns occupied by a given story or newspaper department. It may blanket both text and pictures.

Bleed – When printed matter is trimmed so that the illustrations run off the edges of the sheet it is said to bleed.

Blind interviews – An interview story in which the interviewee is not revealed, e.g. 'a highly placed official' or 'a spokesman for . . .'. Also called a lamp-post interview.

Blow up – Increase the size of any visual item by photographic reproduction.

Body type – The type in which the greater part of the newspaper text is set, generally 7 or 8 point.

Boil it down – A copy desk expression for reducing wordage of a story.

Bold face type – A blacker, heavier type than its regular or medium counterpart in any given type face.

Booklet – A printed piece of six or more pages with a paper cover prepared as a bound unit, usually by stappling.

Box story – A news story or feature enclosed by a 'box'.

Broadside – A sheet of paper printed on one side for quick reading and motivation.

Brochure – A printed piece of six or more pages. More elaborate than a booklet.

Bureau – A subsidiary news gathering organization set-up.

Byline – A signature to precede a news story, as 'By John Smith'.

Byline story – Any signed story in the newspaper.

Campaign – An organized effort to convert the opinion of any group or groups on a subject.

Caps – Abbreviation for capital letters.

Caption – Literally any heading, but used specifically in regard to picture headings and accompanying text. Usually over a picture, whereas a cutline goes under a picture.

Catchline – A guideline or slugline.

Circulation – Average number of copies sold and distributed free per publishing day.

Col. – Abbreviation for column.

Common ownership unit – A newspaper establishment owning two or more news interest newspapers, at least one of which is a daily.

Copy – The term applied to all news manuscript; also, any illustrations to be reproduced by photo engraving.

Copy reader – Copy editor, the editor who puts the copy in final shape before it is set and who writes headlines.

Correspondent – A person, often working on a string, who is authorized to send news from out-of-town points.

Cover – To get all available news about an event.

Coverage – Extent of distribution of publicity or opinion-affecting material.

Credit line – A line giving the source of copy or illustration.

Cropping – Eliminating unnecessary or undesirable background in an illustration.

Cub – A beginning reporter.

Daily – A newspaper issued at least four times a week (UNESCO definition).

Dateline – A line at the top of each page, giving the date on which the newspaper is published; also the line giving the point of origin of a telegraph, cable, or radio story.

Deadline – The last moment to get copy in for an edition.

Delete – 'Take out' or 'omit' from copy.

Desk editor – An editor directing reporters or copy editors.

Dope – Advance news story material, mostly gossip and rumours.

Dummy – Diagram or layout of a newspaper or magazine page, showing the position each story and picture is to have.

Embossing – Pressing a piece of paper between two dyes so that an impression is made to stand above the surface of the rest of the sheet.

Exchanges – Where one newspaper exchanges copies with another, these copies are called exchanges.

Exclusive – A news story is exclusive when it is the property of only one newspaper; a scoop.

Fake – Falsified story.

Facsimile – An exact copy or reproduction of something produced by a mechanical or photographic process.

Feature – To give special prominence to a story. Any story that may not be strictly regarded as news, yet is timely and interesting, may be called a feature. The word is also used to denominate the most important or interesting element in a story.

File – (i) A correspondent files a story when he dispatches it by wire or by radio. (ii) All newspapers keep files of their back copies.

Filler – Short items that may be placed almost anywhere on the page, as distinguished from stories bearing top heads.

Flash – A bulletin by telephone, telegraph, or radio that conveys the first brief word of an event that has just taken place.

Folder – A printed piece of four pages.

Folio – A page; the page number.

Follow, follow-up – A follow story is one based on a story previously published; it gives later developments. Same as a second-day story. Also, a subsidiary story following a big lead, and relating to the same or a similar subject.

Font – An assortment of type faces in one size.

Format – Size, shape, and general make-up of a publication.

Galley proofs – Proofs not made in page form, but drawn from the type as it stands in galley trays following composition.

Glossy – A shiny photographic print, preferred by photo engravers.

Hold for release – Term endorsed on copy that is not to be published until a specified time.

Human interest – Any pleasant little news oddity about people, stories with conversation and action, but not necessarily straight news.

Index – An index of the day's news, usually on the front page.

Input – Information fed into a data processing system.

Inserts – Printed matter prepared for enclosure with letters.

Interview – A story based on an interview.

Kill – Type is killed when it is discarded as useless and thrown into the hell-box. To kill copy is to destroy it.

L.C. – Abbreviation for lower case, meaning small letters, not capitals.

Layout – An outline for presentation of material for publication or reproduction within the confines of the previously designated format.

Lead – Introductory sentences or paragraphs of news story; the big news story of the day.

Leaflet – A printed piece, usually of four pages.

Letterpress – A printing process in which the ink is applied to raised types and then applied to the paper by direct pressure.

Lithographic printing – Transferring an inked image from a smooth surface to paper by a chemical process.

Manual – A compilation of directions and instructions in a book or booklet form.

Masthead – The matter printed in every issue of a newspaper usually at the top of the editorial column, stating the title, publisher, place of publication, etc.; from the nautical term indicating the top of the mast from which a flag is flown, hence also called flag.

Media – Avenues through which PR messages are transmitted, e.g. Radio, TV, newspaper, etc.

Medium newspaper – A paper which has a circulation between 15,001 and 50,000 copies per publishing day.

Mimeographing – A trade-mark process for reproducing typewritten or handwritten material.

More – Written at the bottom of a page of copy indicating more to come.

Morgue – The newspaper's repository for clippings, photos, and all types of reference material.

Morse code – The code used by telegraphers.

Newspaper – Any printed (including cyclostyled) periodical work containing public news or comments on public news.

Newsprint – The paper on which all newspapers are printed. Also used for inexpensive printed material.

Obit, obituary – A biography of a dead person.

Offset – A process of lithography.

Op. ed. – Page opposite the editorial page.

Pad – To make a story long by padding it out with words.

Page proof – The proof of an entire page.

Pamphlet – A printed piece of a few pages, with a proper cover.

Perforating – Cover punching small holes in paper, making it easy to detach a part of the sheet.

Periodical – A newspaper appearing at an interval of a week or more.

Photo-offset – A printing process.

Photostat – Making photographic copies of drawing, map, text, etc.

Pica – Twelve-point type.

Pix – Abbreviation for pictures; any newspaper illustrations.

Planograph – An inexpensive offset printing process.

Play up – To give prominence to.

P.M. – An afternoon paper.

Point – The unit of measurement in which type sizes are designated: approximately 1/72 of an inch.

P.R. – Public relations.

Profile – Biographical sketch.

Proof – An impression of type taken on paper for the purpose of making corrections and alterations.

Public – Any group of individuals that a PR programme seeks to influence.

Public relations – The science and art of attitude control. A public relations man seeks to create public favour for the interest hiring him.

Publicity – A technique of public relations.

Puff – A personal publicity story.

Pull – Proofs are always pulled from the type.

Punch – Stories and headlines with punch are those with vigour, strength, snap, instantaneous appeal.

Quotes – Quotation marks; a part of a story quoted.

Release copy – Copy that is not to be published until a certain release date. Important documents of state, such as the President's message, come to the newspaper in this form.

Reprint – A second or new impression of a printed work.

Round-up – Comprehensive story from several sources.

Run – A story already printed has been run; a reporter's run is his beat or the route he takes on his regular coverage.

Rush – Copy to be handled quickly is so marked.

Scoop – A story that is the exclusive property of one newspaper, possession of which means a victory over a competitor.

Second-day story – A follow-up story based on one that already has appeared. This type of story also carries a second-day head, conveying the hint that it records not a fresh event but developments.

Skyline – Headline across top of page over name plate. Also called over-title and over-the-roof.

Slant – An angle of a story, a story is slanted when a certain aspect is played up for policy or other reasons.

Sleuth – Newspaper slang for reporter who specializes in stories that require exhaustive investigation, detective work.

Slick – A publication published on coated, smooth paper.

Slides – Individual film frames that are projected on to a screen to serve as visual accompaniment of an oral presentation.

Small newspaper – A newspaper having circulation up to 15,000 copies per publishing day.

Spot news – News obtained first-hand of the spot where it happened, hence fresh and live news.

Squib – A short news item; a filler.

Stet – From the Latin, meaning 'let it stand'. Used to indicate that matter marked for correction or omission is to remain as it was originally.

Straight news – A plain recital of news facts with no attempt at featuring or fancy writing or embellishment of any kind.

Stringer – Correspondent, usually paid on space basis.

Style book – Manual setting up standrads for handling copy, i.e. spelling, capitalization, abbreviation, word usages, and so on.

Subhead – A one- or two-line head.

Tabloid – A newspaper format, smaller than standard size, and usually having five columns per page, each page being slightly more than half the size of a standard paper.

Take – A small portion of news manuscript or any copy given out to machine operators by the copy cutter to be set in type; a small portion of a story sent by the copy editor to the composing room.

Telephoto – A photograph transmitted by wire.

Teletype – An electronic system of transmitting information in typewritten form.

Trim – A term used when it is desired to have the story reduced in length, either in manuscript or in type.

Videophone – Combined telephone and television transmission by which voice and sight of the two parties are received at each end.

Yellow journalism – A sensationalized story; a yellow journal specializes in sensationalized stories.

APPENDIX 2

International Code of Ethics for Public Relations*

Considering that all member-countries of the United Nations Organization have agreed to abide by its Charter which reaffirms "its faith in fundamental human rights, in the dignity and worth of the human person" and that having regard to the very nature of their profession, Public Relations practitioners in these countries should undertake to ascertain and observe the principles set out in this Chapter;

Considering that apart from "rights", human beings have not only physical or material needs but also intellectual, moral and social needs, and that their rights are of real benefit to them only in so far as these needs are essentially met;

Considering that, in the course of their professional duties and depending on how these duties are performed, public relations practitioners can substantially help to meet these intellectual, moral and social needs;

And lastly, considering that the use of techniques enabling them to come simultaneously into contact with millions of people gives public relations practitioners a power that has to be restrained by the observance of a strict moral code;

On all these grounds the Public Relations Society of India hereby declares that it accepts, as its moral charter, the principles of the following Code of Ethics and that if, in the light of evidence submitted to the Society, a member of this Society should be found to have infringed this Code in the course of his professional duties, he will be deemed to be guilty of serious misconduct calling for an appropriate penalty.

Accordingly, each Member of this Society—

SHALL ENDEAVOUR

1. To contribute to the achievement of the moral and cultural conditions enabling human beings to reach their full stature and enjoy the indefeasible rights to which they are entitled under the "Universal Declaration of Human Rights";

Code of Athens, presented by Albert Oeckl, President, IPRA. Adopted by International Public Relations Association and European Public Relations Centre in May, 1965, and by Public Relations Society of India at New Delhi on 21 April, 1968.

2. To establish communication patterns and channels which, by fostering the free flow of essential information, will make each member of the group feel that he is being kept informed, and also give him an awareness of his own personal involvement and responsibility and of solidarity with other members;

3. To conduct himself always and in all circumstances in such a manner as to deserve and secure the confidence of those with whom he comes into contact;

4. To bear in mind that, because of the relationship between his profession and the public, his conduct – even in private – will have an impact on the way in which the profession as a whole is appraised.

SHALL UNDERTAKE

5. To observe, in the course of his professional duties, the moral principles and rules of the "Universal Declaration of Human Rights";

6. To pay due regard to, and uphold, human dignity, and to recognize the right of each individual to judge for himself;

7. To establish the moral, psychological and intellectual conditions for dialogue in its true sense, and to recognize the right of the parties involved to state their case and express their views;

8. To act, in all circumstances in such a manner as to take account of the respective interests of the parties involved; both the interests of the organization which he serves and the interests of the publics concerned;

9. To carry out his undertakings and commitments which shall always be so worded as to avoid any misunderstanding, and to show loyalty and integrity in all circumstances so as to keep the confidence of his clients or employers, past or present, and of all the publics that are affected by his actions.

SHALL REFRAIN FROM

10. Subordinating the truth to other requirements;

11. Circulating information which is not based on established and ascertainable facts;

12. Taking part in any venture or undertaking which is unethical or dishonest or capable of impairing human dignity and integrity;

13. Using any "manipulative" methods or techniques designed to create subconscious motivations which the individual cannot control of his own free will and so can not be held accountable for the action taken on them.

APPENDIX 3

Specimens of Types

NEW TIMES ROMAN

30 Point

INHERENT enjoying

24 Point

MOTION PICTURE

Several Foreign Stars 58

18 Point

MODERN TYPES DESIGNED 58

Firm received largest shipment above

14 Point

MODEL PRESS PRIVATE LIMITED

6-E, Rani Jhansi Road, New Delhi-110055.

12 Point

HONESTY IS THE BEST POLICY

a story about a bandit who terrified the citizens

10 Point

KNOWLEDGE TAKEN BY CHANCE. ALMOST EVERYONE

you meet knows more on some subject than you do. Turn that

8 Point

EDUCATING HORSES FOR THE CAVALRY HORSES USED BY THE

United States cavalry must be thoroughly trained in war work. The horses not

6 Point

MODEL PRESS PRIVATE LIMITED, 6-E, Rani Jhansi Road

Jhandewalan, New Delhi-110055.

TIMES NEW ROMAN BOLD

36 Point

MODEST maidens

24 Point

MYSTERIOUS HEROINE 2

this is no mean achievement

18 Point

FOREIGN SONGBIRD ARRIVES 32

Country folk great famous singer 65

14 Point

MERCHANTS SALESMEN USED NEW 12

method to secure smarter business hands in depot

12 Point

EVERYTHING FOR PRINTERS TYPOGRAPHIC

Borders are still in popular demand having acquired it

10 Point

BEAUTIFUL MUSICAL COMPOSITIONS SOMEBODY HAS

that practically all the music of humanity might perish without

8 Point

EDUCATING HORSES FOR THE CAVALRY HORSES USED BY THE

States cavalry must be thoroughly trained in war work. The horses not only

TIMES ROMAN ITALIC

24 Point

IMPORTED 1875 Delights

18 Point

LEASED Gigantic corporation near

14 Point

THE ROAD TO GREATNESS Many people say

12 Point

THE ROAD TO GREATNESS Many people say

10 Point

MODEL PRESS PRIVATE LTD., 6-E, Rani Jhansi Road,

8 Point

A GOOD NATURED COUNTENANCE REALLY Good nature is really more

APPENDIX 4

Proof-reader's Marks

Marginal Mark	*Explanation*	*How indicated in the Copy*
1. Marks of Instruction		
ꝺ	Delete, take out	He sent the coppy.
stet.	Let it stand	~~He sent the copy.~~
sp.	Spell out	He sent (10) copies.
tr.	Transpose	He the sent copy.
¶	Paragraph	read. He sent the copy.
no ¶	No paragraph— run in	read. He sent the copy.
(sent/?)	Query to the author	He the copy.
2. Marks Regarding Type Style		
ital.	Set in *italic*	He sent the copy.
s.c.	Set in SMALL CAPITALS	He sent the copy.
caps.	Set in CAPITALS	he sent the copy.
c.+s.c.	Set in CAPITALS AND SMALL CAPITALS	he sent the copy.
b.f. or bf.	Set in boldface	He sent the copy.
rom.	Change from *italic* to roman	He sent the *copy*.
l.c.	Set in lower case	He Sent the Copy.
u.+l.c. or c.+l.c.	Set in Upper and Lower Case	he sent the copy.
3. Marks Regarding Defects in the Type		
⊗	Broken letters	He sent the copy.
w.f.	Wrong font	He sent the copy.
9	Turn inverted letters	He sent the copy.
//	Straighten marked lines	He sent the copy. He sent the copy.

Marginal Mark	*Explanation*	*How indicated in the Copy*
=	Out of alignment—straighten	He sent the copy.
↓	Push down space	He sent the copy.

4. Marks Regarding Spacing

Marginal Mark	*Explanation*	*How indicated in the Copy*
⁀	Close up	He sent the copy.
ℨ	Delete and close up	He sent the copy.
#	Insert space	He sent thecopy.
eq. #	Equalize the spacing	He sent the copy.
□	Indent one em	□He sent the copy.
□□	Indent two ems	□□He sent the copy.
□□□	Indent three ems	□□□He sent the copy.
[	Move left as indicated	[He sent the copy.
]	Move right as indicated	He sent the copy.]
⌐¬	Raise as indicated	He sent the copy.
⌊⌋	Lower as indicated	He sent the copy.
ld. >	Insert lead between lines	

5. Marks of Punctuation

Marginal Mark	*Explanation*	*How indicated in the Copy*
⊙	Period	He sent the copy
∧	Comma	He sent the copy
;/	Semicolon	He sent the copy
:/	Colon	He sent the copy thus
=/	Hyphen	He was copyediting.
∨	Apostrophe	It is the authors copy.
∨ ∨	Open and close quotes	He said: Send the copy
!/	Exclamation	Send the copy
?/	Question mark	Did he send the copy
1/N or en	One-en dash	Copy, 17, 34, 227–8
1/M or em	One-em dash	We went—with copy.
(/)	Open and close parens	It the copy was sent.
[/]	Open and close brackets	He send *sic* the copy.
∧	Inferior figure	H_2O
∨	Superior figure	xy^2

APPENDIX 5

Broadcasting Code

The nine-point code for broadcasts by individuals prohibits the following:

1. Criticism of friendly countries.
2. Attack on religion or communities.
3. Anything obscene or defamatory.
4. Incitement to violence or anything against maintenance of law and order.
5. Aspersions on the integrity of the President, Governors, and judiciary.
6. Anything amounting to contempt of court.
7. Attack on a political party by name.
8. Hostile criticism of any State or the Centre.
9. Anything showing disrespect to the Constitution or advocating change in the Constitution by violence; but advocating changes in a constitutional way should not be debarred.

This code applies to criticism in the nature of personal tirade, either of a friendly government or of a politcal party or of the Central Government or any State government. But it does not debar reference to any dispassionate discussion of policies pursued by any of them.

The Station Director is competent to draw the individual's attention to the passages in the broadcast talk which violates the code. If the broadcaster refuses to accept the Station Director's suggestions and modify his script accordingly, the Station Director has the authority to refuse him to broadcast. In the case of unresolved differences of opinion between the Minister of a State government and the Station Director, about the interpretation of the code, the matter will be referred to the Minister of Information and Broadcasting who will decide whether or not any change in the broadcast talk is necessary to conform it to the code.

APPENDIX 6

Commercial Broadcasting - Useful Information

Right to Rotate Spots

The AIR Commercial Broadcasting Service reserves the right to rotate spots through the relevant time period for which the charge is made, unless they are fixed spots and specific times of broadcast are pre-arranged.

Two Commercials in one Spot

If a commercial contains reference to products or services belonging to two different advertisers, it will be charged at a rate equivalent to that for two announcements each half the amount of time of the commercial; if no contract exists, the charge will be made at the casual rate. If half of the time booked is not a standard category the advertisement will be charged at the appropriate rate for the next higher time category.

If a commercial contains reference to products or services belonging to the same advertiser but unrelated in their use or function, it will be charged as two separate commercials, each at the rate for an announcement half the time of the commercial; if no contract exists, the charge will be at the casual rates. If half the time booked is not standard category, the advertisements will be charged at the appropriate rate for the next higher time category.

If such tie-ups are intended in the advertisements during sponsored programmes, a written request for inclusion of the tie-up should be made in advance and upon considering the merits of each such request, the additional payment to be made will be intimated to the advertiser.

Procedure for Payments

Except advertising agencies accredited to AIR who are allowed 45 days' credit period as per clause 17 of the contract, all other agencies/canvassers/direct advertisers are required to pay in advance of broadcast. Payments are to be made in cash or by crossed cheques/demand draft on Bombay bank drawn in favour of Reserve Bank of India, Account - All India Radio'.

Booking for Advertisements

For booking time for Bombay-Pune-Nagpur stations, the Director of

Sales, Central Sales Unit, Commercial Broadcasting Service, All India Radio, Broadcasting House, Backbay Reclamation, Post Box No. 11106, Bombay-400020 should be contacted.

Stations other than Bombay/Pune/Nagpur are authorized to book some time directly at their stations. Correspondence relating to such bookings may be addressed to the respective Station Directors (Commercial), All India Radio, Delhi/Calcutta/Chandigarh/Ahmedabad/Bangalore/Hyderabad/Madras/Kanpur/Bhopal/Patna/Jaipur/Trivandrum/Cuttack/Srinagar.

Technical Specifications for Recordings

Commercial announcements recorded on magnetic recording tape shall conform to the following standard:

1. The recording shall be confined to a full track recorded on professional quality tape at velocity of 7.5 inches per second.
2. The tape spool size shall not be less than 5 inches in diameter.
3. The tape recording shall comply with the international standards, in respect of noise level, frequency response, etc.
4. The tape recording shall contain spoken identification announcement as follows:

   (a) An announcement giving the name of the advertiser, products, the number of commercials and the duration of each in the order of recording.

   (b) A label shal be attached to the carton containing the tape giving the following details: tape number, name of client, product, agency, and spot number.

5. Spacing:

   (a) The margin from the start of the tape should be at least ten seconds.

   (b) Spacing in between two advertisements should be 10 to 15 seconds.

   (c) The playback level should be at least 4 MW ($6V_u$) across 600 ohms or 0.707 volts.

Information on rates for spots advertisements, and sponsored programmes, time classification, etc. for different AIR stations are given in the Rate Card issued by CBS Central Sales Unit, Bombay.

APPENDIX 7

Technical Specifications and Rates of T.V. Advertisements

1. Acceptable Formats

Advertisement material for television should be prepared in one of the following formats:

(a) Standard slide with sound as tape.
(b) Caption/graphic on grey cardboard, with sound on tape.
(c) 16 mm positive film with optical/magnetic sound.

2. Contents of Advertisement

Sound part of advertisement should either be in the form of specially composed background instrumental music or verbal message which should preferably be of some special significance. The advertisement may include, besides the credit title of the sponsor, the brand name of the product manufactured or marketed by him and prices of the products.

3. Specification (Picture)

3.1. *Slides*

Slides shall be mounted in standard 50 mm (2″ × 2″) mounts having picture aspect ratio of 4 horizontal : 3 vertical. Any written material or titles should be restricted to TV safe title area.

3.2. *Captions*

Caption card size shall be 305 (12″) horizontal × 228 (9″). Matter should be plain written words or graphic design, in white letters on a dull background. In the case of pictures or photographs contrast range shall be limited to 1 : 30. This matter should be restricted to an area of 6″ × 8″ in the centre of the card.

3.3. 16 *mm Film*/35 *mm Film*

16 mm or 35 mm/print on a film spool may be given. The spool hub shall be as per the standard used at the respective Doordarshan kendras. Material shall be photographic positive with film density range restricted to 0.35 to 1.6 for proper TV reproduction. Any written words or titles, etc. should be within the TV safe title area. The film shall be free from dust/dirt or scratches. A protective leader of a length of not less than 3.5 metres shall be provided on both sides of the film. Identification of the advertisement, name of the company, and duration at 25 frames per second, shall be written on the leader. In the case of 16 mm optical sound film (Comopt) emulsion position should also be indicated. Labels indicating the same information shall also be affixed on the film spool and film box, if any.

4. Sound Specifications

Audible matter in the advertisement shall be recorded in the manner specified below, and shall not be excessively noisy or strident.

4.1. *Sound for Caption or Slide*

Sound accompanying slides or captions shall be on 6.25 mm (1/4″) tape on 178 mm (7″) plastic reel with standard hubs. A leader tape or black tape about 5 mm shall be provided before the start of the recording.

The recording shall be full track on standard professional quality audio tape at a speed of (19.05) 7-1/2 m per second. The recording shall comply with the CCIR standard in respect of frequency response, distortion and noise level, etc.

Before the start of the recording, a spoken word identification announcement shall be recorded giving details of corresponding caption, name of the sponsored programme to which it relates.

Labels should be affixed on to the tape reel and the caption containing the tape giving the following details: tape number, advertiser, product/service advertised, and duration.

4.2. *Film Sound*

Sound on 35 mm film shall be married optical side track (Comopt). Variable area recording is preferred. The location and dimension of picture frames and sound track should conform to appropriate international standards. Useful frequency range should be 40 to 8000 hz.

16 mm film sound shall be married optical side track (Comopt) or married magnetic side track (Commag). Carriable area optical recording is preferred.

The location and dimension of picture frames and sound track should conform to appropriate international standard.

The magnetic sound recording characteristic should be the same as those for magnetic tape recording at a speed of 19.05 (7.5″ per second.

APPENDIX 8

Excerpts from Code of Ethics for Advertising in India

Introduction

Along with the development of a very complex distribution system, the requirements of a market economy, faced with the need for ensuring a regular flow of mass production, have given rise to the development of new techniques of sales promotion.

Of these, advertising has proved itself to be of inestimable value for producers and distributors as well as for consumers. It enables the former to maintain contact with customers who are widely scattered and often unknown, and it assists the latter in choosing those goods and services that are best suited to their particular requirements.

Recognizing that the legitimate function of advertising is the advocacy of the merits of particular products or services, this code is intended to be applied in spirit as well as in letter and should be taken to set out the minimum standards to be observed by the parties concerned. This code does override all ethical standards in advertising laid down by individual organizations, but it does not supersede the standards of practice laid down by individual organizations as incumbent upon their own members and applying to their own particular trade or industry.

General Rules of Conduct

1. Advertising should be so designed as to conform not only to the laws but also to the moral, aesthetic, and religious sentiments of the country in which it is published.
2. No advertisement likely to bring advertising into contempt or disrepute should be permitted. Advertising should not take advantage of the superstition or ignorance of the general public.
3. No advertisements of talismans, charms, and character reading from photographs or such other matter as will trade on the superstition of the general public shall be permitted.
4. Advertising should be truthful, avoid distorting facts and misleading the public by means of implications and omissions. For instance, it should not mislead the consumer by false statements as to:

(a) the character of the merchandise, i.e., its utility, materials, ingredients, origin, etc.;
(b) the price of the merchandise, its value, its suitability, terms of purchase;
(c) the services accompanying purchase, including delivery, exchange, returns, repair, upkeep, etc.;
(d) personal recommendations of the article or service; testimonials which are fictitious and/or fraudulent or the originals of which cannot be produced must not be used; anyone using testimonials in advertisements is as responsible for the statements made in them as he would be if he had made them himself;
(e) the quality of the value of competing goods or the trustworthiness of statements made by others.

5. No advertisement should be permitted to contain any claim so exaggerated as to lead inevitably to disappointment in the mind of the public. Special care is called for in the following cases:

(a) Advertisement addressed to those suffering from illness. In this respect the Code of Standards of Advertising in relation to medicine must be adhered to. The Code sets out general principles to be followed in relation to the advertising of medicines and treatments particularly in respect of cure; illness; misleading or exaggerated claims; appeals to fear; diagnosis or treatment by correspondence; disparaging references; incorrect information about clinics, institutes, laboratories, doctors, hospitals; products offered particularly to women; family planning; natural remedies; special claims; sexual weakness; premature ageing; and loss of virility; slimming; weight reduction or limitations or figure control; tonics; hypnosis; materials meant for distribution in educational institutions.
(b) Advertisements inviting the public to invest money. Such advertisements should not contain statements which may mislead the public in respect of the security offered, rates of return, or terms of amortization.
(c) Advertisements inviting the public to take part in lotteries or such competitions as are permitted by law or which hold out the prospects of gifts. Such advertisements should state clearly all the conditions for the lottery or competition or the conditions for the distribution of the gifts.
(d) The publication of employment notices requiring fees for application forms, prospectus, etc., and security deposits should be forbidden except when such advertisements emanate from governmental or quasi-governmental sources.

6. Methods of advertising designed to create confusion in the mind of the consumer as between goods by one maker and another maker are

unfair and should not be used. Such methods may consist in:

(a) the imitation of the trademark or name of competitor or the packaging or labelling of goods; or
(b) the imitations of advertising devices, copy, layouts or slogans.

7. Advertising should endeavour to gain the goodwill of the public on the basis of the merits of the goods or services advertised. Direct comparison with competing goods or firms and disparaging references are in no circumstances permitted.
8. Indecent, vulgar, suggestive, repulsive, or offensive themes or treatment should be avoided in all advertisements. This also applies to such advertisements which in themselves are not objectionable as defined above, but which advertise objectionable books, photographs, or other matter and thereby lead to their sale and circulation.
9. No advertisements should offer to refund money paid.
10. The use of National Emblem is prohibited by law in advertisements, trademarks, etc., except by governmental agencies. Also, the use of the picture of Gandhi, the President, the Vice-President, and the Prime Minister of India is forbidden in such advertisements, trademarks, etc., except by previous permission. This rule does not apply to advertising of books, films, or other items in which these personages form the chief subject.

APPENDIX 9

New World Information and Communication Order – MacBride Commission's Guidelines

The International Commission for the Study of Communication Problems (MacBride Commission), set up by UNESCO, has set out major guidelines for the development of a new world information and communication order.

Its appraisal on the communication problems and conclusions reflect the consensus of the 16-member commission presided over by Mr. Sean MacBride, former minister for foreign affairs of Ireland and president of the International Peace Bureau.

The commission was set up in November 1977 in pursuance of the UNESCO conference in Nairobi in 1976 and the final 484 page report, together with the director-general's comments, will go to the forthcoming session of the UNESCO general conference in Belgrade in September-October this year. The members of the commission included Mr. B.G. Verghese from India. The full report has just been made available in India.

Mr. MacBride says in a foreword to the report that his concern was how to achieve "a balanced, non-partisan, objective analysis of today's communication scene". Despite the large area of consensus reached on most major issues, many questions remained open and required further analysis, he noted.

Following is a summary of the commission's recommendations:

A better, more just and more democratic social order in the realisation of fundamental human rights can be achieved only through understanding and tolerance, gained in large part by free, open, and balanced communications.

Utmost importance should be given to eliminating imbalances and disparities in communication and its structures, particularly in information flows. Developing countries need to reduce their dependence, and claim a new more just and more equitable order in the field of communication.

Communication is a basic individual right, and freedom of information a fundamental human right. It is essential to develop comprehensive national communication policies linked to overall social, cultural and economic development objectives. National governments should recognise the urgency of according communications higher priority in planning and funding.

Communication can no longer be regarded merely as an incidental service and its development left to chance. Recognition of its potential warrants the formulation by all nations, and particularly developing countries, of comprehensive communication policies linked to overall social, cultural, economic and political goals.

Strong national news agencies are vital for improving each country's national and international reporting where viable regional networks should be set up to increase news flows and serve all the major language groups in the area. Nationally, the agencies should buttress the growth of both urban and rural newspapers to serve as the core of a country's news collection and distribution system.

National book production should be encouraged and accompanied by the establishment of a distribution network for books, newspapers and periodicals.

The development of comprehensive national radio networks, capable of reaching remote areas should take priority over the development of television, which, however, should be encouraged, where appropriate.

There should be a major international research and development effort to increase the supply of paper. The worldwide shortage of paper, including newsprint, and its escalating cost imposing crushing burdens upon struggling newspapers, periodicals and publication industry, above all in the developing countries.

The technological explosion in communication has both great potential and great danger. The outcome depends on crucial decisions and on where and by whom they are taken. Thus it is a priority to organise the decision-making process in a participatory manner on the basis of a full awareness of the social impact of different alternatives.

The concentration of communications technology in a relatively few developed countries and transnational corporations has led to virtual monopoly situations in this field. To counteract these tendencies, national and international measures are required, among them reform of existing patent laws and conventions, appropriate legislation and international agreements.

For the journalist, freedom and responsibility are indivisible. Freedom without responsibility invites distortion and other abuses. But in the absence of freedom there can be no exercise of responsibility. The concept of freedom with responsibility necessarily includes a concern for professional ethics, demanding an equitable approach to events, situations or processes with due attention to their diverse aspects. This is not always the case today.

Codes of professional ethics exist in all parts of the world, adopted voluntarily in many countries by professional groups. The adoption of codes of ethics at national and, in some cases, at the regional level is desirable, provided that such codes are prepared and adopted by the profession itself – without governmental interference.

All countries should take steps to assure admittance of foreign correspondents and facilitate their collection and transmission of news. Special obligations in this regard, undertaken by the signatories to the final act of the Helsinki conference, should be honoured and, indeed, liberally applied.

Free access to news sources by journalists is an indispensable requirement for accurate, faithful and balanced reporting. This necessarily involves access to unofficial, as well as official, sources of information, that is, access to the entire spectrum of opinion within any country.

Conventional standards of news selection and reporting, and many accepted news values, need to be reassessed if readers and listeners around the world are to receive a more faithful and comprehensive account of events, movements and trends in both developing and developed countries.

All countries should adopt measures to enlarge sources of information needed by citizens in their everyday life. A careful review of existing laws and regulations should be undertaken with the aim of reducing limitations, secrecy provision and other constraints in information practices.

Censorship or arbitrary control of information should be abolished. In areas where reasonable restrictions may be considered necessary, these should be provided for by law, subject to judicial review and in line with the principles enshrined in the United Nations charter, the universal declaration of human rights and the international covenants relating to human rights, and in other instruments adopted by the community of nations.

Developing countries have a primary responsibility for undertaking necessary changes to overcome their dependence in the field of communications. The actions needed begin at the national level, but must be complemented by forceful and decisive agreements at the bilateral, sub-regional, regional, and inter-regional levels. Collective self-reliance is the cornerstone of a new world information and communication order.

The establishment within UNESCO of an international centre for the study and planning of information and communication has been suggested. Its main task would be, among other things, to promote the development of national communication systems in developing countries and the balance and reciprocity in international information flows, and mobilise resources for that purpose and manage the funds put at its disposal. It should also keep under review communications technology transfers between developed and developing countries so that they are carried out in the most suitable conditions.

National communication policies should be consistent with adopted international communication principle and should seek to create a climate of mutual understanding and peaceful coexistence among nations. The media should also be encouraged to refrain from advocating national, racial or religious hatred, and incitement to discrimination, hostility, violence, or war.

(14 July, 1980)

APPENDIX 10

Revised Terms of Reference of the Second Press Commission

The Press Commission shall inquire into the growth and status of the Press since the first Press Commission reported and suggest how best it should develop in future.

It shall, in particular, examine and make recommendations on:

1. The role of the Press in a developing democratic society.
2. The present constitutional guarantee with regard to the freedom of speech and expression, whether this is adequate to ensure freedom of the press; adequacy and efficacy of the laws, rules and regulations for maintaining this freedom.
3. Constitutional and legal safeguards to protect the citizen's right to privacy.
4. Means of safeguarding the independence of the Press against economic and political pressures and pressures from proprietors and management.
5. Role of the Press and the responsibilities it should a ssume in developmental policies.
6. The Press as industry, a social institution and a forum for informed discussion of public affairs.
7. Ownership patterns, management practices and financial structures of the Press; their relation to growth, editorial independence and professional integrity.
8. Chain newspapers; links with industry, their effect on competition and on the readers' right to objective news and free comments.
9. Economics of the newspaper industry; newsprint, printing machinery and other inputs for newspapers.
10. Advertising – Government and private, educational and commercial.
11. Government-Press relations and the role of official agencies.
12. Relations that should subsist between different elements of the press, namely, publishers, managers, editors and professional journalists and others.
13. Growth of small and medium papers and of the language press.
14. Development of the periodical press and specialized journals.
15. News coverage and news values; structure and functioning of news agencies and feature agencies; flow of news to and from India.

16. Training of professional manpower; steps to improve professional standards and performance; research in journalism and mass communication.
17. Journalism as a means of better mutual understanding in the context of proposals for a new international information order.
18. Perspective of newspaper development.

(24 July, 1980)

A Select Bibliography

Books

Angoff, Allen, ed. Public Relations for Libraries. 1973. Greenwood.

Black Sam. Practical Public Relations. London, English Language Book Society. 1975.

Black Sam. The Role of Public Relations in Management. Pitman. 1972.

Bernays, Edward L. Your Future in Public Relations (Careers in Depth Series). 1969. Resen Press.

Bhumenthal, L.R. Practice and Public Relations. London, Macmillan. 1972.

Biddleecombe, Peter. International Public Relations Encyclopedia. London, Grant Helen. 1968.

Biddleecombe, Peter, ed. Goodwill, The Wasted Assets. London. Business Books. 1971.

Cutlip, Scott M., ed. Public Relations Bibliography, 2nd ed. 1965. University of Wisconsin Press.

Derriman, J.P. Public Relations in Business Management. University of London Press. 1964.

Derriman, J.P. Company-Investor Relations : An Introduction to Financial Public Relations for British Companies. University of London Press. 1969.

Dhenkney, V.M. Public Relations in Business and Public Administration in India. Poona, Vaishali. 1972.

Ellis, N. and Bowman, P. Manual of Public Relations. Heinemann. 1969.

Furtode R. Det. Public Relations. Bombay, New Book Co. 1965.

A Guide to the Practice of Public Relations. The Institute of Public Relations and Newman Neame. 1958.

Howard Stephenson, ed. Handbook of Public Relations. New York.

Jefkins, Frank. Planned Public Relations. Inter-textbooks. 1969.

Jefkins, Frank. Press Relations Practice. London, Inter-textbooks. 1968.

Jefkins, Frank. Planned Press and Public Relations. London, Inter-textbook Co. 1977.

Kaul, J.M. Public Relations in India. Calcutta, Naya Prakash. 1976.

Kelley, Stanley, Jr. Professional Public Relations and Political Power. 19 5. Johns Hopkins.

Kurtz, Harold P. Public Relations for Hospitals : A Practical Handbook (Illus.). 1969.

Lasswell, Harold D., ed. Propaganda and Promotional Activities : An Annotated Bibliography. 1969. University of Chicago Press.

Lesly, Phillip, ed. Lesly's Public Relations Handbook. Bombay, Super Book House.

Lewis, Geoffrey A. Public Relations for Local Government. 1973. Chaners.

Lewis, H. Gordon. How to Handle Your Own Public Relations. Chicago, Nelson Hall. 1977.

Lloyds, Herbert. Teach Yourself Public Relations. English Universities Press. 1963.

Marx, Jerry. Officer, Tell Your Story : A Guide to Police Public Relations (Illus.). 1967. G.C. Thomas.

Monghan, Patrick. Public Relations Careers in Business and the Community. 1972. Fairchild.

Norris, Donald F. Police Community Relations (Illus.). 1973. Lexington Books.

Norton, Alice, ed. Public Relations Information Sources. 1970.

The Police and the Community. 1973. Lexington Books.

Reiss, Albert J. The Police and the Public, 2nd ed. 1973. Yale University Press.

Rice, Betty. Public Relations for Public Libraries. 1972. Wilson.

Roalman, Arthur R. Profitable Public Relations. Bombay, Taraporewalla. 1972.

Unruh & Willier. Public Relations for Schools. 1974. Fearon.

Woodress, Fred A. Public Relations for Community and Junior Colleges. 1976. Interstate Textbooks.

Periodicals

PLUS-PROFIT PUBLICITY (M): the public relations views letter, 1956. Milton Riback Inc., New York.

PRACTICAL PUBLIC RELATIONS, 1960 (Fortnightly). Current Information Service, Inc., Rochester, New York.

PRESS AND PUBLIC RELATIONS (M): for decision makers and publicists (Text in English), 1969. Press and Public Relations Association, New Delhi.

PR REPORTERS: the weekly public relations letter, 1958. PR Publishing Co. Inc., Meriden.

PERISCOPE: a look around the world of publicity in the north-east, 1970. North East Publicity Association, C/o Repro Services Ltd., Portland Terrace, Newcastle.

PUBLIC RELATIONS (M). Institute of Public Relations, London.

PUBLIC RELATIONS JOURNAL (M): a journal of opinion in the field of public relations practice, 1945. Public Relations Society of America, New York.

PUBLIC RELATIONS QUARTERLY, 1955. Ed. and Pub. Howard Penn Hudson. Rhinbeck, New York.

PUBLIC RELATIONS JOURNAL OF INDIA (Bi-monthly) (Text in English), 1970. MSPR Publications, Karol Bagh, New Delhi-5.

Index